PRECIOUS REMEDIES AGAINST
SATAN'S DEVICES

PRECIOUS REMEDIES
AGAINST
SATAN'S DEVICES

Thomas Brooks

Lest Satan should get an advantage of us: for we are not ignorant of his devices.
—2 Cor. 2:11

THE BANNER OF TRUTH TRUST

THE BANNER OF TRUTH TRUST

Head Office
3 Murrayfield Road
Edinburgh
EH12 6EL
UK

North America Office
PO Box 621
Carlisle
PA 17013
USA

banneroftruth.org

First published 1652
This edition reprinted from the Works of Thomas Brooks (1866)
in the Nichol Series, 1968.
Reprinted 1984, 1987, 1990, 1993, 1997, 2000, 2008, 2011
Re-typeset 2019

© The Banner of Truth Trust 2019

*

ISBN
Print: 978 1 84871 862 3
Epub: 978 1 84871 863 0
Kindle: 978 1 84871 864 7

*

Typeset in 10.5/13.5 Adobe Garamond Pro
at The Banner of Truth Trust, Edinburgh

Printed in the USA by
Versa Press Inc.,
East Peoria, IL.

CONTENTS

———

A BRIEF BIOGRAPHY OF THOMAS BROOKS

━━━

I F readers of Puritan literature were set the task of listing thirty of the 'mighties' among Puritan preachers, the name of Thomas Brooks would certainly appear among them, though few would be inclined to include him among 'the first three.' His name and his works are sufficiently esteemed to secure for him an enduring place in the hearts of knowledgeable Christians, and some few might even award him a topmost niche among the choicest spirits of the seventeenth century. His reputation as a writer of treatises for the heart has never been clouded. His literary style is always lively. Like many of his contemporaries he drew his sermon illustrations from the Scriptures themselves, from everyday life, and from ancient classical literature and history. The amalgam is invariably interesting and edifying.

Brooks is a preacher and writer whose biography, had it been written by himself or by a contemporary, would have possessed no small measure of interest. Unfortunately what can be gleaned of his life-story is scanty in the extreme. Alexander B. Grosart, in the Memoir printed in the Nichol's reprint of Brooks' Works (1866), spins it out to sixteen pages, but he had to search far and wide for elusive information, and the basic facts which he brings to light are few indeed. College and ecclesiastical records—all too brief—can be supplemented by an occasional personal reference in Brooks' own writings, and Grosart, to his considerable joy, discovered and printed the Last Will and Testament of our Puritan. Then, too, Brooks' various treatises survive in their earliest editions and are dated. No portrait of him is known to exist. Of the man himself and his strong personality a clear picture is readily formed in the reader's mind. Our author lives in his writings. Apart from these he is a mere shadow.

Born in 1608—place and county unknown—he matriculated as a 'pensioner' at Emmanuel College, Cambridge, that 'nest of the Puritans,' on the 7th July, 1625, the year of Charles I's accession to the throne of England and Scotland. The term 'pensioner' does not indicate poverty and there is reason to believe that the youth was the son of well-to-do parents. In Emmanuel College he would probably rub shoulders with such men as John Milton and the famed New England trio—Thomas Shepard, John Cotton and Thomas Hooker. His love for and skill in Hebrew, Greek and Latin was nurtured, if not inculcated, during his College days.

After 1625 the veil falls again and for twenty or more years nothing is known of our writer beyond the fact that, before he re-emerges from obscurity, he had become a preacher of the Gospel. London seems to have been the sphere of his ministry. There is little doubt that he held strongly with the Parliamentary cause during the stormy Civil War (1642–48), and it is virtually certain that he acted as chaplain to Parliamentary commanders both on land and sea during this period. There is reason to think that he was on terms of some intimacy with Thomas Fairfax, the Commander-in-Chief of the Parliament's military forces. His horizons were greatly extended during these fateful years, for he lets fall the remark in one of his treatises that he had been abroad 'in other nations and countries.' And again: 'I have been some years at sea, and through grace I can say that I would not exchange my sea experiences for England's riches.' 'Some terrible storms I have been in,' he adds.

By the end of the Civil War, Parliament or rather the New Model Army being victorious—Parliament and Army fell apart—Brooks was Preacher of the Gospel at Thomas Apostles, London. He was accounted sufficiently outstanding as a man of God to preach before the House of Commons (the Rump of the Long Parliament) in the same year (December 26). His sermon was afterwards published under the title, 'God's Delight in the Progress of the Upright,' the text being Psalm 44:18: 'Our heart is not turned back, neither have our steps declined from Thy way.' His second sermon before Parliament was preached on the 8th October, 1650, a thanksgiving day for Cromwell's victory over the Scots at Dunbar on September 3rd. On this occasion the text was, significantly, Isaiah 10:6, which we forbear to quote.

Two years later Brooks transferred from Thomas Apostles to another London Church, St. Margaret's, Fish-Street Hill, not without much opposition from some members of his future congregation. Those who objected to his settlement complained that he had refused to administer the sacraments to certain folk whom he judged to be unworthy, an oblique testimony to Brooks' firmness of conscience. St. Bartholomew's

gloomy Day (1662) found him among the ministers evicted
from their livings and driven into nonconformity. But he
did not leave London, and apparently managed to reside and
preach, as occasion offered, not far from St. Margaret's. He
escaped imprisonment, was eminent among ministers who
refused to flee in the Year of Plague (1665), and was at his
post to comfort the afflicted during and after the Great Fire
of 1666. A lengthy treatise entitled London's Lamentations
(based upon Isaiah 42:24-5) appears in Vol. VI of Brooks'
Works (Nichol's Series). It runs to 312 pages and 'is per-
haps the most remarkable contemporary memorial' of the
calamitous event. It is described on its title-page as 'A serious
discourse concerning that late fiery dispensation that turned
our (once renowned) city into a ruinous heap: also the several
lessons that are incumbent upon those whose houses have
escaped the consuming flames.'

Little of a biographical nature remains to be added. The
years 1652–80 were occupied by preaching and writing, a suc-
cession of treatises appearing at frequent intervals, of which
Precious Remedies against Satan's Devices (1652) was the first.
In 1676 his wife Martha (née Burgess) died. To her he bore the
eloquent testimony: 'She was always best when she was most
with God in a corner. She has many a whole day been pouring
out her soul before God for the nation, for Sion, and the great
concerns of her own soul, when them about her did judge it
more expedient that she had been in her bed, by reason of
some bodily infirmity that did hang upon her; but the divine
pleasures that she took in her [corner] did drown the sense
of pain.' We may judge that much of the success of Brooks'
ministry assuredly resulted from his wife's support of him

in prayer. Let Puritan wives be given their due; assuredly the 'price' of some of them was 'above rubies.' There seem to have been no children of the marriage.

After Martha's death three more years of life remained to Thomas. In the course of them he contracted a second marriage. His 'dear and honoured' second wife was a certain Patience Cartwright of whom he says that she made 'all relations to meet in one,' by which we may judge that, despite her youthfulness (and perhaps because of it), she was a not unworthy successor to Martha.

Six months after making his Will in March, 1680, Brooks entered into the joy of his Lord, gathered 'like as a shock of corn ascendeth in his season.'

Brooks' works certainly follow him. Not only did he serve his own generation by the will of God, but all generations since have seen reason to call him blessed. His writings have 'built up in their most holy faith' not a few of the Lord's stalwarts, besides the many who have made less impact on the Church of God. An admixture of 'salt' (in the apostolic sense) has given outlet to their savour. The first printed work which Spurgeon gave to the Church, his Sermons apart, was *Smooth Stones taken from Ancient Brooks*, a compilation from Brooks' writings in the choosing of which his fiancée, Susannah Thompson, had collaborated. It may well be judged that something of the spiritual wealth of the 'heir of the Puritans' (as Spurgeon is entitled in a recent biography) was derived from this quarter.

Grosart, in an Editorial Postcript which prefaces Vol. VI of Brooks' Works, quotes Calamy as saying that our author was 'a very affecting preacher and useful to many.' To this sombre word of praise he adds his own weighty verdict: 'His slightest "Epistle" is "Bread of Life"; his most fugitive 'Sermon' a full cup of 'Living Water'; ... his one dominating aim to make dead hearts warm with the Life of the Gospel of Him who is Life; his supreme purpose to "bring near" the very Truth of God. Hence his directness, his urgency, his yearning, his fervour, his fulness of Bible citation, his wistfulness, his intensity, his emotion. ... His desire to be "useful" to souls, to achieve the holy success of serving Christ, to win a sparkling crown to lay at His feet, breathes and burns from first to last.'

Few who know Brooks' writings will wish to quarrel with Grosart. Our author is one of the select circle whose praise is 'in all churches of the saints,' or at least in those churches which place value upon legacies of abiding spiritual worth. John Milton is often quoted as saying in his Areopagitica that 'a good book is the precious life-blood of a master spirit, embalmed and treasured up on purpose to a life beyond life.' Better still can we say of Thomas Brooks that, if not a master spirit, he possessed (which is of much greater worth) the Spirit of his Master.

S. M. HOUGHTON

EPISTLE DEDICATORY

———

To his most dear and precious ones, the sons and daughters of the Most High God, over whom the Holy Ghost hath made him a Watchman.

Beloved in our dearest Lord, Christ, the Scripture, your own hearts, and Satan's devices, are the four prime things that should be first and most studied and searched. If any cast off the study of these, they cannot be safe here, nor happy hereafter. It is my work as a Christian, but much more as I am a Watchman, to do my best to discover the fullness of Christ, the emptiness of the creature, and the snares of the great deceiver; which I have endeavoured to do in the following discourse, according to that measure of grace which I have received from the Lord. God once accepted a handful of meal for a sacrifice (Lev. 2:2; 5:12), and a gripe[1] of goat's hair for an oblation; and I know that you have not so 'learned the Father,' as to despise 'the day of small things' (Zech. 4:10).

Beloved, Satan being fallen from light to darkness, from felicity to misery, from heaven to hell, from an angel to a devil,

---

[1] Gripe or 'handful.' Cf. Exod. 25:4; 35:26.

is so full of malice and envy that he will leave no means un-attempted, whereby he may make all others eternally miserable with himself; he being shut out of heaven, and shut up 'under the chains of darkness till the judgment of the great day' (Jude 6), makes use of all his power and skill to bring all the sons of men into the same condition and condemnation with himself. Satan hath cast such sinful seed into our souls, that now he can no sooner tempt, but we are ready to assent; he can no sooner have a plot upon us, but he makes a conquest of us. If he doth but show men a little of the beauty and bravery¹ of the world, how ready are they to fall down and worship him!

Whatever sin the heart of man is most prone to, that the devil will help forward. If David be proud of his people, Satan will provoke him to number them, that he may be yet prouder (2 Sam. 24).

If Peter be slavishly fearful, Satan will put him upon rebuking and denying of Christ, to save his own skin (Matt. 16:22; 26:69-75). If Ahab's prophets be given to flatter, the devil will straightway become a lying spirit in the mouths of four hundred of them, and they shall flatter Ahab to his ruin (1 Kings 22). If Judas will be a traitor, Satan will quickly enter into his heart, and make him sell his master for money, which some heathens would never have done (John 13:2). If Ananias will lie for advantage, Satan will fill his heart that he may lie, with a witness, to the Holy Ghost (Acts 5:3). Satan loves to sail with the wind, and to suit men's temptations to their conditions and inclinations. If they be in prosperity, he will tempt them to deny God (Prov. 30:9); if they be in adversity, he will tempt them to distrust God; if their knowledge

¹ Finery.

be weak, he will tempt them to have low thoughts of God; if their conscience be tender, he will tempt to scrupulosity; if large, to carnal security; if bold-spirited, he will tempt to presumption; if timorous, to desperation; if flexible, to inconstancy; if stiff, to impenitency.

From the power, malice and skill of Satan, doth proceed all the soul-killing plots, devices, stratagems and machinations, that be in the world. Several devices he hath to draw souls to sin, and several plots he hath to keep souls from all holy and heavenly services, and several stratagems he hath to keep souls in a mourning, staggering, doubting and questioning condition.

He hath several devices to destroy the great and honourable, the wise and learned, the blind and ignorant, the rich and the poor, the real and the nominal saints.

One while he will restrain from tempting, that we may think ourselves secure, and neglect our watch; another while he will seem to fly, that he may make us proud of the victory; one while he will fix men's eyes on others' sins than their own, that he may puff them up; another while he may fix their eyes more on others' graces than their own, that he may overwhelm them.

A man may as well tell the stars, and number the sands of the sea, as reckon up all the Devices of Satan; yet those which are most considerable, and by which he doth most mischief to the precious souls of men, are in the following Treatise discovered, and the Remedies against them prescribed.

Beloved, I think it necessary to give you and the world a faithful account of the reasons moving me to appear in print, in these days, wherein we may say, there was never more writing and yet never less practising, and they are these that follow;

Reason 1. Because Satan hath a greater influence upon men, and higher advantages over them (having the wind and the hill, as it were), than they think he hath, and the knowledge of his high advantage is the highway to disappoint him, and to render the soul strong in resisting, and happy in conquering.

Reason 2. Your importunity, and the importunity of many other 'precious sons of Sion' (Lam. 4:2), hath after much striving with God, my own heart, and others, made a conquest of me, and forced me to do that at last, which at first was not a little contrary to my inclination and resolution.

Reason 3. The strange opposition that I met with from Satan, in the study of this following discourse, hath put an edge upon my spirit, knowing that Satan strives mightily to keep those things from seeing the light, that tend eminently to shake and break his kingdom of darkness, and to lift up the kingdom and glory of the Lord Jesus Christ, in the souls and lives of the children of men.[1]

Reason 4. Its exceeding usefulness to all sorts, ranks and conditions of men in the world. Here you have salve for every sore, and a plaster for every wound, and a remedy against every disease, especially against those that tend most to the undoing of souls, and the ruin of the State.

Reason 5. I know not of any one or other that have writ of this subject; all that ever I have seen have only touched upon this string, which hath been no small provocation to me, to

---

[1] Pirates make the strongest and the hottest opposition against those vessels that are most richly laden. So doth Satan, that arch-pirate, against those truths that have most of God, Christ, and heaven in them.

attempt to do something this way, that others, that have better heads and hearts, may be the more stirred to improve their talents in a further discovery of Satan's *Devices*, and in making known of such choice Remedies, as may enable the souls of men to triumph over all his plots and stratagems.

Reason 6. I have many precious friends in several countries, who are not a little desirous that my pen may reach them, now my voice cannot. I have formerly been, by the help of the mighty God of Jacob, a weak instrument of good to them, and cannot but hope and believe that the Lord will also bless these labours to them; they being, in part, the fruit of their desires and prayers.

Reason 7. Lastly, not knowing how soon my glass may be out, and how soon I may be cut off by a hand of death from all opportunities of doing further service for Christ or your souls in this world, I was willing to sow a little handful of spiritual seed among you; that so, when I put off this earthly tabernacle, my love to you, and that dear remembrance of you, which I have in my soul, may strongly engage your minds and spirits to make this book your companion, and under all external or internal changes, to make use of this heavenly salve, which I hope will, by the blessing of the Lord, be as effectual for the healing of all your wounds, as their looking up to the brazen serpent was effectual to heal theirs that were bit and stung with fiery serpents, I shall leave this book with you as a legacy of my dearest love, desiring the Lord to make it a far greater and sweeter legacy than all those carnal legacies that are left by the high and mighty ones of the earth to their nearest and dearest relations.

Beloved, I would not have affection carry my pen too much beyond my intention. Therefore, only give me leave to signify my desires for you, and my desires to you, and I shall draw to a close.

My desires for you are. 'That he would grant you, according to the riches of his glory, to be strengthened with might by his Spirit in the inner man; that Christ may dwell in your hearts by faith, that ye, being rooted and grounded in love, may be able to comprehend with all saints what is the breadth, and length, and depth, and height; and to know the love of Christ that passeth knowledge, that ye might be filled with all the fullness of God' (Eph. 3:16-19); and 'That ye might walk worthy of the Lord unto all pleasing, being fruitful in every good work, and increasing in the knowledge of God, strengthened with all might according to his glorious power, unto all patience and long-suffering, with joyfulness' (Col. 1:10, 11); 'That ye do no evil' (2 Cor. 13:7); 'That your love may abound yet more and more in knowledge, and in all judgment'; 'That ye may approve things that are excellent, that ye may be sincere, and without offence till the day of Christ' (Phil. 1:27; 1:9, 10); and that 'our God would count you worthy of this calling, and fulfil all the good pleasure of his goodness, and the work of faith with power'; 'That the name of our Lord Jesus Christ may be glorified in you, and ye in him, according to the grace of our God and the Lord Jesus Christ' (2 Thess. 1:11, 12). And that you may be eminent in sanctity, sanctity being Zion's glory (Psa. 93:5); that your hearts may be kept upright, your judgments sound, and your lives unblameable. That as ye are now 'my joy,' so in the day of Christ you may be 'my crown'; that I may see my labours in your lives; that your conversation may not be earthly, when the things you hear are heavenly; but that it may be 'as becomes the gospel' (Phil. 1:27). That as the fishes which live in the salt sea yet are fresh, so you, though you live in an uncharitable world, may yet be charitable and loving; that ye may, like the bee, suck honey out of every flower; that ye may shine in a sea of troubles, as the pearl shines in the sky, though it grows in the sea; that in all your trials you may shine like the stone in Thracia, that neither burneth in the fire nor sinketh in the water; that ye may be like the heavens, excellent in substance and beautiful in appearance; that so you may meet me with joy in that day wherein Christ shall say to his Father, 'Lo, here am I, and the children that thou hast given me' (Isa. 8:18).

My desires to you are, That you would make it your business to study Christ, his word, your own hearts, Satan's plots, and eternity, more than ever; That ye would endeavour more to be inwardly sincere than outwardly glorious; to live, than to have a name to live; That ye would labour with all your might to be thankful under mercies, and faithful in your places, and humble under divine appearances, and fruitful under precious ordinances; That as your means and mercies are greater than others 'so your account before God may not prove a worse than others'; That ye would pray for me, who am not worthy to be named among the saints, that I may be a precious instrument in the hand of Christ to bring in many souls unto him, and to build up those that are brought in in their most holy faith; and 'that utterance may be given to me, that I may make known all the will of God' (Eph. 6:19); that I may be sincere, faithful, frequent, fervent and constant in the work of the Lord, and that my labour be not in vain in the Lord; that my labours may be accepted in the Lord and his saints, and I may daily see the travail of my soul.

But, above all, pray for me, that I may more and more find the power and sweet of those things upon my own heart, that I give out to you and others: that my soul may be so visited with strength from on high, that I may live up fully and constantly to those truths that I hold forth to the world; and that I may be both in life and doctrine 'a burning and a shining light,' that so, when the Lord Jesus shall appear, 'I may receive a crown of glory which he shall give to me in that day, and not only to me, but to all that love his appearing' (John 5:35 and 2 Tim. 4:8).

For a close, remember this, that your life is short, your duties many, your assistance great, and your reward sure; therefore faint not, hold on and hold up, in ways of well-doing, and heaven shall make amends for all.

I shall now take leave of you, when my heart hath by my hand subscribed, that I am.

Your loving pastor under Christ, according to all pastoral affections and engagements in our dearest Lord,

THOMAS BROOKS

A WORD TO THE READER

———

Dear Friend!

Solomon bids us buy the truth (Prov. 23:23), but doth not tell us what it must cost, because we must get it though it be never so dear. We must love it both shining and scorching. Every parcel of truth is precious as the filings of gold; we must either live with it, or die for it. As Ruth said to Naomi, 'Whither thou goest I will go, and where thou lodgest I will lodge, and nothing but death shall part thee and me' (Ruth 1:16, 17); so must gracious spirits say, Where truth goes I will go, and where truth lodges I will lodge, and nothing but death shall part me and truth. A man may lawfully sell his house, land and jewels, but truth is a jewel that exceeds all price, and must not be sold; it is our heritage: 'Thy testimonies have I taken as an heritage for ever' (Psa. 119:111). It is a legacy that our forefathers have bought with their bloods, which should make us willing to lay down anything, and to lay out anything, that we may, with the wise merchant in the Gospel (Matt. 13:45), purchase this precious pearl, which is more worth than heaven and earth, and which will make a man live happily, die comfortably, and reign eternally.

And now, if thou pleasest, read the work, and receive this counsel from me.

First, Thou must know that every man cannot be excellent, that yet may be useful. An iron key may unlock the door of a golden treasure, yea, iron can do some things that gold cannot.

Secondly, Remember, it is not hasty reading, but serious meditating upon holy and heavenly truths, that make them prove sweet and profitable to the soul. It is not the bee's touching of the flower that gathers honey, but her abiding for a time upon the flower that draws out the sweet. It is not he that reads most, but he that meditates most, that will prove the choicest, sweetest, wisest and strongest Christian.

Thirdly, Know that it is not the knowing, nor the talking, nor the reading man, but the doing man, that at last will be found the happiest man. 'If you know these things, blessed and happy are you if you do them.' 'Not every one that saith. Lord, Lord, shall enter into the kingdom of heaven, but he that doeth the will of my Father that is in heaven' (John 13:7; Matt. 7:21). Judas called Christ Lord, Lord, and yet betrayed him, and is gone to his place. Ah! how many Judases have we in these days, that kiss Christ, and yet betray Christ; that in their words profess him, but in their works deny him; that bow their knee to him, and yet in their hearts despise him; that call him Jesus, and yet will not obey him for their Lord.

Reader, if it be not strong upon thy heart to practise what thou readest, to what end dost thou read? To increase thy own condemnation?[1] If thy light and knowledge be not turned into practice, the more knowing man thou art, the more miserable

---

[1] The heathen philosopher, Seneca, liked not such as are *semper victuri,* always about to live, but never begin.

man thou wilt be in the day of recompense; thy light and knowledge will more torment thee than all the devils in hell. Thy knowledge will be that rod that will eternally lash thee, and that scorpion that will for ever bite thee, and that worm that will everlastingly gnaw thee; therefore read, and labour to know, that thou mayest do, or else thou art undone for ever.[1] When Demosthenes was asked, what was the first part of an orator, what the second, what the third ? he answered, Action; the same may I say. If any should ask me, what is the first, the second, the third part of a Christian? I must answer. Action; as that man that reads that he may know, and that labours to know that he may do, will have two heavens—a heaven of joy, peace and comfort on earth, and a heaven of glory and happiness after death.

Fourthly and lastly, If in thy reading thou wilt cast a serious eye upon the margent,[2] thou wilt find many sweet and precious notes, that will oftentimes give light to the things thou readest, and pay thee for thy pains with much comfort and profit. So desiring that thou mayest find as much sweetness and advantage in reading this Treatise as I have found, by the overshadowings of heaven, in the studying and writing of it, I recommend thee 'to God, and to the word of his grace, which is able to build thee up, and to give thee an inheritance among them which are sanctified' (Acts 20:32), And rest, reader.

Thy soul's servant in every office of the gospel,

THOMAS BROOKS

[1] God loves, saith Luther, *curistas*, not *queristas* the runner, not the questioner.

[2] Margin, transferred here and throughout in this edition to the foot of page.

INTRODUCTION

———

Lest Satan should get an advantage of us: for we are not ignorant of his devices.—2 Cor. 2:11

In the fifth verse, the apostle shows, that the incestuous person had by his incest sadded those precious souls that God would not have sadded.[1] Souls that walk sinfully are Hazaels to the godly (2 Kings 8:12-15), and draw many sighs and tears from them. Jeremiah weeps in secret for Judah's sins (Jer. 9:1); and Paul cannot speak of the belly-gods with dry eyes (Phil. 3:18, 19). And Lot's righteous soul was burdened, vexed and racked by the filthy Sodomites (2 Pet. 2:7, 8). Every sinful Sodomite was a Hazael to his eyes, a Hadad-rimmon to his heart (Zech. 12:11). Gracious souls use to mourn for other men's sins as well as their own, and for their souls and sins who make a mock of sin, and a jest of damning their own souls. Guilt or grief is all that gracious souls get by communion with vain souls (Psa. 119:136, 158).

In the 6th verse, he shows that the punishment that was inflicted upon the incestuous person was sufficient, and

---

[1] Saddened.

therefore they should not refuse to receive him who had repented and sorrowed for his former faults and follies. It is not for the honour of Christ, the credit of the gospel, nor the good of souls, for professors to be like those bloody wretches, that burnt some that recanted at the stake, saying, 'That they would send them into another world whiles they were in a good mind.'

In the 7th, 8th, 9th, and 10th verses, the apostle stirs up the church to forgive him, to comfort him, and to confirm their love towards him, lest he should be 'swallowed up with overmuch sorrow,' Satan going about to mix the detestable darnel (Matt. 13:25) of desperation with the godly sorrow of a pure penitent heart. It was a sweet saying of Jerome, 'Let a man grieve for his sin, and then joy for his grief.' That sorrow for sin that keeps the soul from looking towards the mercy-seat, and that keeps Christ and the soul asunder, or that shall render the soul unfit for the communion of saints, is a sinful sorrow.

In the 11th verse, he lays down another reason to work them to show pity and mercy to the penitent sinner, that was mourning and groaning under his sin and misery; *i.e.* lest Satan should get an advantage of us: for we are not ignorant of his devices. A little for the opening of the words.

Lest Satan should get an *advantage* of us; lest Satan overreach us. The word in the Greek signifieth to have more than belongs to one. The comparison is taken from the greedy merchant, that seeketh and taketh all opportunities to beguile and deceive others. Satan is that wily merchant, that devoureth, not widows' houses, but most men's souls.

'We are not ignorant of Satan's *devices*,' or plots, or machinations, or stratagems. He is but a titular Christian that hath not personal experience of Satan's stratagems, his set and composed machinations, his artificially moulded methods, his plots, darts, depths, whereby he outwitted our first parents, and fits us a pennyworth still, as he sees reason.

The main observation that I shall draw from these words is this:

That Satan hath his several devices to deceive, entangle, and undo the souls of men. I shall—

1. Prove the point.
2. Show you his several devices.
3. Show the remedies against his devices.
4. Show how it comes to pass that he hath so many several devices to deceive, entangle, and undo the souls of men.
5. Lay down some propositions concerning Satan's devices.

I.

THE PROOF OF THE POINT

———

For the *proof of the point*, take these few Scriptures: (Eph. 6:11), 'Put on the whole armour of God, that ye may be able to stand against the *wiles* of the devil.' The Greek word that is here rendered 'wiles' is a notable emphatical word.

(1) It signifies such snares as are laid behind one, such treacheries as come upon one's back at unawares. It notes the methods or waylayings of that old subtle serpent, who, like Dan's adder 'in the path,' biteth the heels of passengers, and thereby transfuseth his venom to the head and heart (Gen. 49:17). The word signifies an ambushment or stratagem of war, whereby the enemy sets upon a man at unawares.

(2) It signifies such snares as are set to catch one in one's road. A man walks in his road, and thinks not of it; on the sudden he is catched by thieves, or falls into a pit, etc.

(3) It signifies such as are purposely, artificially,[1] and craftily set for the taking the prey at the greatest advantage that can

---

[1] 'Artificially.' Here used with the sense of 'by the use of an artifice or trick.'

be. The Greek signifies properly a waylaying, circumvention, or going about, as they do which seek after their prey. Julian,[1] by his craft, drew more from the faith than all his persecuting predecessors could do by their cruelty. So doth Satan more hurt in his sheep's skin than by roaring like a lion.

Take one scripture more for the proof of the point, and that is in 2 Tim. 2:26, 'And that they might recover themselves out of the snare of the devil, who are taken captive by him at his will.' The Greek word that is here rendered recover themselves, signifies to awaken themselves. The apostle alludeth to one that is asleep or drunk, who is to be awakened and restored to his senses; and the Greek word that is here rendered 'taken captive,' signifies to be taken alive. The word is properly a warlike word, and signifies to be taken alive, as soldiers are taken alive in the wars, or as birds are taken alive and ensnared in the fowler's net. Satan hath snares for the wise and snares for the simple; snares for hypocrites, and snares for the upright; snares for generous souls, and snares for timorous souls; snares for the rich, and snares for the poor; snares for the aged, and snares for youth. Happy are those souls that are not taken and held in the snares that he hath laid!

Take one proof more, and then I will proceed to the opening of the point, and that is in Rev. 2:24, 'But unto you I say, and unto the rest in Thyatira, as many as have not this doctrine, and which have not known the depths of Satan, as they speak, I will put upon you no other burden but to hold fast till I come.' These poor souls called their opinions the depths of God, when indeed they were the depths of Satan. You call your opinions depths, and so they are, but they are such depths as

[1] Julian the Apostate, Roman Emperor in the 4th Century, shortly after Constantine.

Satan hath brought out of hell. They are the whisperings and hissings of that serpent, not the inspirations of God.

II.

SATAN'S DEVICES TO DRAW THE SOUL TO SIN

———

Now, the second thing that I am to show you is, his *several devices*; and herein I shall first show you the several devices that he hath to draw the soul to sin. I shall instance in these twelve, which may bespeak our most serious consideration.

DEVICE 1. *To present the bait and hide the hook*; to present the golden cup, and hide the poison; to present the sweet, the pleasure, and the profit that may flow in upon the soul by yielding to sin, and by hiding from the soul the wrath and misery that will certainly follow the committing of sin. By this device he took our first parents: 'And the serpent said unto the woman, Ye shall not surely die: for God doth know, that in the day ye eat thereof, then your eyes shall be opened; and ye shall be as gods, knowing good and evil' (Gen. 3:4, 5). Your eyes shall be opened, and you shall be as gods! Here is the bait, the sweet, the pleasure, the profit. Oh, but he hides the hook,—the shame, the wrath, and the loss that would certainly follow![1]

[1] So to reduce Dr Rowland Taylor, martyr, they promised him not only his pardon, but a bishopric. Acts & Mon, Foxe.

There is an opening of the eyes of the mind to contemplation and joy, and there is an opening of the eyes of the body to shame and confusion. He promiseth them the former, but intends the latter, and so cheats them—giving them an apple in exchange for a paradise, as he deals by thousands now-a-days.

Satan with ease puts fallacies upon us by his golden baits, and then he leads us and leaves us in a fool's paradise. He promises the soul honour, pleasure, profit, but pays the soul with the greatest contempt, shame, and loss that can be. By a golden bait he laboured to catch Christ (Matt. 4:8, 9). He shows him the beauty and the bravery of a bewitching world, which doubtless would have taken many a carnal heart; but here the devil's fire fell upon wet tinder, and therefore took not. These tempting objects did not at all win upon his affections, nor dazzle his eyes, though many have eternally died of the wound of the eye, and fallen for ever by this vile strumpet the world, who, by laying forth her two fair breasts of profit and pleasure, hath wounded their souls, and cast them down into utter perdition.[1] She hath, by the glistening of her pomp and preferment, slain millions; as the serpent Scytale, which, when she cannot overtake the fleeing passengers, doth, with her beautiful colours, astonish and amaze them, so that they have no power to pass away till she have stung them to death. Adversity hath slain her thousand, but prosperity her ten thousand.

[1] This world at last shall be burnt for a witch, saith one. Many are miserable by loving hurtful things, but they are more miserable by having them. *Augustine* in Psa. 16. Men had need pray with Bernard, 'Grant us, Lord, that we may so partake of temporal felicity, that we may not lose eternal.'

Remedy (1). *First, keep at the greatest distance from sin, and from playing with the golden bait that Satan holds forth to catch you*; for this you have (Rom. 12:9), 'Abhor that which is evil, cleave to that which is good.' When we meet with anything extremely evil and contrary to us, nature abhors it, and retires as far as it can from it. The Greek word that is there rendered 'abhor,' is very significant; it signifies to hate it as hell itself, to hate it with horror.

Anselm used to say, 'That if he should see the shame of sin on the one hand, and the pains of hell on the other, and must of necessity choose one, he would rather be thrust into hell without sin, than to go into heaven with sin, so great was his hatred and detestation of sin. It is our wisest and our safest course to stand at the farthest distance from sin; not to go near the house of the harlot, but to fly from all appearance of evil (Prov. 5:8; 1 Thess. 5:22). The best course to prevent falling into the pit is to keep at the greatest distance; he that will be so bold as to attempt to dance upon the brink of the pit, may find by woeful experience that it is a righteous thing with God that he should fall into the pit. Joseph keeps at a distance from sin, and from playing with Satan's golden baits, and stands. David draws near, and plays with the bait, and falls, and swallows bait and hook with a witness,[1] David comes near the snare, and is taken in it, to the breaking of his bones, the wounding of his conscience, and the loss of his God.[2]

---

[1] 'with a witness'—used in the sense of, 'And no mistake!'

[2] It was a divine saying of a heathen, 'That if there were no God to punish him, no devil to torment him, no hell to burn him, no man to see him, yet would he not sin for the ugliness and filthiness of sin, and the grief of his own conscience.' (*Seneca*)

Sin is a plague, yea, the greatest and most infectious plague in the world; and yet, ah! how few are there that tremble at it, that keep at a distance from it! (1 Cor. 5:6): 'Know ye not that a little leaven leaveneth the whole lump?' As soon as one sin had seized upon Adam's heart, all sin entered into his soul and overspread it. How hath Adam's one sin spread over all mankind! (Rom. 5:12): 'Wherefore as by one man sin entered into the world, and death by sin, and so death passed upon all men, for that all have sinned.' Ah, how doth the father's sin infect the child, the husband's infect the wife, the master's the servant! The sin that is in one man's heart is able to infect a whole world, it is of such a spreading and infectious nature.

The story of the Italian, who first made his enemy deny God, and then stabbed him, and so at once murdered both body and soul, declares the perfect malignity of sin; and oh! that what hath been spoken upon this head may prevail with you, to stand at a distance from sin!

Remedy (2). To consider, *that sin is but a bitter sweet.* That seeming sweet that is in sin will quickly vanish, and lasting shame, sorrow, horror, and terror will come in the room thereof 'Though wickedness be sweet in his mouth, though he hide it under his tongue; though he spare it, and forsake it not, but keep it still within his mouth; yet his meat in his bowels is turned, it is the gall of asps within him' (Job 20:12-14). Forbidden profits and pleasures are most pleasing to vain men, who count madness mirth. Many long to be meddling with the murdering morsels of sin, which nourish not, but rend and consume the belly, the soul that receives them. Many eat that on earth that they digest in hell. Sin's murdering morsels will deceive those that devour them. Adam's apple was a bitter sweet; Esau's mess was a bitter sweet; the Israelites' quails a bitter sweet; Jonathan's honey a bitter sweet; and Adonijah's dainties a bitter sweet. After the meal is ended, then comes the reckoning. Men must not think to dance and dine with the devil, and then to sup with Abraham, Isaac, and Jacob in the kingdom of heaven; to feed upon the poison of asps, and yet that the viper's tongue should not slay them.[1]

When the asp stings a man, it doth first tickle him so as it makes him laugh, till the poison, by little and little, gets to the heart, and then it pains him more than ever it delighted him. So doth sin; it may please a little at first, but it will pain the soul with a witness at last; yea, if there were the least real delight in sin, there could be no perfect hell, where men shall most perfectly be tormented with their sin.

Remedy (3). Solemnly to consider, *that sin will usher in the greatest and the saddest losses that can be upon our souls.* It will usher in the loss of that divine favour that is better than life, and the loss of that joy that is unspeakable and full of glory, and the loss of that peace that passeth understanding, and the loss of those divine influences by which the soul hath been refreshed, quickened, raised, strengthened, and gladded, and the loss of many outward desirable mercies, which otherwise the soul might have enjoyed.[2]

---

[1] When the golden bait is set forth to catch us, we must say as Demosthenes the orator did of the beautiful Lais, when he was asked an excessive sum of money to behold her, 'I will not buy repentance so dear'; I am not so ill a merchant as to sell eternals for temporals. If intemperance could afford more pleasure than temperance Heliogabalus should have been more happy than Adam in paradise. (*Plutarch*)

[2] Chron. 15:3, 4; Psa. 51:12; Isa. 59:8; Jer. 5:2, 17, 18.

It was a sound and savoury reply of an English captain at the loss of Calais, when a proud Frenchman scornfully demanded, 'When will you fetch Calais again,' replied, 'When your sins shall weigh down ours.' Ah, England! my constant prayer for thee is, that thou mayest not sin away thy mercies into their hands that cannot call mercy mercy, and that would joy in nothing more than to see thy sorrow and misery, and to see that hand to make thee naked, that hath clothed thee with much mercy and glory.

Remedy (4). Seriously to consider, *that sin is of a very deceitful and bewitching nature.*[1] Sin is from the greatest deceiver, it is a child of his own begetting, it is the ground of all the deceit in the world, and it is in its own nature exceeding deceitful. 'But exhort one another daily, while it is called Today, lest any of you be hardened through the deceitfulness of sin.' Heb. 3:13. It will kiss the soul, and pretend fair to the soul, and yet betray the soul for ever. It will with Delilah smile upon us, that it may betray us into the hands of the devil, as she did Samson into the hands of the Philistines. Sin gives Satan a power over us, and an advantage to accuse us and to lay claim to us, as those that wear his badge; it is of a very bewitching nature; it bewitches the soul, where it is upon the throne, that the soul cannot leave it, though it perish eternally by it.[2] Sin so bewitches the soul, that it makes the soul call evil good, and good evil; bitter sweet and sweet bitter, light darkness and

[1] In Sardis there grew a herb, called *Appium Sardis*, that would make a man lie laughing when he was deadly sick; such is the operation of sin.

[2] Which occasioned Chrysostom to say, when Eudoxia the empress threatened him, 'Go tell her, "*Nil nisi peccatum timeo,*" I fear nothing but sin.'

darkness light; and a soul thus bewitched with sin will stand it out to the death, at the sword's point with God; let God strike and wound, and cut to the very bone, yet the bewitched soul cares not, fears not, but will still hold on in a course of wickedness, as you may see in Pharaoh, Balaam, and Judas. Tell the bewitched soul that sin is a viper that will certainly kill when it is not killed, that sin often kills secretly, insensibly, eternally, yet the bewitched soul cannot, and will not, cease from sin.

When the physicians told Theotimus that except he did abstain from drunkenness and uncleanness he would lose his eyes, his heart was so bewitched to his sins, that he answered. 'Then farewell, sweet light'; he had rather lose his eyes than leave his sin. So a man bewitched with sin had rather lose God, Christ, heaven, and his own soul than part with his sin. Oh, therefore, for ever take heed of playing with or nibbling at Satan's golden baits.

DEVICE 2. *By painting sin with virtue's colours.* Satan knows that if he should present sin in its own nature and dress, the soul would rather fly from it than yield to it; and therefore he presents it unto us, not in its own proper colours, but painted and gilded over with the name and show of virtue, that we may the more easily be overcome by it, and take the more pleasure in committing of it. Pride, he presents to the soul under the name and notion of neatness and cleanliness, and covetousness (which the apostle condemns for idolatry) to be but good husbandry;[1] and drunkenness to be good fellowship, and riotousness under the name and notion of liberality, and wantonness as a trick of youth.

---

[1] Thrift, 'economy.'

Remedy (1). Consider, *that sin is never a whit the less filthy, vile, and abominable, by its being coloured and painted with virtue's colours.* A poisonous pill is never a whit the less poisonous because it is gilded over with gold; nor a wolf is never a whit the less a wolf because he hath put on a sheep's skin; nor the devil is never a whit the less a devil because he appears sometimes like an angel of light. So neither is sin any whit the less filthy and abominable by its being painted over with virtue's colours.

Remedy (2). *That the more sin is painted forth under the colour of virtue, the more dangerous it is to the souls of men.* This we see evident in these days, by those very many souls that are turned out of the way that is holy—and in which their souls have had sweet and glorious communion with God—into ways of highest vanity and folly, by Satan's neat colouring over of sin, and painting forth vice under the name and colour of virtue. This is so notoriously known that I need but name it. The most dangerous vermin is too often to be found under the fairest and sweetest flowers, the fairest glove is often drawn upon the foulest hand, and the richest robes are often put upon the filthiest bodies. So are the fairest and sweetest names upon the greatest and the most horrible vices and errors that be in the world. Ah! that we had not too many sad proofs of this amongst us!

Remedy (3). *To look on sin with that eye [with] which within a few hours we shall see it.* Ah, souls! when you shall lie upon a dying bed, and stand before a judgment-seat, sin shall be unmasked, and its dress and robes shall then be taken off, and then it shall appear more vile, filthy, and terrible than hell itself; then, that which formerly appeared most sweet will appear most bitter, and that which appeared most beautiful will appear most ugly, and that which appeared most delightful will then appear most dreadful to the soul.[1] Ah, the shame, the pain, the gall, the bitterness, the horror, the hell that the sight of sin, when its dress is taken off, will raise in poor souls! Sin will surely prove evil and bitter to the soul when its robes are taken off. A man may have the stone who feels no fit of it. Conscience will work at last, though for the present one may feel no fit of accusation. Laban showed himself at parting. Sin will be bitterness in the latter end, when it shall appear to the soul in its own filthy nature. The devil deals with men as the panther doth with beasts; he hides his deformed head till his sweet scent hath drawn them into his danger. Till we have sinned, Satan is a parasite; when we have sinned, he is a tyrant.[2] O souls! the day is at hand when the devil will pull off the paint and garnish that he hath put upon sin, and present that monster, sin, in such a monstrous shape to your souls, that will cause your thoughts to be troubled, your countenance to be changed, the joints of your loins to be loosed, and your knees to be dashed one against another, and your hearts to be so terrified, that you will be ready, with Ahithophel and Judas,[3] to strangle and hang your bodies on earth, and your souls in hell, if the Lord hath not more mercy on you than he had on them. Oh! therefore, look upon sin now as you must

[1] Tacitus speaks of Tiberius, that when his sins did appear in their own colours, they did so terrify and torment him that he protested to the Senate that he suffered daily.

[2] Satan, that now allures thee to sin, will ere long make thee to see that *peccatum est deicidium*, sin is a murdering of God; and this will make thee murder two at once, thy soul and thy body, unless the Lord in mercy holds thy hands.

[3] 2 Sam. 17:23 and Matt. 27:5.

look upon it to all eternity, and as God, conscience, and Satan will present it to you another day!

Remedy (4). Seriously to consider, *that even those very sins that Satan paints, and puts new names and colours upon, cost the best blood, the noblest blood, the life-blood, the heart-blood of the Lord Jesu*s.[1] That Christ should come from the eternal bosom of his Father to a region of sorrow and death; that God should be manifested in the flesh, the Creator made a creature; that he that was clothed with glory should be wrapped with rags of flesh; he that filled heaven and earth with his glory should be cradled in a manger; that the power of God should fly from weak man, the God of Israel into Egypt; that the God of the law should be subject to the law, the God of the circumcision circumcised; the God that made the heavens working at Joseph's homely trade; that he that binds the devils in chains should be tempted; that he, whose is the world, and the fullness thereof, should hunger and thirst; that the God of strength should be weary, the Judge of all flesh condemned, the God of life put to death; that he that is one with his Father should cry out of misery, 'My God, my God, why hast thou forsaken me?' (Matt. 27:46); that he that had the keys of hell and death at his girdle should lie imprisoned in the sepulchre of another, having in his lifetime nowhere to lay his head, nor after death to lay his body; that that head, before which the angels do cast down their crowns, should be crowned with thorns, and those eyes, purer than the sun, put out by the darkness of death; those ears, which hear nothing

---

[1] *Una guttula plus valet quam coelum et terra; i.e.* one little drop (speaking of the blood of Christ) is more worth than heaven and earth. (*Luther*)

but hallelujahs of saints and angels, to hear the blasphemies of the multitude; that face, that was fairer than the sons of men, to be spit on by those beastly wretched Jews; that mouth and tongue, that spake as never man spake, accused for blasphemy; those hands, that freely swayed the sceptre of heaven, nailed to the cross; those feet, 'like unto fine brass,' nailed to the cross for man's sins; each sense annoyed: his feeling or touching, with a spear and nails; his smell, with stinking flavour, being crucified about Golgotha, the place of skulls; his taste, with vinegar and gall; his hearing, with reproaches, and sight of his mother and disciples bemoaning him; his soul, comfortless and forsaken; and all this for those very sins that Satan paints and puts fine colours upon! Oh! how should the consideration of this stir up the soul against it, and work the soul to fly from it, and to use all holy means whereby sin may be subdued and destroyed![1]

After Julius Caesar was murdered, Antonius brought forth his coat, all bloody and cut, and laid it before the people, saying, 'Look, here you have the emperor's coat thus bloody and torn': whereupon the people were presently in an uproar, and cried out to slay those murderers; and they took their tables and stools that were in the place, and set them on fire, and ran to the houses of them that had slain Caesar, and burnt them. So that when we consider that sin hath slain our Lord

---

[1] One of the Rabbins, when he read what bitter torments the Messias should suffer when he came into the world, cried out, *Veniat Messias et ego non videam*, *i.e.*, Let the Messias come, but let not me see him! Dionysius being in Egypt at the time of Christ's suffering, and seeing in eclipse of the sun, and knowing it to foe contrary to nature, cried out, *Aut Deus naturbe patitur, aut mundi machina dissolvitur*, Either the God of nature suffers, or the frame of the world will be dissolved.

Jesus, ah, how should it provoke our hearts to be revenged on sin, that that hath murdered the Lord of glory, and hath done that mischief that all the devils in hell could never have done?[1]

It was good counsel one gave, 'Never let go out of your minds the thoughts of a crucified Christ.'[2] Let these be meat and drink unto you; let them be your sweetness and consolation, your honey and your desire, your reading and your meditation, your life, death, and resurrection. thoughts of a crucified Christ. Let these be meat and drink unto you; let them be your sweetness and consolation, your honey and your desire, your reading and your meditation, your life, death, and resurrection.

DEVICE 3. *By extenuating and lessening of sin.* Ah! saith Satan, it is but a little pride, a little worldliness, a little uncleanness, a little drunkenness, etc. As Lot said of Zoar, 'It is but a little one, and my soul shall live' (Gen. 19:20). Alas! saith Satan, it is but a very little sin that you stick so at. You may commit it without any danger to your soul. It is but a little one; you may commit it, and yet your soul shall live.

Remedy (1). First, solemnly consider, *that those sins which we are apt to account small, have brought upon men the greatest wrath of God,* as the eating of an apple, gathering a few sticks on the Sabbath day, and touching the ark. Oh! the dreadful wrath that these sins brought down upon the heads and

---

[1] It is an excellent saying of Bernard, *Quanto pro nobis vilior, tanto nobis charior.* The more vile Christ made himself for us, the more dear he ought to be to us.

[2] *Nolo vivere sine vulnere cum te video vulneratum.* (O my God!) as long as I see thy wounds, I will never live without wounds, said Bonaventure.

hearts of men![1] The least sin is contrary to the law of God, the nature of God, the being of God, and the glory of God; and therefore it is often punished severely by God; and do not we see daily the vengeance of the Almighty falling upon the bodies, names, states, families, and souls of men, for those sins that are but little ones in their eyes? Surely if we are not utterly left of God, and blinded by Satan, we cannot but see it. Oh! therefore, when Satan says it is but a little one, do thou say, 'Oh! but those sins that thou callest little, are such as will cause God to rain hell out of heaven upon sinners as he did upon the Sodomites.'

Remedy (2). Seriously to consider, *that the giving way to a less sin makes way for the committing of a greater.* He that, to avoid a greater sin, will yield to a lesser, ten thousand to one but God in justice will leave that soul to fall into a greater. If we commit one sin to avoid another, it is just we should avoid neither, we having not law nor power in our own hands to keep off sin as we please; and we, by yielding to the lesser, do tempt the tempter to tempt us to the greater. Sin is of an encroaching nature; it creeps on the soul by degrees, step by step, till it hath the soul to the very height of sin.[2] David gives way to his wandering eye, and this led him to those foul sins that caused God to break his bones, and to turn his day into

[1] Draco, the rigid lawgiver, being asked why, when sins were not equal, he appointed death to all, answered, he knew that all sins were not equal, but he knew the least deserved death. So, though the sins of men be not all equal, yet the least of them deserve eternal death.

[2] Psa. 137:9, 'Happy shall he be that taketh and dasheth thy little ones against the stones.' Hugo's gloss as pious, *Sit nihil in te Babylonicum*, Let there be nothing in thee of Babylon; not only the grown men, but the little ones must be dashed against the stones; not only great sins, but little sins must be killed, or they will kill the soul for ever.

night, and to leave his soul in great darkness, Jacob and Peter, and other saints, have found this true by woeful experience, that the yielding to a lesser sin hath been the ushering in of a greater. The little thief will open the door, and make way for the greater, and the little wedge knocked in will make way for the greater. Satan will first draw thee to sit with the drunkard, and then to sip with the drunkard, and then at last to be drunk with the drunkard. He will first draw thee to be unclean in thy thoughts, and then to be unclean in thy looks, and then to be unclean in thy words, and at last to be unclean in thy practices. He will first draw thee to look upon the golden wedge, and then to like the golden wedge, and then to handle the golden wedge, and then at last by wicked ways to gain the golden wedge, though thou runnest the hazard of losing God and thy soul for ever; as you may see in Gehazi, Achan, and Judas, and many in these our days. Sin is never at a stand (Psa. 1:1), first ungodly, then sinners, then scorners. Here they go on from sin to sin, till they come to the top of sin, viz. to sit in the seat of scorners, or as it is in the Septuagint—to affect the honour of the chair of pestilence.

Austin,[1] writing upon John, tells a story of a certain man, that was of an opinion that the devil did make the fly, and not God. Saith one to him, If the devil made flies, then the devil made worms, and God did not make them, for they are living creatures as well as flies. True, said he, the devil did make worms. But, said the other, if the devil did make worms, then he made birds, beasts, and man. He granted all. Thus, saith Austin, by denying God in the fly, became to deny God in man, and to deny the whole creation.[2]

[1] Austin—a shortened form of Augustine.
[2] An Italian having found his enemy at advantage, promised him

By all this we see, that the yielding to lesser sins draws the soul to the committing of greater.[1] Ah! how many in these days have fallen, first to have low thoughts of Scripture and ordinances, and then to slight Scripture and ordinances, and then to make a nose of wax of Scripture and ordinances, and then to cast off Scripture and ordinances, and then at last to advance and lift up themselves, and their Christ-dishonouring and soul-damning opinions, above Scripture and ordinances. Sin gains upon man's soul by insensible degrees (Eccles. 10:13): 'The beginning of the words of his mouth is foolishness, and the end of his talking is mischievous madness.' Corruption in the heart, when it breaks forth, is like a breach in the sea, which begins in a narrow passage, till it eat through, and cast down all before it. The debates of the soul are quick, and soon ended, and that may be done in a moment that may undo a man for ever. When a man hath begun to sin, he knows not where, or when, or how he shall make a stop of sin. Usually the soul goes on from evil to evil, from folly to folly, till it be ripe for eternal misery. Men usually grow from being naught to be very naught, and from very naught to be stark naught, and then God sets them at nought for ever.

Remedy (3). The third remedy against this third device that Satan hath to draw the soul to sin, is solemnly to consider, *that it is sad to stand with God for a trifle.* Dives would not give

---

if he would deny his faith, he would save his life. He, to save his life, denied his faith, which having done, he stabbed him, rejoicing that by this he had at one time taken revenge both on body and soul.

[1] A young man being long tempted to kill his father, or lie with his mother, or be drunk, he thought to yield to the lesser, viz. to be drunk, that he might be rid of the greater; but when he was drunk, he did both kill his father, and lie with his mother.

a crumb, therefore he should not receive a drop (Luke 16:21). It is the greatest folly in the world to adventure the going to hell for a small matter. 'I tasted but a little honey,' said Jonathan, 'and I must die' (1 Sam. 14:29). It is a most unkind and unfaithful thing to break with God for a little. Little sins carry with them but little temptations to sin, and then a man shows most viciousness and unkindness, when he sins on a little temptation. It is devilish to sin without a temptation; it is little less than devilish to sin on a little occasion. The less the temptation is to sin, the greater is that sin.[1] Saul's sin in not staying for Samuel, was not so much in the matter, but it was much in the malice of it; for though Samuel had not come at all, yet Saul should not have offered sacrifice; but this cost him dear, his soul and kingdom.

It is the greatest unkindness that can be showed to a friend, to adventure the complaining, bleeding, and grieving of his soul upon a light and a slight occasion. So it is the greatest unkindness that can be showed to God, Christ, and the Spirit, for a soul to put God upon complaining, Christ upon bleeding, and the Spirit upon grieving, by yielding to little sins. Therefore, when Satan says it is but a little one, do thou answer, that oftentimes there is the greatest unkindness showed to God's glorious majesty, in the acting of the least folly, and therefore thou wilt not displease thy best and greatest friend, by yielding to his greatest enemy.

Remedy (4). The fourth remedy against this device of Satan, is seriously to consider, *that there is great danger, yea, many*

---

[1] It was a vexation to king Lysimachus, that his staying to drink one small draught of water lost him his kingdom; and so it will eternally vex some souls at last that for one little sin, compared with great transgressions, they have lost God, heaven, and their souls for ever. (*Plutarch*)

times most danger, in the smallest sins. 'A little leaven leaveneth the whole lump' (1 Cor. 5:6). If the serpent wind in his head, he will draw in his whole body after. Greater sins do sooner startle the soul, and awaken and rouse up the soul to repentance, than lesser sins do. Little sins often slide into the soul, and breed, and work secretly and undiscernibly in the soul, till they come to be so strong, as to trample upon the soul, and to cut the throat of the soul. There is oftentimes greatest danger to our bodies in the least diseases that hang upon us, because we are apt to make light of them, and to neglect the timely use of means for removing of them, till they are grown so strong that they prove mortal to us. So there is most danger often in the least sins. We are apt to take no notice of them, and to neglect those heavenly helps whereby they should be weakened and destroyed, till they are grown to that strength, that we are ready to cry out, the medicine is too weak for the disease; I would pray, and I would hear, but I am afraid that sin is grown up by degrees to such a head, that I shall never be able to prevail over it; but as I have begun to fall, so I shall utterly fall before it, and at last perish in it, unless the power and free grace of Christ doth act gloriously, beyond my present apprehension and expectation. The viper is killed by the little young ones that are nourished and cherished in her belly; so are many men eternally killed and betrayed by the little sins, as they call them, that are nourished in their own bosoms.[1]

---

[1] Caesar was stabbed with bodkins. Pope Adrian was choked with a gnat. A scorpion is little, yet able to sting a lion to death. A mouse is but little, yet killeth an elephant, if he gets up into his trunk. The leopard being great, is poisoned with a head of garlic. The smallest errors prove many times most dangerous. It is as much treason to coin pence as bigger pieces.

I know not, saith one, whether the maintenance of the least sin be not worse than the commission of the greatest: for this may be of frailty, that argues obstinacy. A little hole in the ship sinks it; a small breach in a sea-bank carries away all before it; a little stab at the heart kills a man; and a little sin, without a great deal of mercy, will damn a man.[1]

Remedy (5). The fifth remedy against this device of Satan, is solemnly to consider, *that other saints have chosen to suffer the worst of torments, rather than they would commit the least sin, i.e.* such as the world accounts.[2] So as you may see in Daniel and his companions, that would rather choose to burn, and be cast to the lions, than they would bow to the image that Nebuchadnezzar had set up. When this peccadillo, in the world's account, and a hot fiery furnace stood in competition, that they must either fall into sin, or be cast into the fiery furnace, such was their tenderness of the honour and glory of God, and their hatred and indignation against sin, that they would rather burn than sin; they knew that it was far better to burn for their not sinning, than that God and conscience should raise a hell, a fire in their bosoms for sin.[3]

I have read of that noble servant of God, Marcus Aurelius minister of a church in the time of Constantine, who in

[1] One little miscarriage doth, in the eyes of the world, overshadow all a Christian's graces, as one cloud doth sometimes overshadow the whole body of the sun.

[2] It is better to die with hunger, than to eat that which is offered to idols. (*Augustine*)

[3] Many heathens would rather die than cozen or cheat one another so faithful were they one to another. Will not these rise in judgment against many professors in these days who make nothing of over-reaching one another?

Constantine's time had been the cause of overthrowing an idol's temple; afterwards, when Julian came to be emperor, he would force the people of that place to build it up again. They were ready to do it, but he refused; whereupon those that were his own people, to whom he preached, took him, and stripped him of all his clothes, and abused his naked body, and gave it up to the children, to lance it with their pen-knives, and then caused him to be put in a basket, and anointed his naked body with honey, and set him in the sun, to be stung with wasps. And all this cruelty they showed, because he would not do anything towards the building up of this idol temple; nay, they came to this, that if he would do but the least towards it, if he would give but a halfpenny to it, they would save him. But he refused all, though the giving of a halfpenny might have saved his life; and in doing this, he did but live up to that principle that most Christians talk of, and all profess, but few come up to, viz. that we must choose rather to suffer the worst of torments that men and devils can invent and inflict, than to commit the least sin whereby God should be dishonoured, our consciences wounded, religion reproached, and our own souls endangered.

Remedy (6). The sixth remedy against this device of Satan is, seriously to consider, *that the soul is never able to stand under the guilt and weight of the least sin, when God shall set it home upon the soul.* The least sin will press and sink the stoutest sinner as low as hell, when God shall open the eyes of a sinner, and make him see the horrid filthiness and abominable vileness that is in sin. What so little, base, and vile creatures as lice or gnats, and yet by these little poor creatures, God so plagued stout-hearted Pharaoh, and all Egypt, that, fainting under it, they were forced to cry out, 'This is the finger of God' (Exod. 8:19). When little creatures, yea, the least creatures, shall be armed with a power from God, they shall press and sink down the greatest, proudest, and stoutest tyrants that breathe.[1] So when God shall cast a sword into the hand of a little sin, and arm it against the soul, the soul will faint and fall under it. Some, who have but projected adultery, without any actual acting it; and others, having found a trifle, and made no conscience to restore it, knowing, by the light of natural conscience, that they did not do as they would be done by; and others, that have had some unworthy thought of God, have been so frightened, amazed, and terrified for those sins, which are small in men's account, that they have wished they had never been; that they could take no delight in any earthly comfort, that they have been put to their wits' end, ready to make away themselves, wishing themselves annihilated.[2]

William Perkins mentions a good man, but very poor, who, being ready to starve, stole a lamb, and being about to eat it with his poor children, and as his manner was afore meat, to crave a blessing, durst not do it, but fell into a great perplexity of conscience, and acknowledged his fault to the owner, promising payment if ever he should be able.

Remedy (7). The seventh remedy against this device is, solemnly to consider, *that there is more evil in the least sin than in the greatest affliction*; and this appears as clear as the sun,

---

[1] The tyrant Maximinus, who had set forth his proclamation engraved in brass for the utter abolishing of Christ and his religion, was eaten of lice.

[2] One drop of an evil conscience swallows up the whole sea of worldly joy. How great a pain, not to be borne, comes from the prick of this small thorn, said one.

by the severe dealing of God the Father with his beloved Son, who let all the vials of his fiercest wrath upon him, and that for the least sin as well as for the greatest.

'The wages of sin is death' (Rom. 6:23); of sin indefinitely, whether great or small.[1] Oh! how should this make us tremble, as much at the least spark of lust as at hell itself; considering that God the Father would not spare his bosom Son, no, not for the least sin, but would make him drink the dregs of his wrath!

And so much for the remedies that may fence and preserve our souls from being drawn to sin by this third device of Satan.

DEVICE 4. *By presenting to the soul the best men's sins, and by hiding from the soul their virtues; by showing the soul their sins, and by hiding from the soul their sorrows and repentance*: as by setting before the soul the adultery of David, the pride of Hezekiah, the impatience of Job, the drunkenness of Noah, the blasphemy of Peter, etc., and by hiding from the soul the tears, the sighs, the groans, the meltings, the humblings, and repentings of these precious souls.

Remedy (1). The first remedy against this device of Satan is, seriously to consider, *that the Spirit of the Lord hath been as careful to note the saints' rising by repentance out of sin, as he hath to note their falling into sins.* David fails fearfully, but by repentance he rises sweetly: 'Blot out my transgressions, wash me thoroughly from my iniquity, cleanse me from my sin; for

---

[1] Death is the heir of the least sin; the best wages that the least sin gives his soldiers is, death of all sorts. In a strict sense, there is no little sin, because no little God to sin against.

I acknowledge my transgressions, and my sin is ever before me. Purge me with hyssop, and I shall be clean; wash me, and I shall be whiter than snow; deliver me from blood-guiltiness, O God, thou God of my salvation.' It is true, Hezekiah's heart was lifted up under the abundance of mercy that God had cast in upon him; and it is as true that Hezekiah humbled himself for the pride of his heart, so that the wrath of the Lord came not upon him, nor upon Jerusalem, in the days of Hezekiah. It is true, Job curses the day of his birth, and it is as true that he rises by repentance; 'Behold, I am vile,' saith he; 'what shall I answer thee? I will lay my hand upon my mouth. Once have I spoken, but I will not answer; yea twice, but I will proceed no further. I have heard of thee by the hearing of the ear, but now mine eye seeth thee; wherefore I abhor myself, and repent in dust and ashes' (Job 40:4, 5; 42:5, 6).[1] Peter falls dreadfully, but rises by repentance sweetly; a look of love from Christ melts him into tears. He knew that repentance was the key to the kingdom of grace. As once his faith was so great that he leapt, as it were, into a sea of waters to come to Christ; so now his repentance was so great that he leapt, as it were, into a sea of tears, for that he had gone from Christ. Some say that, after his sad fall, he was ever and anon weeping, and that his face was even furrowed with continual tears. He had no sooner took in poison but he vomited it up again, ere it got to the vitals; he had no sooner handled this serpent but he turned it into a rod to scourge his soul with remorse for sinning against such clear light, and strong love, and sweet discoveries of the heart of Christ to him.[2]

[1] Tertullian saith that he was (*nulli rei natus nisi poenitentae*) born for no other purpose but to repent.

[2] Luther confesses that, before his conversion, he met not with a more

Clement notes that Peter so repented, that all his life after, every night when he heard the cock crow, he would fall upon his knees, and, weeping bitterly, would beg pardon of his sin. Ah, souls, you can easily sin as the saints, but can you repent with the saints? Many can sin with David and Peter, that cannot repent with David and Peter, and so must perish for ever.

Theodosius the emperor, pressing that he might receive the Lord's supper, excuses his own foul act by David's doing the like: to which Ambrose replies, Thou hast followed David transgressing, follow David repenting, and then think thou of the table of the Lord.

Remedy (2). The second remedy against this device of Satan is, solemnly to consider, *that these saints did not make a trade of sin.* They fell once or twice, and rose by repentance, that they might keep the closer to Christ for ever. They fell accidentally, occasionally, and with much reluctancy;[1] and thou sinnest presumptuously, obstinately, readily, delightfully, and customarily. Thou hast, by thy making a trade of sin, contracted upon thy soul a kind of cursed necessity of sinning, that thou canst as well cease to be, or cease to live, as thou canst cease to sin. Sin is, by custom, become as another nature to thee, which thou canst not, which thou wilt not lay aside, though thou knowest that if thou dost not lay sin aside, God will lay thy soul aside for ever; though thou knowest that if sin and thy soul do not part, Christ and thy soul can never meet. If thou wilt make a trade of sin, and cry out, 'Did not David sin

---

displeasing word in all his study of divinity than repent, but afterward he took delight in the word.

[1] The saints cannot sin with a whole will, but, as it were, with a half will, an unwillingness; not with a full consent, but with a dissenting consent.

thus, and Noah sin thus, and Peter sin thus?' No! their hearts
turned aside to folly one day, but thy heart turns aside to folly
every day (2 Pet. 2:14; Prov. 4:16); and when they were fallen,
they rise by repentance, and by the actings of faith upon a cru-
cified Christ;[1] but thou fallest, and hast no strength nor will
to rise, but wallowest in sin, and wilt eternally die in thy sins,
unless the Lord be the more merciful to thy soul. Dost thou
think, O soul, this is good reasoning? Such a one tasted poison
but once, and yet narrowly escaped; but I do daily drink poi-
son, yet I shall escape. Yet such is the mad reasoning of vain
souls. David and Peter sinned once foully and fearfully; they
tasted poison but once, and were sick to death; but I taste it
daily, and yet shall not taste of eternal death. Remember, O
souls! that the day is at hand when self-flatterers will be found
self-deceivers, yea, self-murderers.

Remedy (3). The third remedy against this device of Satan is,
seriously to consider, *that though God doth not, nor never will,
disinherit his people for their sins, yet he hath severely punished
his people for their sins.* David sins, and God breaks his bones
for his sin: 'Make me to hear joy and gladness, that the bones
which thou hast broken may rejoice' (Psa. 51:8). 'And because
thou hast done this, the sword shall never depart from thy
house, to the day of thy death' (2 Sam. 12:10). Though God
will not utterly take from them his loving-kindness, nor suffer
his faithfulness to fail, nor break his covenant, nor alter the
thing that is gone out of his mouth, yet will he 'visit their
transgression with the rod, and their iniquity with stripes'

---

[1] Though sin do (*habitare*) dwell in the regenerate, as Austin notes,
yet it doth not (*regnare*) reign over the regenerate; they rise by repent-
ance.

(Psa. 89:30, 35). The Scripture abounds with instances of this kind. This is so known a truth among all that know anything of truth, that to cite more scriptures to prove it would be to light a candle to see the sun at noon.[1]

The Jews have a proverb, 'That there is no punishment comes upon Israel in which there is not one ounce of the golden calf'; meaning that that was so great a sin, as that in every plague God remembered it; that it had an influence into every trouble that befell them. Every man's heart may say to him in his sufferings, as the heart of Apollodorus in the kettle, 'I have been the cause of this.' God is most angry when he shows no anger. God keep me from this mercy; this kind of mercy is worse than all other kinds of misery.

One writing to a sick friend hath this expression: 'I account it a part of unhappiness not to know adversity; I judge you to be miserable, because you have not been miserable.'[2] It is mercy that our affliction is not execution, but a correction.[3] He that hath deserved hanging, may be glad if he escape with a whipping. God's corrections are our instructions, his lashes our lessons, his scourges our schoolmasters, his chastisements our advertisements;[4] and to note this, both the Hebrews and the Greeks express chastening and teaching by one and the same word (*musar, paideia*),[5] because the latter is the true end

[1] Josephus reports that, not long after the Jews had crucified Christ on the cross, so many of them were condemned to be crucified, that there were not places enough for crosses, nor crosses enough for the bodies that were to be hung thereon.

[2] *Qui non est cruciatus non est Christianus*, saith Luther, there is not a Christian that carries not his cross.

[3] Psa. 94:12; Prov. 3:12, 13, 16; Obad. 6:13; Isa. 9:1, *et seq.*

[4] Admonitions.

[5] Prov. 3:11, and Heb. 12:5, 7, 8, 11.

of the former, according to that in the proverb, 'Smart makes
wit, and vexation gives understanding.' Whence Luther fitly
calls affliction 'The Christian man's divinity.' So saith Job
(chap. 33:14-19), 'God speaketh once, yea, twice, yet man per-
ceiveth it not. In a dream, in a vision of the night, when deep
sleep falleth upon men, in slumberings upon the bed; then he
openeth the ears of men, and sealeth their instruction, that
he may withdraw man from his purpose and hide pride from
man. He keepeth back his soul from the pit, and his life from
perishing by the sword.' When Satan shall tell thee of other
men's sins to draw thee to sin, do thou then think of the same
men's sufferings to keep thee from sin. Lay thy hand upon thy
heart, and say, 'O my soul! if thou sinnest with David, thou
must suffer with David.'

Remedy (4). The fourth remedy against this device of Satan
is, solemnly to consider, *that there are but two main ends of
God's recording of the falls of his saints.*

And the one is, to keep those from fainting, sinking, and
despair, under the burden of their sins, who fall through
weakness and infirmity.

And the other is, that their falls may be as landmarks to
warn others that stand, to take heed lest they fall. It never
entered into the heart of God to record his children's sins,
that others might be encouraged to sin, but that others might
look to their standings, and hang the faster upon the skirts
of Christ, and avoid all occasions and temptations that may
occasion the soul to fall, as others have fallen, when they have
been left by Christ. The Lord hath made their sins as land-
marks, to warn his people to take heed how they come near
those sands and rocks, those snares and baits, that have been

fatal to the choicest treasures, to wit, the joy, peace, comfort, and glorious enjoyments of the bravest spirits and noblest souls that ever sailed through the ocean of this sinful troublesome world; as you may see in David, Job, and Peter. There is nothing in the world that can so notoriously cross the grand end of God's recording of the sins of his saints, than for any from thence to take encouragement to sin; and wherever you find such a soul, you may write him Christless, graceless, a soul cast off by God, a soul that Satan hath by the hand, and the eternal God knows whither he will lead him.[1]

DEVICE 5. *To present God to the soul as one made up all of mercy.* Oh! saith Satan, you need not make such a matter of sin, you need not be so fearful of sin, not so unwilling to sin; for God is a God of mercy, a God full of mercy, a God that delights in mercy, a God that is ready to show mercy, a God that is never weary of showing mercy, a God more prone to pardon his people than to punish his people; and therefore he will not take advantage against the soul; and why then, saith Satan, should you make such a matter of sin?

Remedy (1). The first remedy is, seriously to consider, *that it is the sorest judgment in the world to be left to sin upon any pretence whatsoever.* O unhappy man! when God leaveth thee to thyself, and doth not resist thee in thy sins.[2] Woe, woe to him at whose sins God doth wink. When God lets the way to hell

---

[1] I have known a good man, saith Bernard, who, when he heard of any that had committed some notorious sin, he was wont to say with himself, '*Ille hodie et ego cras,*' he fell today, so may I tomorrow.

[2] *Humanum est peccare, diabolicum perseverare, et angelicum resurgere* (*Augustine*): *i.e.* it is a human thing to fall into sin, a devilish to persevere therein, and an angelical (or supernatural) to rise from it.

be a smooth and pleasant way, that is hell on this side hell, and
a dreadful sign of God's indignation against a man; a token of
his rejection, and that God doth not intend good unto him.
That is a sad word, 'Ephraim is joined to idols: let him alone'
(Hos. 4:17); he will be uncounsellable and incorrigible; he hath
made a match with mischief, he shall have his bellyful of it;
he falls with open eyes; let him fall at his own peril. And that
is a terrible saying, 'So I gave them up unto their own hearts'
lusts, and they walked in their own counsels' (Psa. 81:12). A
soul given up to sin is a soul ripe for hell, a soul posting to
destruction. Ah Lord! this mercy I humbly beg, that whatever
thou givest me up to, thou wilt not give me up to the ways
of my own heart; if thou wilt give me up to be afflicted, or
tempted, or reproached, I will patiently sit down, and say, 'it
is the Lord; let him do with me what seems good in his own
eyes.' Do anything with me, lay what burden thou wilt upon
me, so thou dost not give me up to the ways of my own heart.[1]

Remedy (2). The second remedy against this device of Satan
is, solemnly to consider, *that God is as just as he is merciful*. As
the Scriptures speak him out to be a very merciful God, so
they speak him out to be a very just God. Witness his casting
the angels out of heaven (2 Pet. 2:4) and his binding them in
chains of darkness[2] till the judgment of the great day; and
witness his turning Adam out of Paradise, his drowning of
the old world, and his raining hell out of heaven upon Sodom;
and witness all the crosses, losses, sicknesses, and diseases,
that be in the world; and witness Tophet, that was prepared

---

[1] *A me, me salva Domine*; Deliver me, O Lord, from that evil man
myself. (*Augustine*)

[2] God hanged them up in gibbets, as it were, that others might hear
and fear, and do no more so wickedly.

of old; witness his 'treasuring up of wrath against the day of wrath, unto the revelation of the just judgments of God'; but above all, witness the pouring forth of all his wrath upon his bosom Son, when he did bear the sins of his people, and cried out, 'My God, my God, why hast thou forsaken me?' (Matt. 27:46).

Remedy (3). The third remedy against this device of Satan is, seriously to consider, *that sins against mercy will bring the greatest and sorest judgments upon men's heads and hearts.* Mercy is Alpha, Justice is Omega. David, speaking of these attributes, placeth mercy in the foreward, and justice in the rearward, saying, 'My song shall be of mercy and judgment' (Psa. 101:1). When mercy is despised, then justice takes the throne.[1] God is like a prince, that sends not his army against rebels before he hath sent his pardon, and proclaimed it by a herald of arms: he first hangs out the white flag of mercy; if this wins men in, they are happy for ever; but if they stand out, then God will put forth his red flag of justice and judgment; if the one is despised, the other shall be felt with a witness.[2]

See this in the Israelites. He loved them and chose them when they were in their blood, and most unlovely. He multiplied them, not by means, but by miracle; from seventy souls they grew in few years to six hundred thousand; the more they were oppressed, the more they prospered. Like camomile, the more you tread it, the more you spread it; or to a palm-tree,

---

[1] *Quanto gradus altior, tanto casus gravior*; the higher we are in dignity, the more grievous is our fall and misery.

[2] *Deus tardus est ad iram, sed tarditatem gravitate poena compensat*: God is slow to anger, but he recompenseth his slowness with grievousness of punishment. If we abuse mercy to serve our lust, then, in Salvian's phrase, God will rain hell out of heaven, rather than not visit for such sins.

the more it is pressed, the further it spreadeth; or to fire, the more it is raked, the more it burneth. Their mercies came in upon them like Job's messengers, one upon the neck of the other: He put off their sackcloth, and girded them with gladness, and 'compassed them about with songs of deliverance'; he 'carried them on the wings of eagles'; he kept them 'as the apple of his eye,' etc.[1] But they, abusing his mercy, became the greatest objects of his wrath. As I know not the man that can reckon up their mercies, so I know not the man that can sum up the miseries that are come upon them for their sins. For as our Saviour prophesied concerning Jerusalem, 'that a stone should not be left upon a stone,' so it was fulfilled forty years after his ascension, by Vespasian the emperor and his son Titus, who, having besieged Jerusalem, the Jews were oppressed with a grievous famine, in which their food was old shoes, leather, old hay, and the dung of beasts. There died, partly of the sword and partly of the famine, eleven hundred thousand of the poorer sort; two thousand in one night were embowelled; six thousand were burned in a porch of the temple; the whole city was sacked and burned, and laid level to the ground; and ninety-seven thousand taken captives, and applied to base and miserable service, as Eusebius and Josephus saith.[2] And to this day, in all parts of the world, are they not the off-scouring of the world? None less beloved, and none more abhorred, than they.[3]

[1] Psa. 32:75; Exod. 19:4; Deut. 32:10.

[2] Vespasian brake into their city at Kedron, where they took Christ, on the same feast day that Christ was taken; he whipped them where they whipped Christ; he sold twenty Jews for a penny, as they sold Christ for thirty pence.

[3] Men are therefore worse, because they ought to be better; and

And so Capernaum, that was lifted up to heaven, was threatened to be thrown down to hell. No souls fall so low into hell, if they fall, as those souls that by a hand of mercy are lifted up nearest to heaven. You slight souls that are so apt to abuse mercy, consider this, that in the gospel days, the plagues that God inflicts upon the despisers and abusers of mercy are usually spiritual plagues; as blindness of mind, hardness of heart, benumbedness of conscience, which are ten thousand times worse than the worst of outward plagues that can befall you. And therefore, though you may escape temporal judgments, yet you shall not escape spiritual judgments: 'How shall we escape, if we neglect so great salvation?' (Heb. 2:3) saith the apostle. Oh! therefore, whenever Satan shall present God to the soul as one made up all of mercy, that he may draw thee to do wickedly, say unto him, that sins against mercy will bring upon the soul the greatest misery; and therefore whatever becomes of thee, thou wilt not sin against mercy.

Remedy (4). The fourth remedy against this device of Satan, is seriously to consider, *that though God's general mercy be over all his works, yet his special mercy is confined to those that are divinely qualified.*[1] So in Exodus 34:6, 7: 'And the Lord passed by before him, and proclaimed. The Lord, the Lord God, merciful and gracious, longsuffering, and abundant in goodness

---

shall be deeper in hell, because heaven was offered unto them; but they would not. Good turns aggravate unkindnesses, and men's offences are increased by their obligations.

[1] Augustus, in his solemn feasts, gave trifles to some, but gold to others that his heart was most set upon. So God, by a hand of general mercy, gives these—poor trifles—outward blessings, to those that he least loves; but his gold, his special mercy, is only towards those that his heart is most set upon.

and truth, keeping mercy for thousands, forgiving iniquity, transgression, and sin, and that will by no means clear the guilty.' Exod. 20:6, 'And showing mercy unto thousands of them that love me, and keep my commandments.' Psa. 25:10, 'All the paths of the Lord are mercy and truth, unto such as keep his covenant and his testimonies.' Psa. 32:10, 'Many sorrows shall be to the wicked: but he that trusteth in the Lord, mercy shall compass him about.' Psa. 33:18, 'Behold, the eye of the Lord is upon them that fear him, upon them that hope in his mercy.' Psa. 103:11, 'For as the heaven is high above the earth, so great is his mercy toward them that fear him.' Verse 17, 'But the mercy of the Lord is from everlasting to everlasting upon them that fear him.' When Satan attempts to draw thee to sin by presenting God as a God all made up of mercy, oh then reply, that though God's general mercy extend to all the works of his hand, yet his special mercy is confined to them that are divinely qualified, to them that love him and keep his commandments, to them that trust in him, that by hope hang upon him, and that fear him; and that thou must be such a one here, or else thou canst never be happy hereafter; thou must partake of his special mercy, or else eternally perish in everlasting misery, notwithstanding God's general mercy.

Remedy (5). The fifth remedy against this device of Satan is, solemnly to consider, *that those that were once glorious on earth, and are now triumphing in heaven, did look upon the mercy of God as the most powerful argument to preserve them from sin, and to fence their souls against sin, and not as an encouragement to sin.* Psa. 26:3-5: 'For thy loving-kindness is before mine eyes, and I have walked in thy truth; I have not sat with vain persons, neither will I go in with dissemblers. I have hated the congregation of evildoers, and will not sit with the wicked.' So Joseph strengthens himself against sin from the remembrance of mercy: 'How then can I,' saith he, 'do this great wickedness, and sin against God?' (Gen. 39:9). He had his eye fixed upon mercy, and therefore sin could not enter, though the irons entered into his soul; his soul being taken with mercy, was not moved with his mistress's impudence. Satan knocked oft at the door, but the sight of mercy would not suffer him to answer or open. Joseph, like a pearl in a puddle, keeps his virtue still.[1] So Paul: 'Shall we continue in sin, that grace may abound? God forbid. How shall we that are dead to sin, live any longer therein?' (Rom. 6:1, 2). There is nothing in the world that renders a man more unlike to a saint, and more like to Satan, than to argue from mercy to sinful liberty; from divine goodness to licentiousness. This is the devil's logic, and in whomsoever you find it, you may write, 'This soul is lost.' A man may as truly say, the sea burns, or fire cools, as that free grace and mercy should make a truly gracious soul to do wickedly. So the same apostle: 'I beseech you therefore, brethren, by the mercies of God, that ye present your bodies a living sacrifice, holy, acceptable unto God, which is your reasonable service' (Rom. 12:1). So John: 'These things I write unto you, that ye sin not' (1 John 2:1, 2). What was it that he wrote? He wrote: 'That we might have fellowship with the Father and his Son; and that the blood of Christ cleanseth us from all sin; and that if we confess our sin, he is faithful and just to forgive us our sins; and that if we do sin, we have an advocate with

---

[1] The stone called *Pontaurus*, is of that virtue, that it preserves him that carries it from taking any hurt by poison. The mercy of God in Christ to our souls is the most precious stone or pearl in the world, to prevent us from being poisoned with sin.

the Father, Jesus Christ the righteous.' These choice favours and mercies the apostle holds forth as the choicest means to preserve the soul from sin, and to keep at the greatest distance from sin; and if this will not do it, you may write the man void of Christ and grace, and undone for ever.

DEVICE 6. *By persuading the soul that the work of repentance is an easy work, and that therefore the soul need not make such a matter of sin.* Why! Suppose you do sin, saith Satan, it is no such difficult thing to return, and confess, and be sorrowful, and beg pardon, and cry, 'Lord, have mercy upon me!' and if you do but this, God will cut the score,[1] and pardon your sins, and save your souls.

By this device Satan draws many a soul to sin, and makes many millions of souls servants or rather slaves to sin.

Remedy (1). The first remedy is, seriously to consider, *that repentance is a mighty work, a difficult work, a work that is above our power.* There is no power below that power that raised Christ from the dead, and that made the world, that can break the heart of a sinner or turn the heart of a sinner. Thou art as well able to melt adamant, as to melt thine own heart; to turn a flint into flesh, as to turn thine own heart to the Lord; to raise the dead and to make a world, as to repent. Repentance is a flower that grows not in nature's garden. 'Can the Ethiopian change his skin, or the leopard his spots? then may ye also do good, that are accustomed to do evil' (Jer. 13:23). Repentance is a gift that comes down from above.[2] Men are not born with

---

[1] To cut the score = to forgive a debt.

[2] Fallen man hath lost the command of himself, and the command of the creatures. And certainly he that cannot command himself cannot repent of himself.

repentance in their hearts, as they are born with tongues in their mouths; (Acts 5:31): 'Him hath God exalted with his right hand to be a Prince and a Saviour, for to give repentance to Israel, and forgiveness of sins.' So in 2 Tim. 2:25: 'In meekness instructing them that oppose themselves; if God peradventure will give them repentance to the acknowledging of the truth.' It is not in the power of any mortal to repent at pleasure.[1] Some ignorant deluded souls vainly conceit that these five words, 'Lord! have mercy upon me,' are efficacious to send them to heaven; but as many are undone by buying a counterfeit jewel, so many are in hell by mistake of their repentance. Many rest in their repentance, though it may be but the shadow of repentance, which caused one to say, 'Repentance damneth more than sin.'

Remedy (2). The second remedy against this device of Satan is, solemnly to consider of *the nature of true repentance.* Repentance is some other thing than what vain men conceive.[2]

Repentance is sometimes taken, in a more strict and narrow sense, for godly sorrow; sometimes repentance is taken, in a large sense, for amendment of life. Repentance hath in it three things, viz.:

The act, subject, terms.

[1] It was a vain brag of king Cyrus, that caused it to be written upon his tombstone. 'I could do all things'; so could Paul too, but it was 'through Christ, which strengthened him.'

[2] The Hebrew word for repentance signifies to return, implying a going back from what a man had done. It notes a turning or converting from one thing to another, from sin to God. The Greeks have two words by which they express the nature of repentance, one signifies to be careful, anxious, solicitous, after a thing is done; the other word denotes afterwit, or after-wisdom, the mind's recovering of wisdom, or growing wiser.

(1) *The formal act of repentance is a changing and converting.* It is often set forth in Scripture by turning. 'Turn thou me, and I shall be turned,' saith Ephraim; 'after that I was turned, I repented,' saith he (Jer. 31:18, 19). It is a turning from darkness to light.

(2) *The subject changed and converted is the whole man*; it is both the sinner's heart and life; first his heart, then his life; first his person, then his practice and conversation. 'Wash you, make you clean,' there is the change of their persons; 'Put away the evil of your doings from before mine eyes; cease to do evil, learn to do well' (Isa. 1:16, 17); there is the change of their practices. So 'Cast away,' saith Ezekiel, 'all your transgressions whereby you have transgressed'; there is the change of the life; 'and make you a new heart and a new spirit' (18:31): there is the change of the heart.

(3) *The terms of this change and conversion, from which and to which both heart and life must be changed; from sin to God.* The heart must be changed from the state and power of sin, the life from the acts of sin, but both unto God; the heart to be under his power in a state of grace, the life to be under his rule in all new obedience; as the apostle speaks, 'To open their eyes and to turn them from darkness to light, and from the power of Satan unto God' (Acts 26:18). So the prophet Isaiah saith, 'Let the wicked forsake his way, and the unrighteous man his thoughts, and let him return unto the Lord' (55:7).

Thus much of the nature of evangelical repentance. Now, souls, tell me whether it be such an easy thing to repent, as Satan doth suggest. Besides what hath been spoken, I desire that you will take notice, that repentance doth include turning from the most darling sin. Ephraim shall say, 'What have I to do any more with idols?' (Hos. 14:8). Yea, it is a turning

from all sin to God (Ezek. 18:30): 'Therefore I will judge you,
O house of Israel, every one according to his ways, saith the
Lord God. Repent, and turn yourselves from your transgres-
sions; so iniquity shall not be your ruin.' Herod turned from
many, but turned not from his Herodias, which was his ruin.
Judas turned from all visible wickedness, yet he would not
cast out that golden devil covetousness, and therefore was cast
into the hottest place in hell. He that turns not from every
sin, turns not aright from any one sin. Every sin strikes at
the honour of God, the being of God, the glory of God, the
heart of Christ, the joy of the Spirit, and the peace of a man's
conscience; and therefore a soul truly penitent strikes at all,
hates all, conflicts with all, and will labour to draw strength
from a crucified Christ to crucify all. A true penitent knows
neither father nor mother, neither right eye nor right hand,
but will pluck out the one and cut off the other. Saul spared
but one Agag, and that cost him his soul and his kingdom
(1 Sam. 15:9). Besides, repentance is not only a turning from
all sin, but also a turning to all good; to a love of all good, to
a prizing of all good, and to a following after all good (Ezek.
18:21): 'But if the wicked will turn from all his sins that he
hath committed, and keep all my statutes, and do that which
is lawful and right, he shall surely live, he shall not die'; that
is, only negative righteousness and holiness is no righteous-
ness nor holiness.[1] David fulfilled *all* the will of God, and had
respect unto all his commandments, and so had Zacharias
and Elizabeth. It is not enough that the tree bears not ill fruit;

[1] It is said of Ithacus, that the hatred of the Priscillian heresy was
all the virtue that he had. The evil servant did not riot out his talent
(Matt. 25:18). Those reprobates (Matt. 25:41-45), robbed not the saints,
but relieved them not; for this they must eternally perish.

but it must bring forth good fruit, else it must be 'cut down and cast into the fire' (Luke 13:7). So it is not enough that you are not thus and thus wicked, but you must be thus and thus gracious and good, else divine justice will put the axe of divine vengeance to the root of your souls, and cut you off for ever. 'Every tree that bringeth not forth good fruit is hewed down and cast into the fire' (Matt. 3:10). Besides, repentance doth include a sensibleness of sin's sinfulness, how opposite and contrary it is to the blessed God. God is light, sin is darkness; God is life, sin is death; God is heaven, sin is hell; God is beauty, sin is deformity.

Also true repentance includes a sensibleness of sin's mischievousness; how it cast angels out of heaven, and Adam out of paradise; how it laid the first corner stone in hell, and brought in all the curses, crosses, and miseries, that be in the world; and how it makes men liable to all temporal, spiritual and eternal wrath; how it hath made men Godless, Christless, hopeless and heavenless.

Further, true repentance doth include sorrow for sin, contrition of heart. It breaks the heart with sighs, and sobs, and groans, for that a loving God and Father is by sin offended, a blessed Saviour afresh crucified, and the sweet Comforter, the Spirit, grieved and vexed.

Again, repentance doth include, not only a loathing of sin, but also a loathing of ourselves for sin. As a man doth not only loathe poison, but he loathes the very dish or vessel that hath the smell of the poison; so a true penitent doth not only loathe his sin, but he loathes himself, the vessel that smells of it; so Ezek. 20:43: 'And there shall ye remember your ways and all your doings, wherein ye have been defiled; and ye shall loathe yourselves in your own sight for all your evils that ye have committed.' True repentance will work your hearts, not only to loathe your sins, but to loathe yourselves.[1]

Again, true repentance doth not only work a man to loathe himself for his sins, but it makes him ashamed of his sin also: 'What fruit had ye in those things whereof ye are now ashamed?' saith the apostle (Rom. 6:21). So Ezekiel: 'And thou shalt be confounded for all that thou hast done, saith the Lord God' (16:63). When a penitent soul sees his sins pardoned, the anger of God pacified, the divine justice satisfied, then he sits down and blushes, as the Hebrew hath it, as one ashamed. Yea, true repentance doth work a man to cross his sinful self, and to walk contrary to sinful self, to take a holy revenge upon sin, as you may see in Paul, the jailor, Mary Magdalene, and Manasseh. This the apostle shows in 2 Cor. 7:10, 11: 'For godly sorrow worketh repentance never to be repented of; but the sorrow of the world worketh death. For behold the self-same thing, that ye sorrowed after a godly sort, what carefulness it wrought in you, yea, what clearing of yourselves, yea, what indignation, yea, what fear, yea, what vehement desire, yea, what zeal, yea, what revenge.'[2] Now souls, sum up all these things together, and tell me whether it would be such an easy thing to repent as Satan would make the soul to believe, and I am confident your heart will answer that it is as hard a thing to repent as it is to make a world, or raise the dead.

---

[1] True repentance is a sorrowing for sin, as it is an offence to God and against God. This both comes from God, and drives a man to God, as it did the church in the Canticles, and the prodigal.

[2] So much the more God hath been displeased with the blackness of sin, the more will he be pleased with the blushing of the sinner (*Bernard*). They that do not burn now in zeal against sin must ere long burn in hell for sin.

I shall conclude this second remedy with a worthy saying of a precious holy man: 'Repentance,' saith he, 'strips us stark naked of all the garments of the old Adam, and leaves not so much as a shirt behind.' In this rotten building it leaves not a stone upon a stone. As the flood drowned Noah's own friends and servants, so must the flood of repenting tears drown our sweetest and most profitable sins.

Remedy (3). The third remedy against this device of Satan is seriously to consider, *that repentance is a continued act. The word repent implies the continuation of it.* True repentance inclines a man's heart to perform God's statutes always, even unto the end. A true penitent must go on from faith to faith, from strength to strength; he must never stand still nor turn back. Repentance is a grace, and must have its daily operation as well as other graces. True repentance is a continued spring, where the waters of godly sorrow are always flowing: 'My sin is ever before me' (Psa. 51:3). A true penitent is often casting his eyes back to the days of his former vanity, and this makes him morning and evening to 'water his couch with his tears.' 'Remember not against me the sins of my youth,' saith one blessed penitent; and 'I was a blasphemer, and a persecutor, and injurious,' saith another penitent.[1] Repentance is a continued act of turning, a repentance never to be repented of, a turning never to turn again to folly. A true penitent hath ever something within him to turn from; he can never get near enough to God; no, not so near him as once he was; and therefore he is still turning and turning that he may get nearer and nearer to him, that is his chiefest good and his only happiness, *optimum maximum*, the best and the greatest.

[1] Psa. 6:6; 23. 5; Tim. 1:13.

They are every day a-crying out, 'O wretched men that we are, who shall deliver us from this body of death!' (Rom. 7:24). They are still sensible of sin, and still conflicting with sin, and still sorrowing for sin, and still loathing of themselves for sin. Repentance is no transient act, but a continued act of the soul. And tell me, O tempted soul, whether it be such an easy thing as Satan would make thee believe, to be every day a-turning more and more from sin, and a-turning nearer and nearer to God, thy choicest blessedness. A true penitent can as easily content himself with one act of faith, or one act of love, as he can content himself with one act of repentance.

A Jewish Rabbi, pressing the practice of repentance upon his disciples, and exhorting them to be sure to repent the day before they died, one of them replied, that the day of any man's death was very uncertain, 'Repent, therefore, every day,' said the Rabbi, 'and then you shall be sure to repent the day before you die.' You are wise, and know how to apply it to your own advantage.

Remedy (4). The fourth remedy against this device of Satan is solemnly to consider, *that if the work of repentance were such an easy work as Satan would make it to be, then certainly so many would not lie roaring and crying out of wrath and eternal ruin under the horrors and terrors of conscience, for not repenting; yea, doubtless, so many millions would not go to hell for not repenting, if it were such an easy thing to repent.*[1] Ah, do not poor souls

---

[1] If thou be backward in the thoughts of repentance, be forward in the thoughts of hell, the flames whereof only the streams of the penitent eye can extinguish (*Tertullian*). Oh, how shalt thou tear and rend thyself! how shalt thou lament fruitless repenting! What wilt thou say? Woe is me, that I have not cast off the burden of sin; woe is me, that I have not washed away my spots, but am now pierced with mine iniquities; now have I lost the surpassing joy of angels! (*Basil*)

under horror of conscience cry out and say, Were all this world a lump of gold, and in our hand to dispose of, we would give it for the least drachm of true repentance! and wilt thou say it is an easy thing to repent? When a poor sinner, whose conscience is awakened, shall judge the exchange of all the world for the least drachm of repentance to be the happiest exchange that ever sinner made, tell me, O soul, is it good going to hell? Is it good dwelling with the devouring fire, with everlasting burnings? Is it good to be for ever separated from the blessed and glorious presence of God, and saints, and to be for ever shut out from those good things of eternal life, which are so many, that they exceed number; so great, that they exceed measure; so precious, that they exceed all estimation? We know it is the greatest misery that can befall the sons of men; and would they not prevent this by repentance, if it were such an easy thing to repent as Satan would have it? Well, then, do not run the hazard of losing God, Christ, heaven, and thy soul for ever, by hearkening to this device of Satan, viz. that it is an easy thing to repent. If it be so easy, why, then, do wicked men's hearts so rise against them that press the doctrine of repentance in the sweetest way, and by the strongest and the choicest arguments that the Scripture doth afford? And why do they kill two at once: the faithful labourer's name and their own souls, by their wicked words and actings, because they are put upon repenting, which Satan tells them is so easy a thing? Surely, were repentance so easy, wicked men would not be so much enraged when that doctrine is, by evangelical considerations, pressed upon them.

Remedy (5). The fifth remedy against this device of Satan is seriously to consider, *that to repent of sin is as great a work of*

grace as not to sin.[1] By our sinful falls the powers of the soul
are weakened, the strength of grace is decayed, our evidences
for heaven are blotted, fears and doubts in the soul are raised
(will God once more pardon this scarlet sin, and show mercy
to this wretched soul?), and corruptions in the heart are more
advantaged and confirmed; and the conscience of a man after
falls is the more enraged or the more benumbed. Now for a
soul, notwithstanding all this, to repent of his falls, this shows
that it is as great a work of grace to repent of sin as it is not
to sin. Repentance is the vomit of the soul; and of all physic,
none so difficult and hard as it is to vomit. The same means
that tends to preserve the soul from sin, the same means works
the soul to rise by repentance when it is fallen into sin. We
know the mercy and loving-kindness of God is one special
means to keep the soul from sin; as David spake, 'Thy lov-
ing-kindness is always before mine eyes, and I have walked in
thy truth, and I have not sat with vain persons, neither will I
go in with dissemblers. I have hated the congregation of evil
doers, and will not sit with the wicked' (Psa. 26:3-5). So by
the same means the soul is raised by repentance out of sin, as
you may see in Mary Magdalene, who loved much, and wept
much, because much was forgiven her (Luke 7:37-39). So those
in Hosea: 'Come, let us return unto the Lord; for he hath
torn, and he will heal; he hath smitten, and he will bind us up.
After two days he will revive us, in the third day he will raise
us up, and we shall live in his sight (or before his face)' (Hos.
6:1, 2); as the Hebrew hath it, 'in his favour.' Confidence in
God's mercy and love, that he would heal them, and bind up

[1] Yet it is better to be kept from sin than cured of sin by repentance,
as if is better for a man to be preserved from a disease than to be aired
of the disease.

their wounds, and revive their dejected spirits, and cause them to live in his favour, was that which did work their hearts to repent and return unto him.

I might further show you this truth in many other particulars, but this may suffice: only remember this in the general, that there is as much of the power of God, and love of God, and faith in God, and fear of God, and care to please God, zeal for the glory of God (2 Cor. 7:11) requisite to work a man to repent of sin, as there is to keep a man from sin; by which you may easily judge, that to repent of sin is as great a work as not to sin. And now tell me, O soul, is it an easy thing not to sin? We know then certainly it is not an easy thing to repent of sin.

Remedy (6). The sixth remedy against this device of Satan is, seriously to consider, *that he that now tempts thee to sin upon this account, that repentance is easy, will, ere long, work thee to despair, and for ever to break the neck of thy soul, present repentance as the difficultest and hardest work in the world*; and to this purpose he will set thy sins in order before thee, and make them to say, 'We are thine, and we must follow thee.' [1] Now, Satan will help to work the soul to look up, and see God angry; and to look inward, and to see conscience accusing and

[1] Bede tells of a certain great man that was admonished in his sickness to repent, who answered that he would not repent yet; for if he should recover, his companions would laugh at him; but, growing more and more sick, his friends pressed him again to repent, but then he told them it was too late, for now, said he, I am judged and condemned.

As one Lamachus, a commander, said to one of his soldiers that was brought before him for a misbehaviour, who pleaded he would do so no more; 'No man must offend twice in war'; so God will not suffer men often to neglect the day of grace.

condemning; and to look downwards, and see hell's mouth
open to receive the impenitent soul: and all this to render the
work of repentance impossible to the soul. What, saith Satan,
dost thou think that that is easy which the whole power of
grace cannot conquer while we are in this world? Is it easy,
saith Satan, to turn from some outward act of sin to which
thou hast been addicted? Dost thou not remember that thou
hast often complained against such and such particular sins,
and resolved to leave them? and yet, to this hour, thou hast
not, thou canst not? What will it then be to turn from every
sin? Yea, to mortify and cut off those sins, those darling lusts,
that are as joints and members, that be as right hands and
right eyes? Hast thou not loved thy sins above thy Saviour?
Hast thou not preferred earth before heaven? Hast thou not
all along neglected the means of grace? and despised the offers
of grace? and vexed the Spirit of grace?

There would be no end, if I should set before thee the
infinite evils that thou hast committed, and the innumerable
good services that thou hast omitted, and the frequent checks
of thy own conscience that thou hast contemned; and there-
fore thou mayest well conclude that thou canst never repent,
that thou shalt never repent. Now, saith Satan, do but a little
consider thy numberless sins, and the greatness of thy sins, the
foulness of thy sins, the heinousness of thy sins, the circum-
stances of thy sins, and thou shalt easily see that those sins that
thou thoughtest to be but motes, are indeed mountains; and
is it not now in vain to repent of them? Surely, saith Satan,
if thou shouldest seek repentance and grace with tears, as
Esau, thou shalt not find it; thy glass is out,[1] thy sun is set, the

---

[1] That is to say, the sand has ran through the hour-glass.

door of mercy is shut, the golden sceptre is taken in, and now
thou that hast despised mercy, shalt be for ever destroyed by
justice. For such a wretch as thou art to attempt repentance is
to attempt a thing impossible. It is impossible that thou, that
in all thy life couldst never conquer one sin, shouldst master
such a numberless number of sins; which are so near, so dear,
so necessary, and so profitable to thee, that have so long bed-
ded and boarded with thee, that have been old acquaintance
and companions with thee. Hast thou not often purposed,
promised, vowed, and resolved to enter upon the practice of
repentance, but to this day couldst never attain it? Surely it is
in vain to strive against the stream, where it is so impossible
to overcome; thou art lost and cast for ever; to hell thou must,
to hell thou shalt. Ah, souls! he that now tempts you to sin, by
suggesting to you the easiness of repentance, will at last work
you to despair, and present repentance as the hardest work in
all the world, and a work as far above man as heaven is above
hell, as light is above darkness. Oh that you were wise, to
break off your sins by timely repentance.[1]

DEVICE 7. *By making the soul bold to venture upon the
occasions of sin.* Saith Satan, You may walk by the harlot's door
though you won't go into the harlot's bed; you may sit and
sup with the drunkard, though you won't be drunk with the
drunkard; you may look upon Jezebel's beauty, and you may
play and toy with Delilah, though you do not commit wick-
edness with the one or the other; you may with Achan handle
the golden wedge, though you do not steal the golden wedge.

---

[1] Repentance is a work that must be timely done, or utterly undone
for ever.

Remedy (1). The first remedy is, *solemnly to dwell upon those scriptures that do expressly command us to avoid the occasions of sin, and the least appearance of evil* (1 Thess. 5:22): 'Abstain from all appearance of evil.' Whatsoever is heterodox, unsound and unsavoury, shun it, as you would do a serpent in your way, or poison in your meat.[1]

Theodosius tare the Arian's arguments presented to him in writing, because he found them repugnant to the Scriptures; and Augustine retracted even ironies only, because they had the appearance of lying.

When God had commanded the Jews to abstain from swine's flesh, they would not so much as name it, but in their common talk would call a sow another thing. To abstain from all appearance of evil, is to do nothing wherein sin appears, or which hath a shadow of sin. Bernard glosseth finely, 'Whatever is of evil show, or of ill report, that he may neither wound conscience nor credit.' We must shun and be shy of the very show and shadow of sin, if either we tender[2] our credit abroad, or our comfort at home.

It was good counsel that Livia gave her husband Augustus: 'It behoveth thee not only not to do wrong, but not to seem to do so'; so Jude 23, 'And others save with fear, pulling them out of the fire, hating even the garment spotted by the flesh.' It is a phrase taken from legal uncleanness, which was contracted by touching the houses, the vessels, the garments, of unclean persons.[3] Under the law, men might not touch a menstruous

---

[1] Epiphanius saith that in the old law, when any dead body was carried by any house, they were enjoined to shut their doors and windows.

[2] To tender = to care for; to have a regard to.

[3] Socrates the ecclesiastical historian, not the philosopher, speaks of two young men that flung away their belts, when, being in an idols'

cloth, nor would God accept of a spotted peace-offering. So we must not only hate and avoid gross sins, but everything that may carry a savour or suspicion of sin; we must abhor the very signs and tokens of sin. So in Prov. 5:8, 'Remove thy way far from her, and come not nigh the door of her house.' He that would not be burnt, must dread the fire; he that would not hear the bell, must not meddle with the rope.[1] To venture upon the occasion of sin, and then to pray, 'Lead us not into temptation,' is all one as to thrust thy finger into the fire, and then to pray that it might not be burnt. So, in Prov. 4:14, 15, you have another command: 'Enter not into the path of the wicked, and go not in the way of evil men: avoid it, pass not by it, turn from it, and pass away.' This triple gradation of Solomon showeth with a great emphasis, how necessary it is for men to flee from all appearance of sin, as the seaman shuns sands and shelves, and as men shun those that have the plague-sores running upon them. As weeds do endanger the corn, as bad humours do endanger the blood, or as an infected house doth endanger the neighbourhood; so doth the company of the bad endanger those that are good. Entireness[2] with wicked consorts is one of the strongest chains of hell, and binds us to a participation of both sin and punishment.

Remedy (2). The second remedy against this device of Satan is, solemnly to consider, *that ordinarily there is no conquest over sin, without the soul turning from the occasion of sin.* It is impossible for that man to get the conquest of sin, that plays

---

temple, the lustrating water fell upon them, detesting, saith the historians' the garment spotted by the flesh.

[1] One said, as oft as I have been among vain men, I returned home less a man than I was before.

[2] Friendship.

and sports with the occasions of sin. God will not remove the temptation, except you turn from the occasion. It is a just and righteous thing with God, that he should fall into the pit, that will adventure to dance upon the brink of the pit, and that he should be a slave to sin, that will not flee from the occasions of sin. As long as there is fuel in our hearts for a temptation, we cannot be secure. He that hath gunpowder about him had need keep far enough off from sparkles. To rush upon the occasions of sin is both to tempt ourselves, and to tempt Satan to tempt our souls. It is very rare that any soul plays with the occasions of sin, but that soul is ensnared by sin.[1] It is seldom that God keeps that soul from the acts of sin, that will not keep off from the occasions of sin. He that adventures upon the occasions of sin is as he that would quench the fire with oil, which is a fuel to maintain it, and increase it. Ah, souls, often remember how frequently you have been overcome by sin, when you have boldly gone upon the occasions of sin; look back, souls, to the day of your vanity, wherein you have been as easily conquered as tempted, vanquished as assaulted, when you have played with the occasions of sin. As you would for the future be kept from the acting of sin, and be made victorious over sin, oh! flee from the occasions of sin.

Remedy (3). The third remedy against this device of Satan is, seriously to consider, *that other precious saints, that were once glorious on earth, and are now triumphing in heaven, have turned from the occasion of sin, as hell itself*; as you may see in Joseph (Gen. 39:10), 'And it came to pass, as she spake to

---

[1] The fable saith, that the butterfly asked the owl how she should deal with the fire which had singed her wings, who counselled her not to behold so much as its smoke.

Joseph day by day, that he hearkened not unto her, to lie by
her, or to be with her.'¹ Joseph was famous for all the four car-
dinal virtues, if ever any were. In this one temptation you may
see his fortitude, justice, temperance, and prudence, in that he
shuns the occasion: for he would not so much as be with her.
And that a man is indeed, that he is in a temptation, which
is but a tap to give vent to corruption. The Nazarite might
not only not drink wine, but not taste a grape, or the husk
of a grape. The leper was to shave his hair, and pare his nails.
The devil counts a fit occasion half a conquest, for he knows
that corrupt nature hath a seed-plot for all sin, which being
drawn forth and watered by some sinful occasion, is soon set
a-work to the producing of death and destruction. God will
not remove the temptation, till we remove the occasion. A bird
whiles aloft is safe, but she comes not near the snare without
danger. The shunning the occasions of sin renders a man most
like the best of men. A soul eminently gracious dares not come
near the trap, though he be far off the blow. So Job 31:1, 'I have
made a covenant with mine eyes; why then should I think
upon a maid?'² I set a watch at the entrance of my senses, that
my soul might not by them be infected or endangered. The eye
is the window of the soul, and if that should be always open,
the soul might smart for it. A man may not look intently upon
that, that he may not love entirely. The disciples were set agog,

---

¹ There are stories of heathens that would not look upon beauties, lest
they should be ensnared. Democritus plucked out his own eyes to avoid
the danger of uncleanness.
² 'I cut a covenant' In making covenants, it was a custom among
the Jews to cut some beast or other in pieces, and to walk between the
pieces, to signify that they desired God to destroy them that should
break the covenant.

by beholding the beauty of the temple. It is best and safest to have the eye always fixed upon the highest and noblest objects; as the mariner's eye is fixed upon the star, when their hand is on the stem. So David, when he was himself, he shuns the occasion of sin (Psa. 26:4, 5): 'I have not sat with vain persons, neither will I go in with dissemblers; I have hated the congregation of evil doers, and will not sit with the wicked.'

Stories speak of some that could not sleep when they thought of the trophies of other worthies that went before them. The highest and choicest examples are to some, and should be to all, very quickening and provoking; and oh that the examples of those worthy saints, David, Joseph, and Job, might prevail with all your souls to shun and avoid the occasions of sin! Every one should strive to be like to them in grace, that they desire to be equal with in glory. He that shooteth at the sun, though he be far short, will shoot higher than he that aimeth at a shrub. It is best, and it speaks out much of Christ within, to eye the highest and the worthiest examples.

Remedy (4). The fourth remedy against this device of Satan is, solemnly to consider, *that the avoiding the occasions of sin, is an evidence of grace, and that which lifts up a man above most other men in the world.*[1] That a man is indeed, which he is in temptation; and when sinful occasions do present themselves before the soul, this speaks out both the truth and the strength of grace; when with Lot, a man can be chaste in Sodom, and with Timothy can live temperate in Asia, among the luxurious Ephesians; and with Job can walk uprightly in the land of Uz,

[1] Plutarch saith of Demosthenes, that he was excellent at praising the worthy acts of his ancestors, but not so at imitating them. Oh that this were not applicable to many professors in our times!

where the people were profane in their lives, and superstitious in their worship; and with Daniel be holy in Babylon; and with Abraham righteous in Chaldea; and with Nehemiah, zealous in Damascus, etc. Many a wicked man is big and full of corruption, but shows it not for want of occasion; but that man is surely good, who in his course will not be bad, though tempted by occasions. A Christless soul is so far from refusing occasions when they come in his way, that he looks and longs after them, and rather than he will go without them he will buy them, not only with love or money, but also with the loss of his soul. Nothing but grace can fence a man against the occasions of sin, when he is strongly tempted thereunto. Therefore, as you would cherish a precious evidence in your own bosoms of the truth and strength of your graces, shun all sinful occasions.

DEVICE 8. *By representing to the soul the outward mercies that vain men enjoy, and the outward miseries that they are freed from, whilst they have walked in the ways of sin.* Saith Satan, Dost thou see, O soul, the many mercies that such and such enjoy, that walk in those very ways that thy soul startles to think of, and the many crosses that they are delivered from, even such as makes other men, that say they dare not walk in such ways, to spend their days in sighing, weeping, groaning, and mourning? and therefore, saith Satan, if ever thou wouldst be freed from the dark night of adversity, and enjoy the sunshine of prosperity, thou must walk in their ways.[1]

[1] It was a weighty saying of Seneca, 'There is nothing more unhappy than he who never felt adversity.' Some of the heathens would be wicked as their gods were, counting it a dishonour to their god to be unlike him. (*Lactantius*)

By this stratagem the devil took those in Jer. 44:16-18, 'As for the word that thou hast spoken unto us in the name of the Lord, we will not hearken unto thee: but we will certainly do whatsoever thing goeth forth out of our own mouth, to burn incense unto the queen of heaven, and to pour out drink-offerings unto her, as we have done, we, and our fathers, our kings, and our princes, in the cities of Judah, and in the streets of Jerusalem: for then had we plenty of victuals, and were well, and saw no evil. But since we left off to burn incense to the queen of heaven, and to pour out drink-offerings unto her, we have wanted all things, and have been consumed by the sword and by the famine.' This is just the language of a world of ignorant, profane, and superstitious souls in London, and England, that would have made them a captain to return to bondage, yea, to that bondage that was worse than that the Israelites groaned under. Oh, say they, since such and such persons have been put down, and left off, we have had nothing but plundering and taxing, and butchering of men; and therefore we will do as we, and our kings, and nobles, and fathers have formerly done, for then had we plenty at home, and peace abroad, and there was none to make us afraid.[1]

Remedy (1). The first remedy is, solemnly to consider, *that no man knows how the heart of God stands by his hand.* His hand of mercy may be towards a man, when his heart may be against that man, as you may see in Saul and others; and the hand of God may be set against a man, when the heart of God

---

[1] It is said of one of the emperors, that Rome had no war in his days, because it was plague enough to have such an emperor. You are wise, and know how to apply it. [The allusion, no doubt, is to Charles I., and the agitation for the Restoration of Charles II. Cromwell died Sept. 3. 1658.]

is dearly set upon a man, as you may see in Job and Ephraim.[1] The hand of God was sorely set against them, and yet the heart and bowels of God were strongly working towards them. No man knoweth either love or hatred by outward mercy or misery; for all things come alike to all, to the righteous and to the unrighteous, to the good and to the bad, to the clean and to the unclean. The sun of prosperity shines as well upon brambles of the wilderness as upon fruit-trees of the orchard; the snow and hail of adversity lights upon the best garden as well as upon the stinking dunghill or the wild waste. Ahab's and Josiah's ends concur in the very circumstances. Saul and Jonathan, though different in their natures, deserts, and deportments, yet in their deaths they were not divided. Health, wealth, honours, crosses, sicknesses, losses, are cast upon good men and bad men promiscuously. 'The whole Turkish empire is nothing else but a crust, cast by heaven's great housekeeper to his dogs.' Moses dies in the wilderness as well as those that murmured. Nabal is rich, as well as Abraham; Ahithophel wise, as well as Solomon; and Doeg honoured by Saul, as well as Joseph was by Pharaoh. Usually the worst of men have most of these outward things; and the best of men have least of earth, though most of heaven.

Remedy (2). The second remedy against this device of Satan is, seriously to consider, *that there is nothing in the world that doth so provoke God to be wroth and angry, as men's taking encouragement from God's goodness and mercy to do wickedly.*

[1] Cicero judged the Jews' religion to be naught, because they were so often overcome, and impoverished, and afflicted; and the religion of Rome to be right, because the Romans prospered and became lords of the world; and yet, though the Romans had his hand, yet the Jews had his heart, for they were dearly beloved though sorely afflicted.

This you may see by that wrath that fell upon the old world, and by God's raining hell out of heaven upon Sodom and Gomorrah. This is clear in Jeremiah 44, from verse 20 to 28. The words are worthy of your best meditation. Oh that they were engraven in all your hearts, and constant in all your thoughts! Though they are too large for me to transcribe them, yet they are not too large for me to remember them. To argue from mercy to sinful liberty, is the devil's logic, and such logicians do ever walk as upon a mine of gunpowder ready to be blown up. No such soul can ever avert or avoid the wrath of God. This is wickedness at the height, for a man to be very bad, because God is very good. A worse spirit than this is not in hell. Ah, Lord, doth not wrath, yea, the greatest wrath, lie at this man's door? Are not the strongest chains of darkness prepared for such a soul? To sin against mercy is to sin against humanity. It is bestial; nay, it is worse. To render good for evil is divine, to render good for good is human, to render evil for evil is brutish; but to render evil for good is devilish; and from this evil deliver my soul, O God.[1]

Remedy (3). The third remedy against this device of Satan is, solemnly to consider, *that there is no greater misery in this life, than not to be in misery; no greater affliction, than not to be afflicted.* Woe, woe to that soul that God will not spend a rod upon! This is the saddest stroke of all, when God refuses to strike at all (Hos. 4:17), 'Ephraim is joined to idols; let him alone.' 'Why should you be smitten any more? you will revolt

---

[1] Such souls make God a god of *clouts* [a mere doll], one that will not do as he saith; but they shall find God to be as severe in punishings he is to others gracious in pardoning. Good turns aggravate unkindnesses, and our guilt is increased by our obligations.

more and more' (Isa. 1:5). When the physician gives over the
patient, you say, 'Ring out his knell, the man is dead.' So when
God gives over a soul to sin without control, you may truly say,
'This soul is lost,' you may ring out his knell, for he is twice
dead, and plucked up by the roots. Freedom from punishment
is the mother of security, the step-mother of virtue, the poison
of religion, the moth of holiness, and the introducer of wick-
edness. 'Nothing,' said one, 'seems more unhappy to me, than
he to whom no adversity hath happened.' Outward mercies oft
times prove a snare to our souls. 'I will lay a stumbling- block'
(Ezek. 3:20). Vatablus's note there is, 'I will prosper him in all
things, and not by affliction restrain him from sin.' Prosperity
hath been a stumbling-block, at which millions have stumbled
and fallen, and broke the neck of their souls for ever.[1]

Remedy (4). The fourth remedy against this device of Satan
is, seriously to consider, *that the wants of wicked men, under all
their outward mercy and freedom from adversity, is far greater
than all their outward enjoyments.* They have many mercies, yet
they want more than they enjoy; the mercies which they enjoy
are nothing to the mercies they want. It is true, they have
honours and riches, and pleasures and friends, and are mighty
in power; their seed is established in their sight with them,
and their offspring before their eyes: 'Their houses are safe
from fear, neither is the rod of God upon them'; 'They send
forth their little ones like a flock, and their children dance.
They take the timbrel and harp, and rejoice at the sound of
the organ'; 'They spend their days in wealth, their eyes stand
out with fatness, they have more than heart can wish: and they

---

[1] Religion brought forth riches, and the daughter soon devoured the
mother, said Augustine.

have no bands in their death, but their strength is firm; they are not in trouble as other men,' as David and Job speak.[1] Yet all this is nothing to what they want.[2] They want interest in God, Christ, the Spirit, the promises, the covenant of grace, and everlasting glory; they want acceptation and reconciliation with God; they want righteousness, justification, sanctification, adoption, and redemption; they want the pardon of sin, and power against sin, and freedom from the dominion of sin; they want that favour that is better than life, and that joy that is unspeakable and full of glory, and that peace that passes understanding, and that grace, the least spark of which is more worth than heaven and earth; they want a house that hath foundations, whose builder and maker is God; they want those riches that perish not, the glory that fades not, that kingdom that shakes not. Wicked men are the most needy men in the world, yea, they want those two things that should render their mercies sweet, viz. the blessing of God, and content with their condition, and without which their heaven is but hell on this side hell.[3] When their hearts are lifted up and grown big upon the thoughts of their abundance, if conscience does but put in a word and say, It is true, here is this and that outward mercy—Oh, but where is an interest in Christ? Where is the favour of God? Where are the comforts of the Holy Ghost? Where are the evidences for heaven? This word

[1] Cf. Psa. 49:11; 73:7; Job 21:12.

[2] Lack.

[3] Neither Christ nor heaven can be hyperbolised. A crown of gold cannot cure the headache, a velvet slipper cannot ease the gout; no more can honour or riches quiet and still the conscience. The heart of man is a three-square triangle, which the whole round circle of the world cannot fill, as mathematicians say, but all the corners will complain of emptiness, and hunger for something else.

from conscience makes the man's countenance to change, his thoughts to be troubled, his heart to be amazed, and all his mercies on the right hand and left to be as dead and withered. Ah, were but the eyes of wicked men open to see their wants under their abundance, they would cry out and say, as Absalom did, 'What are all these to me so long as I cannot see the king's face?' (2 Sam. 14:23,32). What is honour, and riches, and the favour of creatures, so long as I want the favour of God, the pardon of my sins, an interest in Christ, and the hopes of glory! O Lord, give me these, or I die; give me these, or else I shall eternally die.

Remedy (5). The fifth remedy against this device of Satan is, solemnly to consider, *that outward things are not as they seem and are esteemed.* They have, indeed, a glorious outside, but if you view their insides, you will easily find that they fill the head full of cares, and the heart full of fears. What if the fire should consume one part of my estate, and the sea should be a grave to swallow up another part of my estate! what if my servants should be unfaithful abroad, and my children should be deceitful at home! Ah, the secret fretting, vexing, and gnawing that doth daily, yea hourly, attend those men's souls whose hands are full of worldly goods!

It was a good speech of an emperor: 'You,' said he, 'gaze on my purple robe and golden crown, but did you know what cares are under it, you would not take it up from the ground to have it.' It was a true saying of Augustine on the 26th Psalm: 'Many are miserable by loving hurtful things, but they are more miserable by having them.' It is not what men enjoy, but the principle from whence it comes, that makes men happy. Much of these outward things do usually cause great distraction, great vexation, and great condemnation at last, to the possessors of them. If God gives them in his wrath, and does not sanctify them in his love, they will at last be witnesses against a man, and millstones for ever to sink a man in that day when God shall call men to an account, not for the use, but for the abuse of mercy.

Remedy (6). The sixth remedy against this device of Satan is, seriously to consider *the end and the design of God in heaping up mercy upon the heads of the wicked, and in giving them a 'quietus est,' rest and quiet from those sorrows and sufferings that others sigh under.* David, in Psa. 73:17-20, shows the end and design of God in this. Saith he, 'When I went into the sanctuary of God, then I understood their end: surely thou didst set them in slippery places, thou castedst them down into destruction. How are they brought into desolation as in a moment: they are utterly consumed with terrors. As a dream, when one awaketh, so, O Lord, when thou awakest, thou shalt despise their image.'[1] So in Psa. 92:7, 'When the wicked spring as the grass, and when all the workers of iniquity do flourish, it is that they shall be destroyed for ever.' God's setting them up, is but in order to his casting them down; his raising them high, is but in order to his bringing them low. Exod. 9:16; 'And in very deed, for this cause have I raised thee up, for to show in thee my power, and that my name may be declared throughout all

---

[1] Valerian, the Roman emperor, fell from being an emperor to be a footstool to Sapor, king of Persia. Dionysius, king of Sicily, fell from his kingly glory to be a schoolmaster. The brave Queen Zenobia was brought to Rome in golden chains. Belisarius, a famous general, Henry the Fourth, Bajazet, Pythias, great Pompey, and William the Conqueror, these, from being very high, were brought very low; they all fell from great glory and majesty to great poverty and misery.

the earth.' I have constituted and set thee up as a butt-mark,[1] that I may let fly at thee, and follow thee close with plague upon plague, till I have beaten the very breath out of thy body, and got myself a name, by setting my feet upon the neck of all thy pride, power, pomp, and glory. Ah, souls, what man in his wits would be lifted up that he might be cast down; would he set higher than others, when it is but in order to his being brought down lower than others? There is not a wicked man in the world that is set up with Lucifer, as high as heaven, but shall with Lucifer be brought down as low as hell. Canst thou think seriously of this, O soul, and not say, 'O Lord, I humbly crave that thou wilt let me be little in this world, that I may be great in another world; and low here, that I may be high for ever hereafter.[2] Let me be low, and feed low, and live low, so I may live with thee for ever; let me now be clothed with rags, so thou wilt clothe me at last with thy robes; let me now be set upon a dunghill, so I may at last be advanced to sit with thee upon thy throne. Lord, make me rather gracious than great, inwardly holy than outwardly happy, and rather turn me into my first nothing, yea, make me worse than nothing, rather than set me up for a time, that thou mayest bring me low for ever.'

Remedy (7). The seventh remedy against this device of Satan is solemnly to consider, *that God doth often most plague and punish those whom others think he doth most spare and love;* that is, God doth plague and punish them most with spiritual judgments—which are the greatest, the sorest, and

---

[1] Arrow-mark or target.

[2] Grant us, Lord, that we may so partake of temporal felicity, that we may not lose eternal. (*Bernard*)

the heaviest—whom he least punishes with temporal punish-
ments.[1] There are no men on earth so internally plagued as
those that meet with least external plagues. Oh the blindness
of mind, the hardness of heart, the searedness of conscience,
that those souls are given up to, who, in the eye of the world,
are reputed the most happy men, because they are not out-
wardly afflicted and plagued as other men. Ah, souls, it were
better that all the temporal plagues that ever befell the chil-
dren of men since the fall of Adam should at once meet upon
your souls, than that you should be given up to the least
spiritual plague, to the least measure of spiritual blindness or
spiritual hardness of heart. Nothing will better that man, nor
move that man, that is given up to spiritual judgments. Let
God smile or frown, stroke or strike, cut or kill, he minds it
not, he regards it not; let life or death, heaven or hell, be set
before him, it stirs him not; he is mad upon his sin, and God
is fully set to do justice upon his soul. This man's preservation
is but a reservation unto a greater condemnation; this man can
set no bounds to himself; he is become a brat of fathomless
perdition; he hath guilt in his bosom and vengeance at his
back wherever he goes. Neither ministry nor misery, neither
miracle nor mercy, can mollify his heart, and if this soul be
not in hell, on this side hell, who is?[2]

Remedy (8). The eighth remedy against this device of Satan
is, *to dwell more upon that strict account that vain men must*

---

[1] Psa. 81:12; 78:26-31; 106:15: He gave them their requests, but sent
leanness into their soul. It is a heavy plague to have a fat body and a lean
soul; a house full of gold, and a heart full of sin.

[2] It is better to have a sore than a seared conscience. It is better to
have no heart than a hard heart, no mind than a blind mind.

make for all that good that they do enjoy.[1] Ah! did men dwell more upon that account that they must ere long give for all the mercies that they have enjoyed, and for all the favours that they have abused, and for all the sins they have committed, it would make their hearts to tremble and their lips to quiver, and rottenness to enter into their bones; it would cause their souls to cry out, and say, 'Oh that our mercies had been fewer and lesser, that our account might have been easier, and our torment and misery, for our abuse of so great mercy, not greater than we are able to bear. Oh cursed be the day wherein the crown of honour was set upon our heads, and the treasures of this world were cast into our laps; oh cursed be the day wherein the sun of prosperity shined so strong upon us, and this flattering world smiled so much upon us, as to occasion us to forget God, to slight Jesus Christ, to neglect our souls, and to put far from us the day of our account!'

Philip the Third of Spain, whose life was free from gross evils, professed, That he would rather lose his kingdom than offend God willingly; yet being in the agony of death, and considering more thoroughly of his account he was to give to God, fear struck into him, and these words brake from him: 'Oh! would to God I had never reigned. Oh that those years that I have spent in my kingdom, I had lived a solitary life in the wilderness! Oh that I had lived a solitary life with God! How much more securely should I now have died! How much more confidently should I have gone to the throne of God! What doth all my glory profit me, but that I have so much

---

[1] In that day men shall give an account of good things committed unto them, of good things neglected by them, of evil committed by them, and of evils suffered (allowed) by them. Then shall a good conscience be more worth than all the world's good. (*Bernard*)

the more torment in my death?' God keeps an exact account of every penny that is laid out upon him and his, and that is laid out against him and his; and this in the day of account men shall know and feel, though now they wink and will not understand. The sleeping of vengeance causeth the overflowing of sin, and the overflowing of sin causeth the awakening of vengeance. Abused mercy will certainly turn into fury. God's forbearance is no quittance. The day is at hand when he will pay wicked men for the abuse of old and new mercies. If he seem to be slow, yet he is sure. He hath leaden heels, but iron hands. The farther he stretcheth his bow, or draweth his arrow, the deeper he will wound in the day of vengeance. Men's actions are all in print in heaven, and God will, in the day of account, read them aloud in the ears of all the world, that they may all say Amen to that righteous sentence that he shall pass upon all despisers and abusers of mercy.[1]

DEVICE 9. *By presenting to the soul the crosses, losses, reproaches, sorrows, and sufferings that do daily attend those that walk in the ways of holiness.* Saith Satan, Do not you see that there are none in the world that are so vexed, afflicted, and tossed, as those that walk more circumspectly and holily than their neighbours? They are a byword at home, and a reproach abroad; their miseries come in upon them like Job's messengers, one upon the neck of another, and there is no end of their sorrows and troubles. Therefore, saith Satan, you were better to walk in ways that are less troublesome, and less afflicted,

---

[1] Jerome still thought that voice was in his ears, 'Arise ye dead, and come to judgment.' As oft as I think on that day, how doth may whole body quake, and my heart within me tremble.

though they be more sinful; for who but a madman would spend his days in sorrow, vexation, and affliction, when it may be prevented by walking in the ways that I set before him?

Remedy (1). The first remedy against this device of Satan is, solemnly to consider, *that all the afflictions that do attend the people of God, are such as shall turn to the profit and glorious advantage of the people of God.* They shall discover that filthiness and vileness in sin, that yet the soul hath never seen.

It was a speech of a German divine[1] in his sickness, 'In this disease I have learned how great God is, and what the evil of sin is; I never knew to purpose what God was before, nor what sin meant, till now.' Afflictions are a crystal glass, wherein the soul hath the clearest sight of the ugly face of sin. In this glass the soul comes to see sin to be but a bitter-sweet; yea, in this glass the soul comes to see sin not only to be an evil, but to be the greatest evil in the world, to be an evil far worse than hell itself.

Again, they shall contribute to the mortifying and purging away of their sins (Isa. 1:25 and 27:8, 9). Afflictions are God's furnace, by which he cleanses his people from their dross. Affliction is a fire to purge out our dross, and to make virtue shine; it is a potion to carry away ill humours, better than all the *benedictum medicamentum* (commended remedies), as physicians call them.[2] Aloes kill worms; colds and frosts do destroy vermin; so do afflictions the corruptions that are in our hearts. The Jews, under all the prophets' thunderings, retained their idols; but after their Babylonish captivity, it is observed, there have been no idols found amongst them.

---

[1] Gaspar Olevianus (1586).
[2] In times of peace our armour is rusty, in time of war it is bright.

Again, afflictions are sweet preservatives to keep the saints from sin, which is a greater evil than hell itself. As Job spake, 'Surely it is meet to be said unto God, I have borne chastisement, I will not offend any more; That which I see not, teach thou me; if I have done iniquity, I will do no more. Once have I spoken foolishly, yea, twice, I will do so no more' (Job 34:31, 32; 40:5). The burnt child dreads the fire. Ah! saith the soul under the rod, sin is but a bitter-sweet; and for the future I intend, by the strength of Christ, that I will not buy repentance at so dear a rate.[1]

The Rabbins, to scare their scholars from sin, were wont to tell them, 'That sin made God's head ache'; and saints under the rod have found by woeful experience, that sin makes not only their heads, but their hearts ache also.

Augustine, by wandering out of his way, escaped one that lay in wait to mischief him. If afflictions did not put us out of our way, we should many times meet with some sin or other that would mischief our precious souls.

Again, they will work the saints to be more fruitful in holiness (Heb. 12:10, 11): 'But he afflicts us for our profit, that we might be partakers of his holiness.' The flowers smell sweetest after a shower; vines bear the better for bleeding; the walnut tree is most fruitful when most beaten. Saints spring and thrive most internally when they are most externally afflicted. Afflictions are called by some 'the mother of virtue.' Manasseh's chain was more profitable to him than his crown. Luther could not understand some Scriptures till he was in affliction.

---

[1] Salt brine preserves from putrefaction, and salt marshes keep the sheep from the rot: so do afflictions the saints from sin. The ball in the Emblem saith, the harder you beat me down in affliction, the higher I shall bound in affection towards heaven and heavenly things.

The Christ-cross is no letter, and yet that taught him more than all the letters in the row. God's house of correction is his school of instruction. All the stones that came about Stephen's ears did but knock him closer to Christ, the cornerstone. The waves did but lift Noah's ark nearer to heaven; and the higher the waters grew, the more near the ark was lifted up to heaven. Afflictions do lift up the soul to more rich, clear, and full enjoyments of God (Hos. 2:14): 'Behold, I will allure her into the wilderness, and speak comfortably to her' (or rather, as the Hebrew hath it), 'I will earnestly or vehemently speak to her heart.' God makes afflictions to be but inlets to the soul's more sweet and full enjoyment of his blessed self. When was it that Stephen saw the heavens open, and Christ standing at the right hand of God, but when the stones were about his ears, and there was but a short step betwixt him and eternity?

And when did God appear in his glory to Jacob, but in the day of his troubles, when the stones were his pillows, and the ground his bed, and the hedges his curtains, and the heavens his canopy? Then he saw the angels of God ascending and descending in their glistering robes. The plant in Nazianzen[1] grows with cutting; being cut, it flourisheth; it contends with the axe, it lives by dying, and by cutting it grows.[2] So do saints by their afflictions that do befall them; they gain more experience of the power of God supporting them, of the

---

[1] 'In Nazianzen,' in the writings of Gregory of Nazianzus (329–89), one of the four great 'fathers' of the Eastern church.

[2] It is reported of Tiberius the emperor that, passing by a place where he saw a cross lying in the ground upon a marble stone, and causing the stone to be digged up, he found a great deal of treasure under the cross. So many a precious saint hath found much spiritual and heavenly treasure under the crosses they have met withal.

wisdom of God directing them, of the grace of God refresh-
ing and cheering them, and of the goodness of God quieting
and quickening of them, to a greater love to holiness, and to a
greater delight in holiness, and to a more vehement pursuing
after holiness.

I have read of a fountain, that at noonday is cold, and at
mid-night it grows warm; so many a precious soul is cold
Godwards, and heaven-wards, and holiness-wards, in the day
of prosperity; that grow warm God-wards and heaven-wards,
and holiness-wards, in the midnight of adversity.

Again, Afflictions serve to keep the hearts of the saints
humble and tender (Lam. 3:19, 20): 'Remembering my afflic-
tion and my misery, the wormwood and the gall. My soul
hath them still in remembrance, and is humbled in me,' or
bowed down in me, as the original hath it. So David, when he
was under the rod, could say, 'I was dumb, I opened not my
mouth; because thou didst it' (Psa. 39:9).

I have read of one [Gregory Nazianzen], who, when any-
thing fell out prosperously, would read over the Lamentation
of Jeremiah, and that kept his heart tender, humbled, and low.
Prosperity doth not contribute more to the puffing up the
soul, than adversity doth to the bowing down of the soul. This
the saints by experience find; and therefore they can kiss and
embrace the cross, as others do the world's crown.[1]

Again, they serve to bring the saints nearer to God, and
to make them more importunate and earnest in prayer with
God. 'Before I was afflicted, I went astray; but now have I kept
thy word.' 'It is good for me that I have been afflicted, that I

---

[1] The more precious odours and the purest spices are beaten and
bruised, the sweeter scent and savour they send abroad. So do saints
when they are afflicted.

might learn thy statutes.' 'I will be to Ephraim as a lion, and
as a young lion to the house of Judah. I, even I, will tear and
go away: I will take away, and none shall rescue him.' 'I will
go and return to my place, till they acknowledge their offence,
and seek my face: in their affliction they will seek me early.'
And so they did. 'Come,' say they, 'and let us return unto the
Lord: for he hath torn, and he will heal us; he hath smitten,
and he will bind us up. After two days he will revive us: in the
third day he will raise us up, and we shall live in his sight.'[1] So
when God had hedged up their way with thorns, then they
say, 'I will go and return to my first husband; for then was it
with me better than now' (Hos. 2:6-7). Ah the joy, the peace,
the comfort, the delight, and content that did attend us, when
we kept close communion with God, doth bespeak our return
to God. 'We will return to our first husband; for then was it
with us better than now.'

When Tiribazus, a noble Persian, was arrested, he drew
out his sword, and defended himself; but when they told him
that they came to carry him to the king, he willingly yielded.
So, though a saint may at first stand a little out, yet when he
remembers that afflictions are to carry him nearer to God, he
yields, and kisses the rod. Afflictions are like the prick at the
nightingale's breast, that awakes her, and puts her upon her
sweet and delightful singing.

Again, afflictions serve to revive and recover decayed graces;
they inflame that love that is cold, and they quicken that faith
that is decaying, and they put life into those hopes that are
withering, and spirits into those joys and comforts that are
languishing.[2] Musk, saith one, when it hath lost its sweetness,

---

[1] Psa. 119:67, 71; Hos. 5:14, 15; 6:1, 2.

[2] Most men are like a top, that will not go unless you whip it, and

if it be put into the sink amongst filth it recovers it. So do afflictions recover and revive decayed graces. The more saints are beaten with the hammer of afflictions, the more they are made the trumpets of God's praises, and the more are their graces revived and quickened. Adversity abases the loveliness of the world that might entice us; it abates the lustiness of the flesh within, that might incite us to folly and vanity; and it abets the spirit in his quarrel to the two former, which tends much to the reviving and recovering of decayed graces. Now, suppose afflictions and troubles attend the ways of holiness, yet seeing that they all work for the great profit and singular advantage of the saints, let no soul be so mad as to leave an afflicted way of holiness, to walk in a smooth path of wickedness.

Remedy (2). The second remedy against this device of Satan is, solemnly to consider, *that all the afflictions that do befall the saints, do only reach their worser part; they reach not, they hurt not, their noble part, their best part.* All the arrows stick in the target, they reach not the conscience: 'And who shall harm you, if ye be followers of that which is good?' saith the apostle (1 Pet. 3:13). That is, none shall harm you. They may thus and thus afflict you, but they shall never harm you.[1]

It was the speech of an heathen, whenas by a tyrant he was commanded to be put into a mortar, and to be beaten to

the more you whip it the better it goes. You know how to apply it. They that are in adversity, saith Luther, do better understand Scriptures; but those that are in prosperity, read them as a verse in Ovid. Bees are killed with honey, but quickened with vinegar. The honey of prosperity kills our graces, but the vinegar of adversity quickens our graces.

[1] The Christian soldier shall ever be master of the day. *Mori posset vinci non posse*, said Cyprian to Cornelius; he may suffer death, but never conquest.

pieces with an iron pestle, he cries out to his persecutors: 'You do but beat the vessel, the case, the husk of Anaxarchus, you do not beat me.' His body was to him but as a case, a husk; he counted his soul himself, which they could not reach. You are wise, and know how to apply it.

Socrates said of his enemies, 'They may kill me, but they cannot hurt me.' So afflictions may kill us, but they cannot hurt us; they may take away my life, but they cannot take away my God, my Christ, my crown.

Remedy (3). The third remedy against this device of Satan is, seriously to consider, *that the afflictions that do attend the saints in the ways of holiness, are but short and momentary.* 'Sorrow may abide for a night, but joy comes in the morning' (Psa. 30:5). This short storm will end in an everlasting calm, this short night will end in a glorious day, that shall never have end.[1] It is but a very short time between grace and glory, between our title to the crown and our wearing the crown, between our right to the heavenly inheritance and our possession of the heavenly inheritance. Fourteen thousand years to the Lord is but as one day. What is our life but a shadow, a bubble, a flower, a post, a span, a dream? Yea, so small a while doth the hand of the Lord rest upon us, that Luther cannot get diminutives enough to extenuate it, for he calls it a very little cross that we bear. The prophet in Isaiah 26:20, saith the indignation doth not (*transire*) pass, but (*pertransire*) overpass. The sharpness, shortness, and suddenness of it is set forth by the travail of a woman (John 16:21). And that is a sweet

[1] There are none of God's afflicted ones that have not their intermissions, respites, and breathing whiles, under their short and momentary afflictions. When God's hand is on thy back, let thy hand be on thy mouth, for though the affliction be sharp, it shall be but short.

scripture: 'For ye have need of patience, that after ye have done the will of God, ye might receive the promise.' 'For yet a little while, he that shall come will come, and will not tarry' (Heb. 10:36, 37). 'A little, little, little while.'

When Athanasius's friends came to bewail him, because of his misery and banishment, he said, 'It is but a little cloud, and will quickly be gone.' It will be but as a day before God will give his afflicted ones beauty for ashes, the oil of gladness for the spirit of heaviness; before he will turn all your sighing into singing, all your lamentations into consolations, your sackcloth into silks, ashes into ointments, and your fasts into everlasting feasts.

Remedy (4). The fourth remedy against this device of Satan, is seriously to consider, *that the afflictions that do befall the saints are such as proceed from God's dearest love.*[1] 'As many as I love, I rebuke and chasten' (Rev. 3:19). Saints, saith God, think not that I hate you, because I thus chide you. He that escapes reprehension may suspect his adoption. God had one Son without corruption, but no son without correction. A gracious soul may look through the darkest cloud, and see a God smiling on him. We must look through the anger of his correction to the sweetness of his countenance; even as by the rainbow we see the beautiful image of the sun's light in the midst of a dark and waterish cloud.

When Munster lay sick, and his friends asked him how he did and how he felt himself, he pointed to his sores and ulcers, whereof he was full, and said, 'These are God's gems and

---

[1] Augustine asketh, *Si amatur quo modo infirmatur?* If he were beloved, how came he to be sick? So are wicked men apt to say, because they know not that corrections are pledges of our adoption, and badges of our sonship. God had one Son without sin, but none without sorrow.

jewels, wherewith he decketh his best friends, and to me they are more precious than all the gold and silver in the world.' A soul at first conversion is but rough cast; but God by afflictions doth square and fit, and fashion it for that glory above, which doth speak them out to flow from precious love; therefore the afflictions that do attend the people of God should be no bar to holiness, nor no motive to draw the soul to ways of wickedness.

Remedy (5). The fifth remedy against this device of Satan is, solemnly to consider, *that it is our duty and glory not to measure afflictions by the smart but by the end*. When Israel was dismissed out of Egypt, it was with gold and ear-rings (Exod. 11:3); so the Jews were dismissed out of Babylon with gifts, jewels, and all necessary utensils (Ezra 1:7-11). Look more at the latter end of a Christian than the beginning of his affliction. Consider the patience of Job, and what end the Lord made with him. Look not upon Lazarus lying at Dives's door, but lying in Abraham's bosom. Look not to the beginning of Joseph, who was so far from his dream that the sun and moon should reverence him, that for two years he was cast where he could see neither sun, moon, nor stars; but behold him at last made ruler over Egypt. Look not upon David as there was but a step between him and death, nor as he was envied by some, and slighted and despised by others; but behold him seated in his royal throne, and dying in his bed of honour, and his son Solomon and all his glistering nobles about him. Afflictions, they are but as a dark entry into your Father's house; they are but as a dirty lane to a royal palace. Now tell me, souls, whether it be not very great madness to shun the ways of holiness, and to walk in the ways of wickedness, because of those afflictions that do attend the ways of holiness.[1]

[1] Afflictions, they are but our Father's goldsmiths, who are working

Remedy (6). The sixth remedy against this device of Satan is, seriously to consider, *that the design of God in all the afflictions that do befall them, is only to try them; it is not to wrong them, nor to ruin them, as ignorant souls are apt to think.* 'He knoweth the way that I take; and when he hath tried me, I shall come forth as gold,' saith patient Job 23:10. So in Deut. 8:2, 'And thou shalt remember all the way which the Lord thy God led thee these forty years in the wilderness, to humble thee, and to prove thee, to know what was in thy heart, whether thou wouldest keep his commandments or no.' God afflicted them thus, that he might make known to themselves and others what was in their hearts. When fire is put to green wood, there comes out abundance of watery stuff that before appeared not; when the pond is empty, the mud, filth, and toads come to light.[1] The snow covers many a dunghill, so doth prosperity many a rotten heart. It is easy to wade in a warm bath, and every bird can sing in a sunshine day. Hard weather tries what health we have; afflictions try what sap we have, what grace we have. Withered leaves soon fall off in windy weather, rotten boughs quickly break with heavy weights. You are wise, and know how to apply it.

Afflictions are like pinching frosts, that will search us; where we are most unsound, we shall soonest complain, and where most corruptions lie, we shall most shrink. We try metal by knocking; if it sound well, then we like it. So God tries his

---

to add pearls to our crowns. Tiberius saw paradise when he walked upon hot burning coals. Herodotus said of the Assyrians, Let them drink nothing but wormwood all their life long; when they die, they shall swim in honey. You are wise, and know how to apply it.

[1] The king of Aracam (as Scaliger records), tries her whom he means to marry by sweating. If they be sweet, he marries them; if not, then he rejects them. You may easily make the application.

by knocking, and if under knocks they yield a pleasant sound, God will turn their night into day, and their bitter into sweet, and their cross into a crown; and they shall hear that voice, 'Arise, and shine; for the glory of the Lord is risen upon thee, and the favours of the Lord are flowing in on thee' (Isa. 60:1).[1]

Remedy (7). The seventh remedy against this device of Satan is solemnly to consider, *that the afflictions, wrath, and misery that do attend the ways of wickedness, are far greater and heavier than those are that do attend the ways of holiness.*[2] Oh, the galling, girding, lashing, and gnawing of conscience, that do attend souls in a way of wickedness! 'The wicked,' saith Isaiah, 'are like the troubled sea, when it cannot rest, whose waters cast up mire and dirt.' 'There is no peace to the wicked, saith my God.'[3] There are snares in all their mercies, and curses and crosses do attend all their comforts, both at home and abroad. What is a fine suit of clothes with the plague in it? and what is a golden cup when there is poison at the bottom? or what is a silken stocking with a broken leg in it? The curse of God, the wrath of God, the hatred of God, and the fierce indignation of God, do always attend sinners walking in a way of wickedness. Turn to Deuteronomy 28, and read from verse 15 to the end of the chapter, and turn to Leviticus 26, and read from verse 14 to the end of the chapter, and then you shall see how the curse

[1] Dunghills raked send out a filthy steam, ointments a sweet perfume. This is applicable to sinners and saints under the rod.

[2] Sin oftentimes makes men insensible of the wrath of the Almighty. Sin transforms many a man, as it were, into those bears in Pliny, that could not be stirred with the sharpest prickles; or those fishes in Aristotle, that though they have spears thrust into their sides, yet they awake not.

[3] Isa. 57:20 and 48:22.

of God haunts the wicked, as it were a fury, in all his ways. In
the city it attends him, in the country hovers over him; com-
ing in, it accompanies him; going forth, it follows him, and in
travel it is his comrade. It fills his store with strife, and mingles
the wrath of God with his sweetest morsels. It is a moth in
his wardrobe, murrain among his cattle, mildew in the field,
rot among sheep, and ofttimes makes the fruit of his loins
his greatest vexation and confusion. There is no solid joy, nor
lasting peace, nor pure comfort, that attends sinners in their
sinful ways.[1] There is a sword of vengeance that doth every
moment hang over their heads by a small thread;[2] and what joy
and content can attend such souls, if the eye of conscience be
but so far open as to see the sword? Ah! the horrors and terrors,
the tremblings and shakings, that attend their souls!

DEVICE 10. *By working them to be frequent in comparing
themselves and their ways with those that are reputed or reported
to be worse than themselves.* By this device the devil drew the
proud Pharisee to bless himself in a cursed condition, 'God,
I thank thee that I am not as other men are, extortioners,
unjust, adulterers, or even as this publican' (Luke 18:11). Why,
saith Satan, you swear but pretty oaths, as 'by your faith and
troth,' but such and such swear by wounds and blood; you are
now and then a little wanton, but such and such do daily defile
and pollute themselves by actual uncleanness and filthiness;
you deceive and overreach your neighbours in things that are

---

[1] Sin brings in sorrow and sickness. The Rabbins say, that when
Adam tasted the forbidden fruit, his head ached. Sirens are said to sing
curiously while they live, but to roar horribly when they die. So do the
wicked.

[2] The allusion is to Damocles.

but as toys and trifles, but such and such deceive and over-reach others in things of greatest concernment, even to their ruin and undoings; you do but sit, and chat, and sip with the drunkard, but such and such sit and drink and are drunk with the drunkard; you are only a little proud in heart and habit, in looks and words.

Remedy (1). The first remedy against this device of Satan is, solemnly to consider this, *that there is not a greater nor a clearer argument to prove a man a hypocrite, than to be quick-sighted abroad and blind at home*, than to see 'a mote in another man's eye, and not a beam in his own eye' (Matt. 7:3, 4); than to use spectacles to behold other men's sins rather than look-ing-glasses to behold his own; rather to be always holding his finger upon other men's sores, and to be amplifying and aggra-vating other men's sins than mitigating of his own.[1]

Remedy (2). The second remedy against this device of Satan is, *to spend more time in comparing of your internal and exter-nal actions with the Rule, with the word, by which you must be judged at last, than in comparing of yourselves with those that are worse than yourselves.*[2] That man that, comparing his self with others that are worse than himself, may seem, to himself and others, to be an angel; yet comparing himself with the word, may see himself to be like the devil, yea, a very devil. 'Have

[1] History speaks of a kind of witches that, stilting abroad, would put on their eyes, but returning home they boxed them up again. So do hypocrites.

[2] The nearer we draw to God and his word, the more rottenness we shall find in our bones. The more any man looks into the body of the sun, the less he seeth when he looks down again. It is said of the basilisk, that if he look into a glass he presently dieth; so will sin, and a sinner (in a spiritual sense), when the soul looks into the word, which is God's glass.

not I chosen twelve, and one of you is a devil?' (John 6:70). Such men are like him, as if they were spit out of his mouth.

Satan is called 'the god of this world' (2 Cor. 4:4), because, as God at first did but speak the word, and it was done, so, if the devil doth but hold up his finger, give the least hint, they will do his will, though they undo their souls for ever. Ah, what monsters would these men appear to be, did they but compare themselves with a righteous rule, and not with the most unrighteous men; they would appear to be as black as hell itself.

Remedy (3). The third remedy against this device of Satan is, seriously to consider, *that though thy sins be not as great as those of others, yet without sound repentance on thy side and pardoning mercy on God's, thou wilt be as certainly damned as others, though not equally tormented with others.*[1] What though hell shall not be so hot to thee as to others, yet thou must as certainly go to hell as others, unless the glorious grace of God shines forth upon thee in the face of Christ. God will suit men's punishments to their sins; the greatest sins shall be attended with the greatest punishments, and lesser sins with lesser punishments. Alas, what a poor comfort will this be to thee when thou comest to die, to consider that thou shalt not be equally tormented with others, yet must be for ever shut out from the glorious presence of God, Christ, angels, and saints, and from those good things of eternal life, that are so many that they exceed number, so great that they exceed measure, so precious that they exceed estimation! Sure it is, that the tears of heaven[2] are not sufficient to bewail the loss of

---

[1] As in heaven one is more glorious than another, so in hell one shall be more miserable than another. (*Augustine*)

[2] [Brooks seems to have written 'heaven' by mistake for 'hell.']

heaven; the worm of grief gnaws as painful as the fire burns; if those souls (Acts 20:37) wept because they should see Paul's face no more, how deplorable is the eternal deprivation of the beatifical vision![1]

But this is not all: thou shalt not be only shut out of heaven, but shut up in hell for ever; not only shut out from the presence of God and angels, but shut up with devils and damned spirits for ever; not only shut out from those sweet, surpassing, unexpressible, and everlasting pleasures that be at God's right hand, but shut up for ever under those torments that are ceaseless, remediless and endless.[2] Ah, souls, were it not ten thousand times better for you to break off your sins by repentance, than to go on in your sins till you feel the truth of what now you hear?

The God of Israel is very merciful. Ah, that you would repent and return, that your souls might live for ever! Remember this, grievous is the torment of the damned for the bitterness of the punishments, but most grievous for the eternity of the punishments. For to be tormented without end, this is that which goes beyond the bounds of all desperation. Ah, how do the thoughts of this make the damned to roar and cry out for unquietness of heart, and tear their hair, and gnash their teeth, and rage for madness, that they must dwell in 'everlasting burnings' for ever![3]

---

[1] The gate of indulgence, the gate of hope, the gate of mercy, the gate of glory, the gate of consolation, and the gate of salvation, will be for ever shut against them (Matt. 25:10).

[2] It was a good saying of Chrysostom, speaking of hell: Let us not seek where it is, but how we shall escape it.

[3] Surely one good means to escape hell is to take a turn or two in hell by our daily meditations.

DEVICE 11. *By polluting and defiling the soul and judg-ments of men with such dangerous errors, that do in their proper tendency tend to carry the souls of men to all looseness and wick-edness, as woeful experience doth abundantly evidence.* Ah, how many are there filled with these and suchlike Christ-dishon-ouring and soul-undoing opinions, viz. that ordinances are poor, low, carnal things, and not only to be lived above, but without also; that the Scriptures are full of fallacies and uncer-tainties, and no further to be heeded than they agree with that spirit that is in *them*; that it is a poor, low thing, if not idolatry too, to worship God in a Mediator; that the resurrection is already past; that there was never any such man or person as Jesus Christ, but that all is an allegory, and it signifies nothing but light and love, and such good frames born in men; that there is no God nor devil, heaven nor hell, but what is within us; that there is no sin in the saints, they are under no law but that of the Spirit, which is all freedom; that sin and grace are equally good, and agreeth to his will,—with a hundred other horrid opinions, which hath caused wickedness to break in as a flood among us..

Remedy (1). The first remedy against this device of Satan is, solemnly to consider, *that an erroneous, vain mind is as odious to God as a vicious life.*[1] He that had the leprosy in his head was to be pronounced utterly unclean (Lev. 13:44). Gross errors make the heart foolish, and render the life loose, and the soul light in the eye of God. Error spreads and frets like a gangrene, and renders the soul a leper in the sight of God.[2]

---

[1] A blind eye is worse than a lame foot.

[2] The breath of the erroneous is infectious, and, like the dogs of Congo, they bite though they bark not.

It was God's heavy and dreadful plague upon the Gentiles, to be given up to a mind void of judgment, or an injudicious mind, or a mind rejected, disallowed, abhorred of God, or a mind that none have cause to glory in, but rather to be ashamed of (Rom. 1:28). I think that in these days God punisheth many men's former wickednesses by giving them up to soul-ruining errors. Ah, Lord, this mercy I humbly beg, that thou wouldest rather take me into thine own hand, and do anything with me, than give me up to those sad errors to which thousands have married their souls and are in a way of perishing for ever.[1]

Remedy (2). The second remedy against this device of Satan is, *to receive the truth affectionately, and let it dwell in your souls plenteously.*[2] When men stand out against the truth, when truth would enter, and men bar the door of their souls against the truth, God in justice gives up such souls to be deluded and deceived by error, to their eternal undoing (2 Thess. 2:10-12): 'Because they received not the love of the truth, that they might be saved, God shall send them strong delusions (or, as the Greek hath it, "the efficacy of error,") that they should believe a lie; that they all might be damned who believed not the truth, but had pleasure in unrighteousness.' Ah, sirs, as you love your souls, do not tempt God, do not provoke God, by your withstanding truth and out-facing truth, to give you up to believe a lie, that you may be damned. There are no men on earth so fenced against error as those are that receive the truth in the love of it. Such souls are not 'easily tossed to and fro, and carried about with every wind of doctrine by

---

[1] Through animosity to persist in error is diabolical; it were best that we never erred; next to that, that we amended our error.

[2] The greatest sinners are sure to be the greatest sufferers.

the sleight of men and cunning craftiness, wherein they lie in wait to deceive' (Eph. 4:14).[1] It is not he that receives most of the truth unto his head, but he that receives most of the truth affectionately into his heart, that shall enjoy the happiness of having his judgment sound and clear, when others shall be deluded and deceived by them, who make it their business to infect the judgments and to undo the souls of men.

Ah, souls, as you would not have your judgments polluted and defiled with error, 'Let the word of the Lord,' that is more precious than gold, yea than fine gold, 'dwell plenteously in you' (Col. 3:16).[2] Oh, let not the word be a stranger, but make it your choicest familiar! Then will you be able to stand in the day wherein many shall fall on your right hand, and on your left, by the subtlety of those that shall say, 'Lo, here is Christ, or lo, there is Christ.'

There was more wit than grace in his speech that counselled his friends, 'Not to come too nigh unto truth, lest his teeth should be beaten out with its heels.' Ah, souls, if truth dwell plenteously in you, you are happy; if not, you are unhappy under all your greatest felicity.[3]

'It is with truth,' saith Melanchthon, 'as it is with holy water, every one praised it, and thought it had some rare virtue in it; but offer to sprinkle them with it, and they will shut their eyes, and turn away their faces from it.'

[1] The Greek signifies cogging with a die; such sleights as cheaters and false gamesters use at dice.

[2] Dwell in you as an ingrafted word incorporated into your souls, so concocted and digested by you, as that you turn it into a part of yourselves.

[3] *Veritas vincit*, Truth at last triumphs. *Veritas stat in aperto campo*, Truth stands in the open fields; ay, and it makes those souls stand in whom it dwells, when others fell as stars from heaven.

Remedy (3). The third remedy against this device of Satan is, solemnly to consider, *that error makes the owner to suffer loss.* All the pains and labour that men take to defend and maintain their errors, to spread abroad and infect the world with their errors, shall bring no profit, nor no comfort to them in that day, wherein 'every man's work shall be made manifest, and the fire shall try it of what sort it is,' as the apostle shows in that remarkable scripture (1 Cor. 3:11-15). Ah, that all those that rise early and go to bed late, that spend their time, their strength, their spirits, their all, to advance and spread abroad God-dishonouring and soul-undoing opinions, would seriously consider of this, that they shall lose all the pains, cost and charge that they have been, or shall be at, for the propagating of error; and if they are ever saved, it shall be by fire, as the apostle there shows. Ah, sirs, is it nothing to lay out your money for that which is not bread? and your strength for that which will not, which cannot, profit you in the day that you must make up your account, and all your works must be tried by fire?[1] Ah, that such souls would now at last 'buy the truth, and sell it not' (Prov. 23:23). Remember you can never over-buy it, whatsoever you give for it; you can never sufficiently sell it, if you should have all the world in exchange for it.

It is said of Caesar, that 'he had greater care of his books than of his royal robes,' for, swimming through the waters to escape his enemies, he carried his books in his hand above the waters, but lost his robes. Ah, what are Caesar's books to God's books? Well, remember this, that one day, yea, one hour

---

[1] Error as a glass is bright, but brittle, and cannot endure the hammer, or fire, as gold can, which, though rubbed or melted, remains firm and lustrous.

spent in the study of truth, or spreading abroad of truth, will yield the soul more comfort and profit than many thousand years spent in the study and spreading abroad of corrupt and vain opinions, that have their rise from hell, and not from heaven, from the god of this world and not from the God that shall at last judge this world, and all the corrupt opinions of men.

Remedy (4). The fourth remedy against this device of Satan is, *To hate, reject and abominate all those doctrines and opinions that are contrary to godliness, and that open a door to profaneness,[1] and all such doctrines and opinions that require men to hold forth a strictness above what the Scripture requireth; and all such doctrines and opinions that do advance and lift up corrupted nature to the doing of supernatural things, which none can do but by that supernatural power that raised Christ from the grave; and such opinions that do lift our own righteousness in the room of Christ's righteousness, that place good works in the throne of Christ, and makes them co-partners with Christ.* And all those opinions and doctrines that do so set up and cry up Christ and his righteousness, as to cry down all duties of holiness and righteousness, and all those doctrines and opinions that do make the glorious and blessed privileges of believers in the days of the gospel to be lesser, fewer and weaker, than they were in the time of the law. Ah, did your souls arise with a holy hatred, and a strong indignation against such doctrines and opinions, you would stand when others fall, and you

---

[1] One old piece of gold is worth a thousand new counters, and one old truth of God is more than a thousand new errors. True hatred is against all errors; It is sad to frown upon one error and smile upon another.

would shine as the sun in his glory, when many that were once as shining stars may go forth as stinking snuffs.[1]

Remedy (5). The fifth remedy against this device of Satan is, *to hold fast the truth.* As men take no hold on the arm of flesh till they let go the arm of God (Jer. 17:5), so men take no hold on error till they have let go their hold of truth; therefore hold fast the truth (2 Tim. 1:13 and Titus 1:9). Truth is thy crown, hold fast thy crown, and let no man take thy crown from thee. Hath not God made truth sweet to thy soul, yea, sweeter than honey, or the honeycomb? and wilt not thou go on to heaven, feeding upon truth, that heavenly honeycomb, as Samson did of his honeycomb?[2] Ah, souls, have you not found truth sweetening your spirits, and cheering your spirits, and warming your spirits, and raising your spirits, and corroborating your spirits? Have not you found truth a guide to lead you, a staff to uphold you, a cordial to strengthen you, and a plaster to heal you? And will not you hold fast the truth? Hath not truth been your best friend in your worst days? Hath not truth stood by you when friends have forsaken you? Hath not truth done more for you than all the world could do against you, and will you not hold fast the truth?[3] Is not truth your right eye, without which you cannot see for Christ? And your right hand, without which you cannot do for Christ? And your right foot, without which you cannot walk with Christ? And

---

[1] Gideon had seventy sons, and but one bastard, and yet that bastard destroyed all the rest (Judg. 8:29, etc.). One turn may bring a man quite out of the way.

[2] The priests of Mercury, when they ate their figs and honey, cried out, 'Sweet is truth.'

[3] It is with truth as with some plants, which live and thrive but in warm climates.

will you not hold truth fast? Oh! hold fast the truth in your judgments and understandings, in your wills and affections, in your profession and conversation.

Truth is more precious than gold or rubies, 'and all the things thou canst desire are not to be compared to her' (Prov. 3:15). Truth is that heavenly glass wherein we may see the lustre and glory of divine wisdom, power, greatness, love and mercifulness. In this glass you may see the face of Christ, the favour of Christ, the riches of Christ, and the heart of Christ, beating and working sweetly towards your souls. Oh! let your souls cleave to truth, as Ruth did to Naomi (Ruth 1:15, 16), and say, 'I will not leave truth, nor return from following after truth; but where truth goes I will go, and where truth lodgeth I will lodge; and nothing but death shall part truth and my soul.'[1] What John said to the church of Philadelphia I may say to you, 'Hold fast that which thou hast, that no man take thy crown' (Rev. 3:11). The crown is the top of royalties: such a thing is truth: 'Let no man take thy crown.' 'Hold fast the faithful word,' as Titus speaks (chap. 1:9).[2] You were better let go anything than truth; you were better let go your honours and riches, your friends and pleasures, and the world's favours; yea, your nearest and dearest relations, ay, your very lives, than to let go truth. Oh, keep the truth, and truth will make you safe and happy for ever. Blessed are those souls that are kept by truth.

---

[1] Though I cannot dispute for the truth, yet I can die for the truth, said a blessed martyr.

[2] Hold fast as with tooth and nail, against these that would snatch it from us.

Remedy (6). The sixth remedy against this device of Satan is, *to keep humble*. Humility will keep the soul free from many darts of Satan's casting, and erroneous snares of his spreading. As low trees and shrubs are free from many violent gusts and blasts of wind which shake and rend the taller trees, so humble souls are free from those gusts and blasts of error that rend and tear proud, lofty souls. Satan and the world have least power to fasten errors upon humble souls. The God of light and truth delights to dwell with the humble; and the more light and truth dwells in the soul, the further off darkness and error will stand from the soul. The God of grace pours in grace into humble souls, as men pour liquor into empty vessels; and the more grace is poured into the soul, the less error shall be able to overpower the soul, or to infect the soul.[1]

That is a sweet word in Psalm 25:9, 'The meek' (or the humble) 'will he guide in judgment, and the meek will he teach his way.'[2] And certainly souls guided by God, and taught by God, are not easily drawn aside into ways of error. Oh, take heed of spiritual pride! Pride fills our fancies, and weakens our graces, and makes room in our hearts for error. There are no men on earth so soon entangled, and so easily conquered by error, as proud souls. Oh, it is dangerous to love to be wise above what is written, to be curious and unsober in your desire of knowledge, and to trust to your own capacities and abilities

---

[1] I have read of one who, seeing in a vision so many snares of the devil spread upon the earth, he sat down mourning, and said within himself, Who shall pass through these? whereupon he heard a voice answering, Humility shall pass through them.

[2] Psa. 25:9: 'Gnanavim' (Hebrew), which signifies 'the humble or afflicted.' The high ride quickly ebbs, and the highest sun is presently declining. You know how to apply it.

to undertake to pry into all secrets, and to be puffed up with a carnal mind. Souls that are thus a-soaring up above the bounds and limits of humility, usually fall into the very worst of errors, as experience doth daily evidence.[1]

Remedy (7). The seventh remedy against this device of Satan is, solemnly to consider, *the great evils that errors have produced.* Error is a fruitful mother, and hath brought forth such monstrous children as hath set towns, cities and nations on fire.[2] Error is that whorish woman that hath cast down many, wounded many, yea, slain many strong men, many great men, and many learned men, and many professing men in former times and in our time, as is too evident to all that are destitute of the truth, and blinded by Satan. Oh, the graces that error hath weakened, and the sweet joys and comforts that error hath clouded, if not buried! Oh, the hands that error hath weakened, the eyes that error hath blinded, the judgments of men that error hath perverted, the minds that error hath darkened, the hearts that error hath hardened, the affections that error hath cooled, the consciences that error hath seared, and the lives of men that error hath polluted! Ah, souls! can you solemnly consider of this, and not tremble more at error than at hell itself?

DEVICE 12. *To choose wicked company, to keep wicked society.* And oh! the horrid impieties and wickedness that Satan hath drawn men to sin, by moving them to sit and associate themselves with vain persons.

[1] The proud soul is like him that gazed upon the moon, but fell into the pit.

[2] Errors in conscience produce many great evils, not only in men's own souls, but also in human affairs.

Remedy (1). The first remedy against this device of Satan is, *to dwell, till your hearts be affected, upon those commands of God that do expressly require us to shun the society of the wicked* (Eph. 5:11): 'And have no fellowship with the unfruitful works of darkness, but rather reprove them'; (Prov. 4:14-16): 'Enter not into the path of the wicked, and go not in the way of evil men. Avoid it, pass not by it, turn from it, and pass away.' 1 Cor. 5:9-11; 2 Thess. 3:6; Prov. 1:10-15. Turn to these Scriptures, and let your souls dwell upon them, till a holy indignation be raised in your souls against fellowship with vain men. 'God will not take the wicked by the hand,' as Job speaks (8:20; 30:24). Why then should you? God's commands are not like those that are easily reversed, but they are like those of the Medes, they cannot be changed. If these commands be not now observed by thee, they will at last be witnesses against thee, and millstones to sink thee, in that day that Christ shall judge thee.[1]

Remedy (2). The second remedy against this device of Satan is, seriously to consider, *that their company is very infectious and dangerous,* as is clear from the Scripture above mentioned. Ah, how many have lost their names, and lost their estates, and strength, and God, and heaven, and souls, by society with wicked men! As ye shun a stinking carcase, as the seaman shuns sands and rocks, and shoals, as ye shun those that have the plague-sores running upon them, so should you shun the society of wicked men. As weeds endanger the corn, as bad humours endanger the blood, or as an infected house the neighbourhood, so doth wicked company the soul[2] (Prov. 13:20).

---

[1] The commands of God must outweigh all authority and example of men. (*Jerome*)

[2] Eusebius reports of John the Evangelist, that he would not suffer

Bias, a heathen man, being at sea in a great storm, and per-
ceiving many wicked men in the ship calling upon the gods:
'Oh,' said he, 'forbear prayer, hold your tongues; I would not
have the gods take notice that you are here; they sure will
drown us all if they should.' Ah, sirs, could a heathen see so
much danger in the society of wicked men, and can you see
none?

Remedy (3). The third remedy against this device of Satan is,
*to look always upon wicked men under those names and notions
that the Scripture doth set them out under.* The Scripture calls
them lions for their fierceness, and bears for their cruelty, and
dragons for their hideousness, and dogs for their filthiness,
and wolves for their subtleness. The Scripture styles them scor-
pions, vipers, thorns, briars, thistles, brambles, stubble, dirt,
chaff, dust, dross, smoke, scum, as you may see in the margin.[1]
It is not safe to look upon wicked men under those names
and notions that they set out themselves by, or that flatterers
set them out by; this may delude the soul, but the looking
upon them under those names and notions that the Scrip-
ture sets them out by, may preserve the soul from frequenting
their company and delighting in their society. Do not tell me
what this man calls them, or how such and such count them;
but tell me how doth the Scripture call them, how doth the
Scripture count them? As Nabal's name was, so was his nature
(1 Sam. 25:25), and, as wicked men's names are, so are their

Cerinthus, the heretic, in the same bath with him, lest some judgment
should abide them both. A man that keepeth ill company is like him
that walketh in the sun, tanned insensibly.

[1] 2 Tim. 4:17; Isa. 11:7; Ezek. 3:10; Matt. 7:6; Rev. 22:15; Luke 13:32;
Isa. 10:17; Ezek. 2:6; Judg. 9:14; Job 21:18; Psa. 83:13; Psa. 18:42; Ezek.
22:18, 19; Isa. 65:5; Ezek. 24:6.

natures. You may know well enough what is within them, by the apt names that the Holy Ghost hath given them.[1]

Remedy (4). The fourth remedy against this device of Satan, is, solemnly to consider, *that the society and company of wicked men have been a great grief and burden to those precious souls that were once glorious on earth, and are now triumphing in heaven* (Psa. 120:5, 6): 'Woe is me, that I sojourn in Mesech, that I dwell in the tents of Kedar! My soul hath long dwelt with him that hateth peace.' So Jeremiah; 'Oh, that I had in the wilderness a lodging-place of wayfaring men, that I might leave my people, and go from them! for they be all adulterers, an assembly of treacherous men' (Jer. 9:2). So they vexed Lot's righteous soul by 'their filthy conversation' (2 Pet. 2:7);[2] they made his life a burden, they made death more desirable to him than life, yea, they made his life a lingering death. Guilt or grief is all that good gracious souls get by conversing with wicked men.

---

[1] Lactantius says of Lucian that he spared neither God nor man; such monsters are wicked men, which should render their company to all that have tasted of the sweetness of divine love, a burden and not a delight.

[2] O Lord, let me not go to hell, where the wicked are; for Lord, thou knowest I never loved their company here, said a gracious gentlewoman, when she was to die, being in much trouble of conscience.

III.

SATAN'S DEVICES TO KEEP SOULS FROM HOLY DUTIES, TO HINDER SOULS IN HOLY SERVICES, AND TO KEEP THEM OFF FROM RELIGIOUS PERFORMANCES

———

T HE second thing to be shown is, the several devices that Satan hath, as to draw souls to sin, so to keep souls from holy duties, to hinder souls in holy services, and to keep them off from religious performances.

> And he showed me Joshua the high priest standing before the angel of the Lord, and Satan standing at his right hand to resist him (Zech. 3:1).

DEVICE 1. *By presenting the world in such a dress, and in such a garb to the soul, as to ensnare the soul, and to win upon the affection of the soul.* He represents the world to them in its beauty and bravery,[1] which proves a bewitching sight to a world of men.[2] (It is true, this took not Christ, because Satan could find no matter in him for his temptation to work upon.) So that he can no sooner cast out his golden bait, but

[1] 'Finery.'
[2] The beauty of the world foils a Christian more than the strength; the flattering sunshine more than the blustering storm. In storms we keep our garments close about us.

we are ready to play with it, and to nibble at it; he can no sooner throw out his golden ball, but men are apt to run after it, though they lose God and their souls in the pursuit. Ah! how many professors in these days have for a time followed hard after God, Christ, and ordinances, till the devil hath set before them the world in all its beauty and bravery, which hath so bewitched their souls that they have grown to have low thoughts of holy things, and then to be cold in their affections to holy things, and then to slight them, and at last, with the young man in the Gospel, to turn their backs upon them. All the time, the thoughts, the spirits, the hearts, the souls, the duties, the services, that the inordinate love of this wicked world doth eat up and destroy, and hath ate up and destroyed. Where one thousand are destroyed by the world's frowns, ten thousand are destroyed by the world's smiles. The world, siren-like, it sings us and sinks us; it kisses us, and betrays us, like Judas; it kisses us and smites us under the fifth rib, like Joab. The honours, splendour, and all the glory of this world, are but sweet poisons, that will much endanger us, if they do not eternally destroy us.[1] Ah! the multitude of souls that have surfeited of these sweet baits and died for ever.

Remedy (1). The first remedy against this device of Satan is, *to dwell upon the impotency and weakness of all these things here below.* They are not able to secure you from the least evil, they are not able to procure you the least desirable good. The crown of gold cannot cure the headache, nor the velvet slipper

---

[1] The inhabitants of Nilus are deaf by the noise of the waters; so the world makes such a noise in men's ears, that they cannot hear the things of heaven. The world is like the swallows' dung that put out Tobias's eyes. The champions could not wring an apple out of Milo's hand by a strong hand, but a fair maid, by fair means, got it presently.

ease the gout, nor the jewel about the neck take away the pain of the teeth. The frogs of Egypt entered into the rich men's houses of Egypt, as well as the poor. Our daily experience doth evidence this, that all the honours and riches that men enjoy, cannot free them from the cholic, the fever, or lesser diseases.[1] Nay, that which may seem most strange, is that a great deal of wealth cannot keep men from falling into extreme poverty. You shall find seventy kings, with their fingers and toes cut off, glad, like whelps, to lick up crumbs under another king's table; and shortly after, the same king that brought them to this penury, is reduced to the same poverty and misery (Judg. 1:6). Why then should that be a bar to keep thee out of heaven, that cannot give thee the least ease on earth?'

Remedy (2). The second remedy against this device of Satan is, *to dwell upon the vanity of them as well as upon the impotency of all worldly good.* This is the sum of Solomon's sermon, 'Vanity of vanities, all is vanity.' This our first parents found, and therefore named their second son Abel, or 'vanity.' Solomon, that had tried these things, and could best tell the vanity of them, he preacheth this sermon over again and again. 'Vanity of vanities, all is vanity.' It is sad to think how many thousands there be that can say with the preacher, 'Vanity of vanities, all is vanity,' nay, swear it, and yet follow after these things as if there were no other glory, nor felicity, but what is to be found in these things they call vanity.[2] Such men will sell Christ,

---

[1] A prior, said Melanchthon, rolled his hand up and down in a basinful of angels, thinking thereby to have charmed his gout, but it would not do, Nugas the Scythian, despising the rich presents and ornaments that were sent unto him by the emperor of Constantinople, asked whether those things could drive away calamities, diseases, or death.

[2] Gilemex, king of Vandals, led in triumph by Belisarius, cried

heaven, and their souls for a trifle, that call these things vanity, but do not cordially believe them to be vanity, but set their hearts upon them as if they were their crown, the top of their royalty and glory. Oh let your souls dwell upon the vanity of all things here below, till your hearts be so thoroughly convinced and persuaded of the vanity of them, as to trample upon them, and make them a footstool for Christ to get up, and ride in a holy triumph in your hearts.[1]

Chrysostom once said, That if he were the fittest in the world to preach a sermon to the whole world, gathered together in one congregation, and had some high mountain for his pulpit, from whence he might have a prospect of all the world in his view, and were furnished with a voice of brass, a voice as loud as the trumpets of the archangel, that all the world might hear him, he would choose to preach upon no other text than that in the Psalms, 'O mortal men, how long will ye love vanity, and follow after leasing?' (Psa. 4:2).

Tell me, you that say all things under the sun are vanity, if you do really believe what you say, why do you spend more thoughts and time on the world, than you do on Christ, heaven and your immortal souls? Why do you then neglect your duty towards God, to get the world? Why do you then so eagerly pursue after the world, and are so cold in your pursuing after God, Christ and holiness? Why then are your hearts

---

out, 'Vanity of vanity, all is vanity?' The fancy of Lucian, who placeth Charon on the top of an high hill, viewing all the affairs of men living, and looking on their greatest cities as little birds' nests, is very pleasant.

[1] Oh the imperfection, the ingratitude, the levity, the inconstancy, the perfidiousness of those creatures we most servilely affect. Ah, did we but weigh man's pain with his payment, his crosses with his mercies, his miseries with his pleasures, we should then see that there is nothing got by the bargain, and conclude, 'Vanity of vanities, all is vanity?'

so exceedingly raised, when the world comes in, and smiles upon you; and so much dejected, and cast down, when the world frowns upon you, and with Jonah's gourd withers before you?

Remedy (3). The third remedy against this device of Satan is, *to dwell much upon the uncertainty, the mutability, and inconstancy of all things under the sun.* Man himself is but the dream of a dream, but the generation of a fancy, but an empty vanity, but the curious picture of nothing, a poor, feeble, dying flash. All temporals are as transitory as a hasty headlong current, a shadow, a ship, a bird, an arrow, a post that passeth by. 'Why shouldst thou set thine eyes upon that which is not?' saith Solomon (Prov. 23:5). And saith the apostle, 'The fashion of this world passeth away'[1] (1 Cor. 7:31). Heaven only hath a foundation, earth hath none, 'but is hanged upon nothing,' as Job speaks (26:7). The apostle willed Timothy to 'charge rich men that they be not high-minded, nor put their trust in uncertain riches' (1 Tim. 6:17).[2] They are like bad servants, whose shoes are made of running leather,[3] and will never tarry long with one master. As a bird hoppeth from tree to tree, so do the honours and riches of this world from man to man. Let Job and Nebuchadnezzar testify this truth, who fell from great wealth to great want. No man can promise himself to be wealthy till night; one storm at sea, one coal of fire, one false friend, one unadvised word, one false witness, may make thee a beggar

---

[1] 1 Cor. 7:31 intimateth, that there is nothing of any firmness, or solid consistence, in the creature.

[2] Riches were never true to any that trusted to them; they have deceived men, as Job's brook did the poor travellers in the summer season (Job 6:15).

[3] A phrase meaning, he is given to rambling about.

and a prisoner all at once. All the riches and glory of this world is but as smoke and chaff that vanisheth; 'As a dream and vision in the night, that tarrieth not' (Job 20:8). 'As if a hungry man dreameth, and like a thirsty man which thinketh he drinketh, and behold when he is awaked, his soul is faint,' as the prophet Isaiah saith (Chap. 29:8). Where is the glory of Solomon? the sumptuous buildings of Nebuchadnezzar? the nine hundred chariots of Sisera? the power of Alexander? the authority of Augustus, that commanded the whole world to be taxed? Those that have been the most glorious, in what men generally account glorious and excellent, have had inglorious ends; as Samson for strength, Absalom for favour, Ahithophel for policy, Haman for favour, Asahel for swiftness, Alexander for great conquest and yet after twelve years poisoned. The same you may see in the four mighty kingdoms, the Chaldean, Persian, Grecian, and Roman: how soon were they gone and forgotten![1] Now rich, now poor, now full, now empty, now in favour, anon out of favour, now honourable, now despised, now health, now sickness, now strength, now weakness.[2]

Remedy (4). The fourth remedy against this device of Satan is, seriously to consider, *that the great things of this world are very hurtful and dangerous to the outward and inward man, through the corruptions that be in the hearts of men.* Oh, the

[1] The most renowned Frederick lost all, and sued to be made but sexton of the church that himself had built. I have read of a poor fisherman, who, while his nets were a-drying, slept upon the rock, and dreamed that he was made a king, on a sudden starts up, and leaping for joy, fell down from the rock, and in the place of his imaginary felicities loses his little portion of pleasures.

[2] The pomp of this world John compareth to the moon, which increaseth and decreaseth (Rev. 12:1).

rest, the peace, the comfort, the content that the things of this world do strip many men of! Oh, the fears, the cares, the envy, the malice, the dangers, the mischiefs, that they subject men to![1] They oftentimes make men carnally confident.[2] The rich man's riches are a strong tower in his imagination. 'I said in my prosperity I should never be moved' (Psa. 30:6). They often swell the heart with pride, and make men forget God, and neglect God, and despise the rock of their salvation. When Jeshurun 'waxed fat, and was grown thick, and covered with fatness, then he forgot God, and forsook God that made him, and lightly esteemed the rock of his salvation,' as Moses spake (Deut. 32:15). Ah, the time, the thoughts, the spirits, that the things of the world consume and spend! Oh, how do they hinder the actings of faith upon God! how do they interrupt our sweet communion with God! how do they abate our love to the people of God! and cool our love to the things of God! and work us to act like those that are most unlike to God! Oh, the deadness, the barrenness that doth attend men under great outward mercies![3] Oh, the riches of the world chokes the word; that men live under the most soul-searching, and soul-enriching means with lean souls! Though they have full purses, though their chests are full of silver, yet their hearts are empty of grace. In Genesis 13:2, it is said, that 'Abram was very rich in cattle, in silver and in gold.' According to the

[1] Henry the Second, hearing Le Mans his chief city to be taken, used this blasphemous speech: I shall never, saith he, love God any more, that suffered a city so dear to me to be taken from me.

[2] When one presented Antipater, king of Macedonia, with a book treating on happiness, his answer was, I have no leisure.

[3] Four good mothers beget four bad daughters: great familiarity begets contempt; truth, hatred; virtue, envy; riches, ignorance (a French proverb).

Hebrew, it is 'Abram was very weary'; to show that riches are a heavy burden, and a hindrance many times to heaven, and happiness.[1]

King Henry the Fourth (of France) asked the Duke of Alva if he had observed the great eclipse of the sun, which had lately happened. No, said the duke, I have so much to do on earth, that I have no leisure to look up to heaven. Ah, that this were not true of most professors in these days! It is very sad to think, how their hearts and time is so much taken up with earthly things, that they have scarce any leisure to look up to heaven, or to look after Christ, and the things that belong to their everlasting peace.

Riches, though well got, yet are but like to manna; those that gathered less had no want, and those that gathered more, it was but a trouble and annoyance to them. The world is troublesome, and yet it is loved; what would it be if it were peaceable? You embrace it, though it be filthy; what would you do if it were beautiful? You cannot keep your hands from the thorns; how earnest would you be then in gathering the flowers? The world may be fitly likened to the serpent Scytale, whereof it is reported, that when she cannot overtake the flying passengers, she doth with her beautiful colours so astonish and amaze them, that they have no power to pass away, till she hath stung them.[2] Ah, how many thousands are there now

---

[1] Polycrates bestowed five talents for a gift upon one Anacreon, who for two nights after was so troubled with care how to keep them, and how to bestow them, as he carried them back again to Polycrates, saying, they were not worth the pains which he had already taken for them.

[2] Sicily is so full of sweet flowers that dogs cannot hunt there. And what do all the sweet contents of this world, but make us lose the scent of heaven!

on earth, that have found this true by experience, that have spun a fair thread to strangle themselves, both temporally and eternally, by being bewitched by the beauty and bravery of this world.

Remedy (5). The fifth remedy against this device of Satan is, to consider, *that all the felicity of this world is mixed. Our light is mixed with darkness, our joy with sorrow, our pleasures with pain, our honour with dishonour, our riches with wants.* If our lights be spiritual, clear and quick, we may see in the felicity of this world our wine mixed with water, our honey with gall, our sugar with wormwood, and our roses with prickles.[1] Sorrow attends worldly joy, danger attends worldly safety, loss attends worldly labours, tears attend worldly purposes. As to these things, men's hopes are vain, their sorrow certain and joy feigned. The apostle calls this world 'a sea of glass,' a sea for the trouble of it, and glass for the brittleness and bitterness of it.[2] The honours, profits, pleasures and delights of the world are true gardens of Adonis, where we can gather nothing but trivial flowers, surrounded with many briars.

Remedy (6). The sixth remedy against this device of Satan is, *to get better acquaintance and better assurance of more blessed and glorious things.*[3] That which raised up their spirits (Heb. 10 and 11) to trample upon all the beauty, bravery and glory of the

[1] Hark, scholar, said the harlot to Apuleius, it is but a bitter sweet you are so fond of. Surely all the things of this world are but bitter sweets.

[2] Qu, *not* this world? Cf. Rev. 4:6; 15:2; 21:18.

[3] Let heaven be a man's object, and earth will soon be his abject. Luther being at one time in some wants, it happened that a good sum of money was unexpectedly sent him by a nobleman of Germany, at which, being something amazed, he said, 'I fear that God will give me my reward here, but I protest I will not be so satisfied.'

world, was the acquaintance with, 'and assurance of better and more durable things.' 'They took joyfully the spoiling of their goods, knowing in themselves that they had in heaven a better and a more durable substance.' 'They looked for a house that had foundations, whose builder and maker was God.' 'And they looked for another country, even an heavenly.' 'They saw him that was invisible, and had an eye to the recompense of reward.'[1] And this made them count all the glory and bravery of this world to be too poor and contemptible for them to set their hearts upon. The main reason why men dote upon the world, and damn their souls to get the world, is, because they are not acquainted with a greater glory. Men ate acorns, till they were acquainted with the use of wheat. Ah, were men more acquainted with what union and communion with God means, what it is to have 'a new name, and a new stone, that none knows but he that hath it' (Rev. 2:17); did they but taste more of heaven, and live more in heaven, and had more glorious hopes of going to heaven, ah, how easily would they have the moon under their feet.

It was an excellent saying of Lewis of Bavaria, emperor of Germany, 'Such goods are worth getting and owning, as will not sink or wash away if a shipwreck happen, but will wade and swim out with us.'[2] It is recorded of Lazarus, that after his resurrection from the dead, he was never seen to laugh, his thoughts and affections were so fixed in heaven, though

[1] Heb. 10:34; 11:10, 16, 26.
[2] There is, saith Augustine, *bona throni*, goods of the throne; and there are *bona scabelli*, goods of the footstool: when Basil was tempted with money and preferment, said he, 'Give me money that may last for ever, and glory that may eternally flourish; for the fashion of this world passeth away, as the waters of a river that runs by a city.'

his body was on earth, and therefore he could not but slight temporal things, his heart being so bent and set upon eternals. There are goods for the throne of grace, as God, Christ, the Spirit, adoption, justification, remission of sin, peace with God, and peace with conscience; and there are goods of the footstool, as honours, riches, the favour of creatures, and other comforts and accommodations of this life. Now he that hath acquaintance with, and assurance of the goods of the throne, will easily trample upon the goods of the footstool. Ah that you would make it your business, your work, to mind more, and make sure more to your own souls, the great things of eternity, that will yield you joy in life and peace in death, and a crown of righteousness in the day of Christ's appearing, and that will lift up your souls above all the beauty and bravery of this bewitching world, that will raise your feet above other men's heads. When a man comes to be assured of a crown, a sceptre and the royal robes, he then begins to have low, mean and contemptible thoughts of those things that before he highly prized. So will assurance of more great and glorious things breed in the soul a holy scorn and contempt of all these poor, mean things, which the soul before did value above God, Christ and heaven.

Remedy (7). The seventh remedy against this device of Satan is, seriously to consider, *that true happiness and satisfaction is not to be had in the enjoyment of worldly good*. True happiness is too big and too glorious a thing to be found in anything below that God that is a Christian's *summum bonum*, chiefest good.[1] The blessed angels, those glittering courtiers, have

[1] True happiness lies only in our enjoyment of a suitable good, a pure good, a total good, and an eternal good; and God only is such a good,

all felicities and blessedness, and yet have they neither gold, nor silver, nor jewels, nor none of the beauty and bravery of this world. Certainly if happiness was to be found in these things, the Lord Jesus, who is the right and royal heir of all things, would have exchanged his cradle for a crown; his birth chamber, a stable, for a royal palace; his poverty for plenty; his despised followers for shining courtiers; and his mean provisions for the choicest delicates. Certainly happiness lies not in those things that a man may enjoy, and yet be miserable for ever. Now a man may be great and graceless with Pharaoh, honourable and damnable with Saul, rich and miserable with Dives: therefore happiness lies not in these things. Certainly happiness lies not in those things that cannot comfort a man upon a dying bed. Is it honours, riches or friends that can comfort thee when thou comest to die? Or is it not rather faith in the blood of Christ, the witness of the Spirit of Christ, the sense and feeling of the love and favour of Christ, and the hopes of eternally reigning with Christ? Can happiness lie in those things that cannot give us health, or strength, or ease, or a good night's rest, or an hour's sleep, or a good stomach? Why, all the honours, riches and delights of this world cannot give these poor things to us, therefore certainly happiness lies not in the enjoyment of them.[1] And surely happiness is not to be found in those things that cannot satisfy the souls of men. Now none of these things can satisfy the soul of man. 'He that loveth silver shall not be satisfied with silver, nor he that loveth abundance with increase; this is also vanity,' said

---

and such a good can only satisfy die soul of man. Philosophers could say, that he was never a happy man that might afterwards become miserable.

[1] Gregory the Great used to say, He is poor whose soul is void of grace, not whose coffers are empty of money. The reasonable soul may be busied about other things but it cannot be filled with them.

the wise man (Eccles. 5:10). The barren womb, the horseleech's daughter, the grave and hell, will as soon be satisfied, as the soul of man will by the enjoyment of any worldly good. Some one thing or another will be for ever wanting to that soul that hath none but outward good to live upon. You may as soon fill a bag with wisdom, a chest with virtue, or a circle with a triangle, as the heart of man with anything here below. A man may have enough of the world to sink him, but he can never have enough to satisfy him.

Remedy (8). The eighth remedy against this device of Satan is, solemnly to consider, *of the dignity of the soul*. Oh, the soul of man is more worth than a thousand worlds! It is the greatest abasing of it that can be to let it dote upon a little shining earth, upon a little painted beauty and fading glory, when it is capable of union with Christ, of communion with God, and of enjoying the eternal vision of God.

Seneca could say, 'I am too great, and born to greater things, than that I should be a slave to my body.' Oh! do you say my soul is too great, and born to greater things, than that I should confine it to a heap of white and yellow earth?[1]

I have been the longer upon the remedies that may help us against this dangerous device of Satan, because he doth usually more hurt to the souls of men by this device than he doth by all other devices. For a close, I wish, as once Chrysostom did, that that sentence (Eccles. 2:11). 'Then I looked on all the

[1] Plutarch tells of Themistocles, that he accounted it not to stand with his state to stoop down to take up the spoils the enemies had scattered in flight; but saith to one of his followers 'You may, for you are not Themistocles.' Oh what a sad thing it is that a heathen should set his feet upon those very things upon which most professors set their hearts, and for the gain of which, with Balaam, many run the hazard of losing their immortal souls for ever.

works that my hands had wrought, and on the labour that I had laboured to do, and behold all was vanity and vexation of spirit, and there was no profit under the sun,' were engraven on the door-posts into which you enter, on the tables where you sit, on the dishes out of which you eat, on the cups out of which you drink, on the bedsteads where you lie, on the walls of the house where you dwell, on the garments which you wear, on the heads of the horses on which you ride, and on the foreheads of all them whom you meet, that your souls may not, by the beauty and bravery of the world, be kept off from those holy and heavenly services that may render you blessed while you live, and happy when you die; that you may breathe out your last into his bosom who lives for ever, and who will make them happy for ever that prefer Christ's spirituals and eternals above all temporal transitory things.

DEVICE 2. The second device that Satan hath to draw the soul from holy duties, and to keep them off from religious services, is, *by presenting to them the danger, the losses, and the sufferings that do attend the performance of such and such religious services*. By this device Satan kept those that believed on Christ from confessing of Christ: in John 12:42, 'Nevertheless among the chief rulers also many believed on him; but because of the Pharisees they did not confess him, lest they should be put out of the synagogue.' I would walk in all the ways of God, I would give up myself to the strictest way of holiness, but I am afraid dangers will attend me on the one hand, and losses, and haply such and such sufferings on the other hand, saith many a man. Oh, how should we help ourselves against this temptation and device of Satan!

Remedy (1). The first remedy against this device of Satan is to consider, t*hat all the troubles and afflictions that you meet with in a way of righteousness shall never hurt you, they shall never harm you. 'And who is he that shall harm you, if you be followers of that which is good?*' saith the apostle, *i.e.* none shall harm you (1 Pet. 3:13).[1] Natural conscience cannot but do homage to the image of God stamped upon the natures, words, works, and life of the godly; as we may see in the carriage of Nebuchadnezzar and Darius towards Daniel. All afflictions and troubles that do attend men in a way of righteousness can never rob them of their treasure, of their jewels. They may rob them of some light slight things, as the sword that is by their side, or the stick in their hand, or of the flowers or ribbons that be in their hats.[2] The treasures of a saint are the presence of God, the favour of God, union and communion with God, the pardon of sin, the joy of the Spirit, the peace of conscience, which are jewels that none can give but Christ, nor none can take away but Christ. Now why should a gracious soul keep off from a way of holiness because of afflictions, when no afflictions can strip a man of his heavenly jewels, which are his ornaments and his safety here, and will be his happiness and glory hereafter? Why should that man be afraid, or troubled for storms at sea, whose treasures are sure in a friend's hand upon land? Why, a believer's treasure is always safe in the hands of Christ; his life is safe, his soul is safe, his grace is safe, his comfort is safe, and his crown is safe in the hand of

---

[1] Nobody is properly hurt but by himself, and by his own fault.

[2] Gordius, that blessed martyr, accounted it a loss to him not to suffer many kinds of tortures. He saith tortures are but tradings with God for glory. The greater the combat is, the greater is the following reward.

Christ.[1] 'I know him in whom I have believed, and that he is able to keep that which I have committed unto him until that day,' saith the apostle (2 Tim. 1:12). The child's most precious things are most secure in his father's hands; so are our souls, our graces, and our comforts in the hand of Christ.

Remedy (2). The second remedy against this device of Satan is to consider, *that other precious saints that were shining lights on earth, and are now triumphing in heaven, have held on in religious services, notwithstanding all the troubles and dangers that have surrounded them.*[2] Nehemiah and Ezra were surrounded with dangers on the left hand and on the right, and yet, in the face of all, they held on building the temple and the wall of Jerusalem. So Daniel, and those precious worthies (Psa. 44:19, 20), under the want of outward encouragements, and in the face of a world of very great discouragements, their souls clave to God and his ways. 'Though they were sore broken in the place of dragons, and covered with the shadow of death, yea, though they were all the day long counted as sheep for the slaughter, yet their hearts were not turned back, neither did their steps decline from his ways.' Though bonds and imprisonments did attend Paul and the rest of the apostles in every place, yet they held on in the work and service of the Lord; and why, then, should you degenerate from their worthy

---

[1] That was a notable speech of Luther, let him that died for my soul see to the salvation of it.

[2] Will Fowler (martyr) said: Heaven will as soon fall as I will forsake my profession or budge in the least degree from it. So Sanctus, being under great torments, cries out, *Christianus sum*, I am a Christian. No torments could work him to decline the service of God. I might produce a cloud of witnesses; but if those do not work you to be noble and brave, I am afraid more will not.

examples, which is your duty and your glory to follow? (2 Cor. 6:5, Heb. 11:36).

Remedy (3). The third remedy against this device of Satan is, solemnly to consider, *that all the troubles and dangers that do attend the performance of all holy duties and heavenly services are but temporal and momentary, but the neglect of them may lay thee open to all temporal, spiritual, and eternal dangers.* 'How shall we escape, if we neglect so great salvation?' (Heb. 2:3). He saith not, if we reject or renounce so great salvation. No; but if we neglect, or shift off so great salvation, how shall we escape?[1] That is, we cannot by any way, or means, or device in the world, escape. Divine justice will be above us, in spite of our very souls. The doing of such and such heavenly services may lay you open to the frowns of men, but the neglect of them will lay you open to the frowns of God; the doing of them may render you contemptible in the eyes of men, but the neglect of them may render you contemptible in the eyes of God; the doing of them may be the loss of thy estate, but the neglect of them may be the loss of God, Christ, heaven, and thy soul for ever; the doing of them may shut thee out from some outward temporal contents, the neglect of them may shut thee out from that excellent matchless glory 'that eye hath not seen, nor ear heard, neither hath it entered into the heart of men' (Isa. 64:4). Remember this, there is no man that breathes but shall suffer more by neglecting those holy and heavenly services that God commands, commends, and rewards, than he can possibly suffer by doing of them.[2]

---

[1] The Greek signifies—disregard, not care for it.

[2] Francis Xavier counselled John the Third, king of Portugal, to meditate every day a quarter of an hour upon that text, 'What shall it profit a man to gain the whole world, and lose his soul!'

Remedy (4). The fourth remedy against this device of Satan is, to consider, *that God knows how to deliver from troubles by troubles, from afflictions by afflictions, from dangers by dangers.* God, by lesser troubles and afflictions, doth oftentimes deliver his people from greater, so that they shall say. We had perished, if we had not perished; we had been undone, if we had not been undone; we had been in danger, if we had not been in danger. God will so order the afflictions that befall you in the way of righteousness, that your souls shall say. We would not for all the world but that we had met with such and such troubles and afflictions: for surely, had not these befallen us, it would have been worse and worse with us. Oh the carnal security, pride, formality, dead-heartedness, lukewarmness, censoriousness, and earthliness that God hath cured us of, by the trouble and dangers that we have met with in the ways and services of the Lord!

I remember a story of a godly man, that, as he was going to take shipping for France, he broke his leg; and it pleased Providence so to order it, that the ship that he should have gone in, at that very instant was cast away, and not a man saved; so by breaking a bone, his life was saved.[1] So the Lord many times breaks our bones, but it is in order to the saving of our lives and our souls for ever. He gives us a portion that makes us heart-sick, but it is in order to the making us perfectly well, and to the purging of us from those ill humours that have made our heads ache, and God's heart ache, and our souls sick, and heavy to the death. Oh therefore let no danger or misery hinder thee from thy duty.[2]

[1] The 'breaking of his leg' on the way saved the life of the saintly Bernard Gilpin from being sacrificed by Bonner, Bishop of London (1558).

[2] Had not these things perished, I could not have been safe, said a philosopher when he saw what great possessions he had lost.

Remedy (5). The fifth remedy against this device of Satan is, solemnly to consider, *that you shall gain more in the service of God, and by walking in righteous and holy ways, though troubles and afflictions should attend you, than you can possibly suffer, or lose, by your being found in the service of God.* 'Godliness is great gain' (1 Tim. 6:6). Oh, the joy, the peace, the comfort, the rest, that saints meet with in the ways and service of God! They find that religious services are not empty things, but things in which God is pleased to discover his beauty and glory to their souls. 'My soul thirsts for God,' saith David, 'that I might see thy beauty and thy glory, as I have seen thee in thy sanctuary' (Psa. 63:2). Oh, the sweet looks, the sweet words, the sweet hints, the sweet joggings, the sweet influences, the sweet love-letters, that gracious souls have from heaven, when they wait upon God in holy and heavenly services, the least of which will darken and outweigh all the bravery and glory of this world, and richly recompense the soul for all the troubles, afflictions, and dangers that have attended it in the service of God.[1] Oh, the saints can say under all their troubles and afflictions, that they have meat to eat, and drink to drink, that the world knows not of; that they have such incomes, such refreshments, such warmings, that they would not exchange for all the honours, riches, and dainties of this world. Ah, let but a Christian compare his external losses with his spiritual, internal, and external gain, and he shall find, that for every penny that he loses in the service of God, he gains a pound; and for every pound that he loses, he gains a hundred; for

---

[1] Tertullian, in his book to the martyrs, had an apt saying. That is right and good merchandise, when something is parted with to gain more. He applieth it to their sufferings, wherein, though the flesh lost something, yet the spirit got much more.

every hundred lost, he gains a thousand. We lose pins in his service, and find pearls; we lose the favour of the creature, and peace with the creature, and haply the comforts and contents of the creature, and we gain the favour of God, peace with conscience, and the comforts and contents of a better life. Ah, did the men of this world know the sweet that saints enjoy in afflictions, they would rather choose Manasseh's iron chain than his golden crown; they would rather be Paul a prisoner, than Paul rapt up in the third heaven. For 'light afflictions,' they shall have 'a weight of glory'; for a few afflictions, they shall have these joys, pleasures, and contents, that are as the stars of heaven, or as the sands of the sea that cannot be numbered; for momentary afflictions, they shall have an eternal crown of glory.[1] 'It is but winking, and thou shalt be in heaven presently,' said the martyr. Oh, therefore, let not afflictions or troubles work thee to shun the ways of God, or to quit that service that should be dearer to thee than a world, yea, than thy very life.

DEVICE 3. *By presenting to the soul the difficulty of performing them.* Saith Satan, it is so hard and difficult a thing to pray as thou shouldst, and to wait on God as thou shouldst, and to walk with God as thou shouldst, and to be lively, warm, and active in the communion of saints as thou shouldst, that you were better ten thousand times to neglect them, than to meddle with them; and doubtless by this device Satan hath

---

[1] When the noble General Zedislaus had lost this hand in the wars of the king of Poland, the king sent him a golden hand for It. What we lose in Christ's service he will make up, by giving us some golden mercies. Though the cross be bitter, yet it is but short; a little storm, as one said of Julian's persecution, and an eternal calm follows.

and doth keep off thousands from waiting on God and from giving to him that service that is due to his name.

Remedy (1). *The first remedy against this device of Satan is, to dwell more upon the necessity of the service and duty, than on the difficulty that doth attend the duty.* You should reason thus with your souls: O our souls, though such and such services be hard and difficult, yet are they exceeding necessary for the honour of God, and the keeping up his name in the world, and the keeping under of sin, and the strengthening of weak graces, and so the reviving of languishing comforts, and for the keeping clear and bright your blessed evidences, and for the scattering of your fears, and for the raising of your hopes, and for the gladdening the hearts of the righteous, and stopping the mouths of unrighteous souls, who are ready to take all advantages to blaspheme the name of God, and throw dirt and contempt upon his people and ways. Oh, never leave thinking on the necessity of this and that duty, till your souls be lifted up far above all the difficulties that do attend religious duties.[1]

Remedy (2). The second remedy against this device of Satan is, solemnly to consider, *that the Lord Jesus will make his services easy to you, by the sweet discovery of himself to your souls, whilst you are in his service.* 'Thou meetest[2] him that rejoiceth and worketh righteousness, those that remember thee in thy ways,'

---

[1] The necessity of doing your duty appears by this, that you are his servants by a threefold right; you are his servants by right of creation, and by right of sustentation, and by right of redemption.

[2] The word in the Hebrew is diversely taken; but most take the word here to signify 'to meet a soul with those bowels of love and tenderness as the father of the prodigal met the prodigal with.' God is *Pater miserationum*, he is all bowels; he is swift to show mercy, as he is slow to anger.

as the prophet Isaiah saith (Isa. 64:5). If meeting with God, who is goodness itself, beauty itself, strength itself, glory itself, will not sweeten his service to thy soul, nothing in heaven or earth will.

Jacob's meeting with Rachel, and enjoying of Rachel, made his hard service to be easy and delightful to him; and will not the soul's enjoying of God, and meeting with God, render his service to be much more easy and delightful? Doubtless it will. The Lord will give that sweet assistance by his Spirit and grace, as shall make his service joyous and not grievous, a delight and not a burden, a heaven and not a hell, to believing souls.[1] The confidence of this divine assistance raised up Nehemiah's spirit far above all those difficulties and discouragements that did attend him in the work and service of the Lord, as you may see in Nehemiah 2:19, 20: 'But when Sanballat the Horonite, and Tobiah the servant, the Ammonite, and Geshem the Arabian, heard it, they laughed us to scorn, and despised us, and said, 'What is this thing that ye do? will ye rebel against the king?' 'Then answered I them, and said unto them.' The God of heaven, he will prosper us; therefore we his servants will arise and build: but you have no right, nor portion, nor memorial, in Jerusalem. Ah, souls, while you are in the very service of the Lord, you shall find by experience, that the God of heaven will prosper you, and support you, and encourage and strengthen you, and carry you through the

[1] Luther speaks excellently to Melanchthon, who was apt to be discouraged with doubts and difficulties, and fear from foes, and to cease the service they had undertaken. 'If the work be not good, why did we ever own it? If it be good, why should we ever decline it? Why, saith he, should we fear the conquered world, that have Christ the conqueror on our side?'

hardest service, with the greatest sweetness and cheerfulness that can be. Remember this, that God will suit your strength to your work, and in the hardest service you shall have the choicest assistance.

Remedy (3). The third remedy against this device of Satan is, *to dwell upon the hard and difficult things that the Lord Jesus hath passed through for your temporal, spiritual, and eternal good*. Ah, what a sea of blood, a sea of wrath, of sin, of sorrow and misery, did the Lord Jesus wade through for your internal and eternal good![1] Christ did not plead, this cross is too heavy for me to bear; this wrath is too great for me to lie under; this cup, which hath in it all the ingredients of divine displeasure, is too bitter for me to sup off,[2] how much more to drink the very dregs of it? No, Christ stands not upon this; he pleads not the difficulty of the service, but resolutely and bravely wades through all, as the prophet Isaiah shows; 'The Lord God hath opened my ear, and I was not rebellious, neither turned away my back. I gave my back to the smiters, and my cheeks to them that plucked off the hair; I hid not my face from shame and spitting' (chap. 50:6). Christ makes nothing of his Father's wrath, the burden of your sins, the malice of Satan, and the rage of the world, but sweetly and triumphantly passes through all. Ah, souls! if this consideration will not raise up your spirits above all the discouragements that you meet with, to own Christ and his service, and to stick and cleave to Christ and his service, I am afraid nothing will. A soul not stirred by this, not raised and lifted up by this, to be resolute and brave

----

[1] It is not fit, since the Head was crowned with thorns, that the members should be crowned with rosebuds, saith Zanchius.

[2] [Qu. 'sip of'?]

in the service of God, notwithstanding all dangers and diffi-
culties, is a soul left of God to much blindness and hardness.[1]

Remedy (4). The fourth remedy against this device of Satan
is to consider, *that religious duties, holy and heavenly exercises,
are only difficult to the worse, to the ignoble, part of a saint. They
are not to the noble and better part of a saint, to the noble part,
the soul, and the renewed affections of a saint.* Holy exercises
are a heavenly pleasure and recreation, as the apostle speaks:
'I delight in the law of God, after the inward man: with my
mind I serve the law of God, though with my flesh the law of
sin' (Rom. 7:22). To the noble part of a saint, Christ's 'yoke is
easy, and his burden is light' (Matt. 11:30).[2] All the commands
and ways of Christ (even those that tend to the pulling out
of right eyes and cutting off of right hands) are joyous, and
not grievous, to the noble part of a saint.[3] All the ways and
services of Christ are pleasantness, in the abstract, to the bet-
ter part of a saint. A saint, so far as he is renewed, is always
best when he sees most of God, when he tastes most of God,
when he is highest in his enjoyments of God, and most warm
and lively in the service of God. Oh, saith the noble part of a
saint, that it might be always thus! Oh that my strength were
the strength of stones, and my flesh as brass, that my worse

[1] Godfrey of Bullen [Bouillon], Crusader King of Jerusalem (1099),
refused to be crowned with a crown of gold, saying, it became not a
Christian there to wear a crown of gold, where Christ for our salvation
had sometime worn a crown of thorns.

[2] The Greek signifies that Christ's yoke is a benign, a gracious, a
pleasant, a good, and a gainful yoke, opposed to that which is painful
and tedious.

[3] As every flower hath its sweet savour, so every good duty carries
meat in the mouth, comfort in the performance of it.

part might be more serviceable to my noble part, that I might act by an untired power in that service, that is a pleasure, a paradise, to me.

Remedy (5). The fifth remedy against this device of Satan is, solemnly to consider, *that great reward and glorious recompence that doth attend those that cleave to the service of the Lord in the face of all difficulties and discouragements.* Though the work be hard, yet the wages are great. Heaven will make amends for all. Ay, one hour's being in heaven will abundantly recompense you for cleaving to the Lord and his ways in the face of all difficulties. This carried the apostle through the greatest difficulties. He had an eye 'to the recompence of reward'; he looked for 'a house that had foundations, whose builder and maker was God,' and for 'a heavenly country.' Yea, this bore up the spirit of Christ in the face of all difficulties and discouragements; 'Looking unto Jesus, the author and finisher of our faith; who, for the joy that was set before him, endured the cross, despising the shame, and is set down at the right hand of the throne of God' (Heb. 12:2).[1]

Christians that would hold on in the service of the Lord, must look more upon the crown than upon the cross, more upon their future glory than upon their present misery, more upon their encouragements than upon their discouragements. God's very service is wages; his ways are strewed with roses, and paved 'with joy that is unspeakable and full of glory,' and with 'peace that passeth understanding.' Some degree of comfort

[1] Basil speaks of some martyrs that were cast out all night naked in a cold, frosty time, and were to be burned the next day, how they comforted themselves in this manner: The winter is sharp, but paradise is sweet; here we shiver for cold, but the bosom of Abraham will make amends for all.

follows every good action, as heat accompanies fire, as beams
and influences issue from the sun; 'Moreover, by them is thy
servant warned, and in keeping of them there is great reward,'
Psa. 19:11. Not only for keeping, but in keeping of them, there
is great reward.[1] The joy, the rest, the refreshing, the comforts,
the contents, the smiles, the incomes[2] that saints now enjoy
in the ways of God, are so precious and glorious in their eyes,
that they would not exchange them for ten thousand worlds.
Ah! if the vails[3] be thus sweet and glorious before pay-day
comes, what will be that glory that Christ will crown his saints
with for cleaving to his sendee in the face of all difficulties;
when he shall say to his Father, 'Lo, here am I, and the chil-
dren which thou hast given me' (Isa. 8:18). If there be so much
to be had in a wilderness, what then shall be had in paradise?

DEVICE 4. *By working them to make false inferences from
those blessed and glorious things that Christ hath done.* As that
Jesus Christ hath done all for us, therefore there is nothing for
us to do but to joy and rejoice. He hath perfectly justified us
and fulfilled the law, and satisfied divine justice, and pacified
his Father's wrath, and is gone to heaven to prepare a place
for us, and in the mean time to intercede for us; and therefore
away with praying, and mourning, and hearing. Ah! what a
world of professors hath Satan drawn in these days from reli-
gious services, by working them to make such sad, wild, and
strange inferences from the sweet and excellent things that the
Lord Jesus hath done for his beloved ones.

[1] This is a reward before the reward, a sure reward of well doing;
in doing thereof not only *for* doing thereof, there is great reward (Psa.
19:11).

[2] 'Incomings.'

[3] 'Gratuities.'

Remedy (1). The first remedy against this device of Satan is, *to dwell as much on those scriptures that show you the duties and services that Christ requires of you, as upon those scriptures that declare to you the precious and glorious things that Christ hath done for you.*[1] It is a sad and dangerous thing to have two eyes to behold our dignity and privileges, and not one to see our duties and services. I should look with one eye upon the choice and excellent things that Christ hath done for me, to raise up my heart to love Christ with the purest love, and to joy in Christ with the strongest joy, and to lift up Christ above all, who hath made himself to be my all; and I should look with the other eye upon those services and duties that the Scriptures require of those for whom Christ hath done such blessed things, as upon that of the apostle: 'What, know ye not that your body is the temple of the Holy Ghost, which is in you, which ye have of God? and ye are not your own: for ye are bought with a price; therefore glorify God in your body, and in your spirit, which are God's' (1 Cor. 6:19, 20). And that: 'Therefore, my beloved brethren, be ye steadfast, unmoveable, always abounding in the work of the Lord, knowing that your labour is not in vain in the Lord' (1 Cor. 15:58). And that: 'And let us not be weary in well-doing, for in due season we shall reap if we faint not' (Gal. 6:9). And that of the apostle: 'Rejoice always' (1 Thess. 5:16), and 'Pray without ceasing' (1 Thess. 5:17). And that in the Philippians: 'Work out your own salvation with fear and trembling' (2:12); and that, 'This do till I come' (1 Tim. 4:13); and that, 'Let us consider one another, to

---

[1] Tertullian hath this expression of the Scriptures: *Adoro plenitudinem Scripturarum,* I adore the fullness of the Scripture. Gregory calls the Scripture the heart and soul of God; and who will not then dwell in it?

provoke one another to love, and to good works, not forsaking the assembling of ourselves together, as the manner of some is, but exhorting one another, and so much the more as you see the day approaching' (Heb. 10:24, 25). Now, a soul that would not be drawn away by this device of Satan, he must not look with a squint eye upon these blessed scriptures, and abundant more of like import, but he must dwell upon them; he must make these scriptures to be his chiefest and his choicest companions, and this will be a happy means to keep him close to Christ and his service in these times, wherein many turn their backs upon Christ, under pretence of being interested in the great glorious things that have been acted by Christ.[1]

Remedy (2). The second remedy against this device of Satan is, to consider, *that the great and glorious things that Jesus Christ hath done, and is a-doing for us, should be so far from taking us off from religious services and pious performances, that they should be the greatest motives and encouragements to the performance of them that may be, as the Scriptures do abundantly evidence.* I will only instance in some, as that, 'That we, being delivered out of the hands of our enemies, might serve him without fear, in holiness and righteousness before him all the days of our life' (1 Pet. 2:9; Luke 1:74, 75). Christ hath freed you from all your enemies, from the curse of the law, the predominant damnatory power of sin, the wrath of God, the sting of death, and the torments of hell; but what is the end and design of Christ in doing these great and marvellous things for his people? It is not that we should throw off duties of

---

[1] The Jews were much in turning over the leaves of the Scripture, but they did not weigh the matter of them (John 5:39): 'You search the Scriptures.' The Greek there seemeth to be indicative rather than imperative.

righteousness and holiness, but that their hearts may be the more free and sweet in all holy duties and heavenly services.[1] So the apostle, 'I will be their God, and they shall be my people': 'And I will be a Father unto you, and ye shall be my sons and daughters, saith the Lord Almighty.' Mark what follows: 'Having therefore these promises, dearly beloved, let us cleanse ourselves from all filthiness of the flesh and spirit, perfecting holiness in the fear of the Lord' (2 Cor. 6:17, 18 and chap. 7:1 compared). And again: 'The grace of God that bringeth salvation hath appeared to all men, teaching us that, denying all ungodliness and worldly lusts, we should live soberly, righteously, and godly in this present world, looking for that blessed hope, and the glorious appearing of the great God and our Saviour Jesus Christ, who gave himself for us, that he might redeem us from all iniquity, and purify us unto himself a peculiar people, zealous of good works' (Titus 2:12-14). Ah, souls! I know no such arguments to work you to a lively and constant performance of all heavenly services, like those that are drawn from the consideration of the great and glorious things that Christ hath done for you; and if such arguments will not take you and win upon you, I do think the throwing of hell fire in your faces will never do it.[2]

Remedy (3). The third remedy against this device of Satan is, seriously to consider, *that those precious souls which Jesus Christ hath done and suffered as much for as he hath for you, have been*

---

[1] This I am sure of, that all man's happiness here is his holiness, and his holiness shall hereafter be his happiness. Christ hath therefore broke the devil's yoke from off our necks, that his Father might have better service from our hearts.

[2] Talk not of a good life, but let thy life speak. Your actions in passing pass not away; for every good work is a grain of seed for eternal life.

exceeding active and lively in all religious services and heavenly performances.[1] He did as much and suffered as much for David as for you, and yet who more in praying and praising God than David? 'Seven times a day will I praise the Lord' (Psa. 119:164). Who more in the studying and meditating on the word than David? 'Thy law is my meditation all the day' (Psa. 119:97). The same truth you may run and read in Jacob, Moses, Job, Daniel, and in the rest of the holy prophets and apostles, whom Christ hath done as much for as for you. Ah, how have all those worthies abounded in works of righteousness and holiness, to the praise of free grace! Certainly Satan hath got the upper hand of those souls that do argue thus—Christ hath done such and such glorious things for us, therefore we need not make any care and conscience of doing such and such religious services as men say the word calls for. If this logic be not from hell, what is? Ah, were the holy prophets and apostles alive to hear such logic come out of the mouths of such as profess themselves to be interested in the great and glorious things that Jesus Christ hath done for his chosen ones, how would they blush to look upon such souls! and how would their hearts grieve and break within them to hear the language and to observe the actings of such souls![2]

Remedy (4). The fourth remedy against this device of Satan is, seriously to consider this, *that those that do not walk in the ways of righteousness and holiness, that do not wait upon God in the several duties and services that are commanded by him,*

[1] The saints' motto in all ages hath been *Laboremus*, let us be doing. God loves the runner, not the questioner or disputer, saith Luther.
[2] He that talks of heaven, but doeth not the will of God, is like him that gazed upon the moon, but fell into the pit.

cannot have that evidence to their own souls of their righteous-
ness before God, of their fellowship and communion with God,
of their blessedness here, and their happiness hereafter, as those
souls have, that love and delight in the ways of the Lord, that are
always best when they are most in the works and service of the
Lord.[1] 'Little children,' saith the apostle, 'let no man deceive
you: he that doeth righteousness is righteous, even as he is
righteous' (1 John 3:7). 'In this,' saith the same apostle, 'the
children of God are manifest, and the children of the devil;
whosoever doeth not righteousness is not of God, neither he
that loveth not his brother' (verse 10). 'If ye know that he is
righteous,' saith the same apostle, 'ye know that every one that
doeth righteousness, is born of him. He that saith, I know
him, and keepeth not his commandments, is a liar, and the
truth is not in him. But whosoever keepeth his word, in him
verily is the love of God perfected: hereby know we that we are
in him. He that saith he abideth in him, ought himself also
so to walk, even as he walked.' 'If we say that we have fellow-
ship with him, and walk in darkness, we lie, and do not the
truth; but if we walk in the light, as he is in the light, we have
fellowship one with another; and the blood of Jesus Christ his
Son cleanseth us from all sin,' saith the same apostle (1 John

---

[1] Certainly it is one thing to judge by our graces, another thing to
rest or put our trust in them. There is a great deal of difference betwixt
declaring and deserving. As David's daughters were known by their
garments of divers colours, so are God's children by their piety and
sanctity, A Christian's emblem should be an house walking towards
heaven. High words surely make a man neither holy nor just; but a vir-
tuous life, a circumspect walking, makes him dear to God. A tree that
is not fruitful is for the fire. Christianity is not a talking, but a walking
with God, who will not be put off with words; if he miss of fruit, he will
take up his axe, and then the soul is cut off for ever.

2:4-6, and 1:6, 7). So (James 2:14-20): 'What doth it profit, my brethren, though a man say he hath faith, and have no works; can faith save him?' i.e. it cannot. 'For as the body without the spirit is dead, so faith without works is dead also.' To look after holy and heavenly works, is the best way to preserve the soul from being deceived and deluded by Satan's delusions, and by sudden flashes of joy and comfort; holy works being a more sensible[1] and constant pledge of the precious Spirit, begetting and maintaining in the soul more solid, pure, clear, strong, and lasting joy. Ah souls! As you would have in yourselves a constant and a blessed evidence of your fellowship with the Father and the Son, and of the truth of grace, and of your future happiness, look that you cleave close to holy services; and that you turn not your backs upon religious duties.

Remedy (5). The fifth remedy against this device of Satan is, solemnly to consider, *that there are other choice and glorious ends for the saint's performance of religious duties, than for the justifying of their persons before God, or for their satisfying of the law or justice of God, or for the purchasing of the pardon of sin; viz. to testify their justification.*[2] 'A good tree cannot but bring forth good fruits' (Matt. 7:17), to testify their love to God, and their sincere obedience to the commands of God; to testify their deliverance from spiritual bondage, to evidence the indwelling of the Spirit, to stop the mouths of the worst of men, and to gladden those righteous souls that God would not have saddened. These, and abundance of other choice ends there be, why those that have an interest in the glorious

---

[1] 'Conscious.'

[2] It is a precious truth, never to be forgotten, that duties are esteemed not by their acts, but by their ends.

doings of Christ, should, notwithstanding that, keep close to the holy duties and religious services that are commanded by Christ. And if these considerations will not prevail with you, to wait upon God in holy and heavenly duties, I am afraid if one should rise from the dead, his arguments would not win upon you, but you would hold on in your sins, and neglect his service, though you lost your souls for ever.[1]

DEVICE 5. *By presenting to them the paucity and poverty of those that walk in the ways of God, that hold on in religious practices.* Saith Satan, do not you see that those that walk in such and such religious ways are the poorest, the meanest, and the most despicable persons in the world? This took with them in John 7:47-49: 'Then answered the Pharisees, Are ye also deceived? Have any of the rulers, or of the Pharisees, believed on him? But this people who knoweth not the law are cursed.'

Remedy (1). The first remedy against this device of Satan is, to consider, *that though they are outwardly poor, yet they are inwardly rich.* Though they are poor in temporals, yet they are rich in spirituals.[2] The worth and riches of the saints is inward. 'The King's daughter is all glorious within' (Psa. 45:13). 'Hearken, my beloved brethren, hath not God chosen the poor of this world, rich in faith, and heirs of the kingdom which

---

[1] The end in view moves to action. Keep thyself within compass, and have an eye always to the end of thy life and actions, was Maximilian the emperor's motto.

[2] Do not you see, saith Chrysostom, the places where treasures are hid are rough and overgrown with thorns? Do not the naturalists tell you, that the mountains that are big with gold within, are bare of grass without? Saints have, as scholars, poor commons (daily fare) here, because they must study hard to go to heaven.

he hath promised to them that love him?' saith James 2:5. 'I know thy poverty, but thou art rich,' saith John to the church of Smyrna (Rev. 2:9). What though they have little in possession, yet they have a glorious kingdom in reversion. 'Fear not, little flock, it is your Father's pleasure to give you a kingdom' (Luke 12:32). Though saints have little in hand, yet they have much in hope. You count those happy, in a worldly sense, that have much in reversion, though they have little in possession; and will you count the saints miserable because they have little in hand, little in possession, though they have a glorious kingdom in reversion of this? I am sure the poorest saint that breathes will not exchange, were it in his power, that which he hath in hope and in reversion, for the possession of as many worlds as there be stars in heaven, or sands in the sea.

Remedy (2). The second remedy against this device of Satan is, to consider, *that in all ages God hath had some that have been great, rich, wise, and honourable, that have chosen his ways, and cleaved to his service in the face of all difficulties.* Though not many wise men, yet some wise men; and though not many mighty, yet some mighty have; and though not many noble, yet some noble have. Witness Abraham, and Jacob, and Job, and several kings, and others that the Scriptures speak of. And ah! how many have we among ourselves, whose souls have cleaved to the Lord, and who have swum to his service through the blood of the slain, and who have not counted their lives dear unto them, that they and others might enjoy the holy things of Christ, according to the mind and heart of Christ.[1]

[1] Good nobles, saith one, are like black swans; and (are) thinly scattered in the firmament of a State, even like stars of the first magnitude: yet some God hath had in all ages, as might be showed out of histories.

Remedy (3). The third remedy against this device of Satan is, solemnly to consider, *that the spiritual riches of the poorest saints do infinitely transcend the temporal riches of all the wicked men in the world; their spiritual riches do satisfy them; they can sit down satisfied with the riches of grace that be in Christ, without honours, and without riches.*[1] 'He that drinks of that water that I shall give him, shall thirst no more' (John 4:13). The riches of poor saints are durable; they will bed and board with them; they will go to the prison, to a sickbed, to a grave, yea, to heaven with them. The spiritual riches of poor saints are as wine to cheer them, and as bread to strengthen them, and as cloth to warm them, and as armour to protect them. Now, all you that know anything, do know that the riches of this world cannot satisfy the souls of men, and they are as fading as a flower, or as the owners of them are.[2]

Remedy (4). The fourth remedy against this device, is seriously to consider, *that though the saints, considered comparatively, are few; though they be 'a little, little flock,' 'a remnant,' 'a garden enclosed,' 'a spring shut up, a fountain sealed'; though they are as 'the summer gleanings'; though they are 'one of a city, and two of a tribe';*[3] *though they be but a handful to a houseful, a spark to a flame, a drop to the ocean, yet consider them simply in themselves, and so they are an innumerable number that cannot be numbered.* As John speaketh: 'After this I beheld, and lo, a great multitude which no man could number, of all nations,

[1] Alexander's vast mind inquired if there were any more worlds to conquer.

[2] Crassus was so rich that he maintained an army with his own revenues; yet he, his great army, with his son and heir, fell together, and left his great estate to others.

[3] Luke 12:32; Isa. 1:9; Song of Sol. 4:12; Judg. 8:2 and Jer. 3:14.

and kindreds, and peoples, and tongues, stood before the throne, and before the Lamb, clothed with white robes, and palms in their hands' (Rev. 7:9). So Matthew speaks: 'And I say unto you, that many shall come from the east and west, and shall sit down with Abraham, Isaac, and Jacob in the kingdom of heaven' (Matt. 8:11). So Paul: 'But ye are come unto mount Sion, and unto the city of the living God, the heavenly Jerusalem, and to an innumerable company of angels, to the general assembly and church of the firstborn, which are written in heaven, and to God the judge of all, and to the spirits of just men made perfect' (Heb. 12:22).[1]

Remedy (5). The fifth remedy against this device of Satan is, seriously to consider, *that it will be but as a day before these poor despised saints shall shine brighter than the sun in his glory.* It will not be long before you will wish. Oh! that we were now among the poor, mean despised ones in the day that God comes to make up his jewels! It will not be long before these poor few saints shall be lifted up upon their thrones to judge the multitude, the world, as the apostle speaks: 'Know ye not that the saints shall judge the world?' (1 Cor. 6:2). And in that day, oh! how will the great and the rich, the learned and the noble, wish that they had lived and spent their days with these few poor contemptible creatures in the service of the Lord! Oh! how will this wicked world curse the day that ever they had such base thoughts of the poor mean saints, and that their poverty became a stumbling-block to keep them off from the ways of sanctity.[2]

[1] When Fulgentius saw the nobility of Rome sit mounted in their bravery (finery), it mounted his meditations to the heavenly Jerusalem.
[2] John Foxe being once asked whether he knew a certain poor man

I have read of Ingo, an ancient king of the Draves, who, making a stately feast, appointed his nobles, at that time pagans, to sit in the hall below, and commanded certain poor Christians to be brought up into his presence-chamber, to sit with him at his table, to eat and drink of his kingly cheer; at which many wondering, he said, 'He accounted Christians, though never so poor, a greater ornament to his table, and more worthy of his company, than the greatest peers unconverted to the Christian faith; for when these might be thrust down to hell, those might be his consorts and fellow-princes in heaven.' You know how to apply it. Although you see the stars sometimes by their reflections in a puddle, or in the bottom of a well, ay, in a stinking ditch, yet the stars have their situation in heaven. So, though you see a godly man in a poor, miserable, low, despised condition for the things of this world, yet he is fixed in heaven, in the region of heaven: 'Who hath raised us up,' saith the apostle, 'and made us sit together in heavenly places in Christ Jesus.' Oh! therefore, say to your own souls, when they begin to decline the ways of Sion because of the poverty and paucity of those that walk in them, The day is at hand when those few, poor, despised saints shall shine in glory, when they shall judge this world, and when all the wicked of this world will wish that they were in their condition, and would give ten thousand worlds, were it in their power, that

---

who had received succour of him in time of trouble, he answered, I remember him well. I tell you I forget lords and ladies to remember such. So will God deal by his poor saints. He will forget the great and mighty ones of the world to remember his few poor despised ones. Though John the Baptist was poor in the world, yet the Holy Ghost calls him the greatest that was born of woman. Ah, poor saints, men that know not your worth, cannot have such low thoughts of you but the Lord will have as high.

they might but have the honour and happiness to wait upon those whom for their poverty and paucity they have neglected and despised in this world.

Remedy (6). The sixth remedy against this device of Satan is, solemnly to consider, *that there will come a time, even in this life, in this world, when the reproach and contempt that is now cast upon the ways of God, by reason of the poverty and paucity of those that walk in those ways, shall be quite taken away, by his making them the head that have days without number been the tail, and by his raising them up to much outward riches, prosperity, and glory, who have been as the outcast because of their poverty and paucity.*[1] John, speaking of the glory of the church, the new Jerusalem that came down from heaven (Rev. 21:24), tells us, 'That the nations of them which are saved shall walk in the light of it, and the kings of the earth do bring their glory into it.' So the prophet Isaiah: 'They shall bring their sons from far, and their silver and their gold with them. For brass I will bring gold, and for iron I will bring silver, and for wood brass, and for stones iron' (chap. 60:17). And so the prophet Zechariah speaks (chap. 14:14): 'And the wealth of all the heathen round about shall be gathered together, gold, and silver, and apparel, in great abundance.' The Lord hath promised that 'the meek shall inherit the earth' (Matt. 5:5);

[1] These following scriptures do abundantly confirm this truth: Jer. 31:12; Isa. 30:23; 62:8, 9; Joel 2:23, 24; Mic. 4:6; Amos 9:13, 14; Zech. 8:12; Isa. 41:18; 19; 55:13; 66:6, 7; 65:21, 22; 61:4; 60:10; Ezek. 36:10. Only take these two cautions: (1.) That in these times the saints' chiefest comforts, delights, and contents will consist in their more clear, full, and constant enjoyment of God. (2.) That they shall have such abundant measure of the Spirit poured out upon them, that their riches and outward glory shall not be snares unto them, but golden steps to a richer living in God.

and 'heaven and earth shall pass away, before one jot or one tittle of his word shall pass unfulfilled' (verse 18). Ah, poor saints! now some thrust sore at you, others look a-squint upon you, others shut the door against you, others turn their backs upon you, and most of men (except it be a few that live much in God, and are filled with the riches of Christ) do either neglect you or despise you because of your poverty; but the day is coming when you shall be lifted up above the dunghill, when you shall change poverty for riches, your rags for robes, your reproach for a crown of honour, your infamy for glory, even in this world.

And this is not all, but God will also mightily increase the number of his chosen ones, multitudes shall be converted to him: 'Who hath heard such a thing? who hath seen such things? shall the earth be made to bring forth in one day? or shall a nation be born at once? for as soon as Sion travailed, she brought forth children. And they shall bring all your brethren for an offering unto the Lord, out of all nations, upon horses, and in chariots, in litters, and upon mules, and upon swift beasts, to my holy mountain Jerusalem, saith the Lord; as the children of Israel bring an offering in a clean vessel into the house of the Lord' (Isa. 66:8, 20). Doth not the Scripture say, that 'the kingdoms of this world must become the kingdoms of our Lord'? (Rev. 11:15). Hath not God given to Christ 'the heathen, and the uttermost parts of the earth for his possession'? (Psa. 2:8). Hath not the Lord said, that in 'the last days the mountain of the Lord's house shall be lifted up above the hills, and shall be established in the top of the mountains, and all nations shall flow unto it, (Isa. 2:2 and 54:14 and 61:9). Pray, read, and meditate upon Isa. 60 and 66 and 2:1-5, and there you shall find the multitudes that shall be converted to Christ.

And oh! that you would be mighty in believing and in wrestling with God, that he would hasten the day of his glory, that the reproach that is now upon his people and ways may cease!

DEVICE 6. *By presenting before them the examples of the greatest part of the world, that walk in the ways of their own hearts, and that make light and slight of the ways of the Lord.*[1] Why, saith Satan, do not you see that the great and the rich, the noble and the honourable, the learned and the wise, even the greatest number of men, never trouble themselves about such and such ways, and why then should you be singular and nice? You were far better do as the most do.

Remedy (1). The first remedy against this device of Satan is, solemnly to consider *of those scriptures that make directly against following the sinful examples of men.* As that in Exodus, 'Thou shalt not follow a multitude to do evil, neither shalt thou speak in a cause to decline after many to wrest judgment' (chapter 23:2). The multitude generally are ignorant, and know not the way of the Lord, therefore they speak evil of that they know not. They are envious and maliciously bent against the service and way of God, and therefore they cannot speak well of the ways of God: 'This way is everywhere spoken against,' saith they (Acts 28:22). So in Numbers 16:21, 'Separate from them, and come out from among them.' So the apostle: 'Have no fellowship with the unfruitful works of darkness' (Eph. 5:11). So Solomon: 'Enter not into the way of the wicked: forsake the foolish, and live' (Prov. 4:14 and 9:6). They that walk with the most shall perish with the most.[2] They that do as the most

---

[1] John 7:48, 49; 1 Cor. 1:26, 28; Mic. 7:2-4.
[2] The way to hell is broad and well beaten. The way to be undone

shall ere long suffer with the most. They that live as the most, must die with the most, and to hell with the most.

Remedy (2). The second remedy against this device of Satan is, seriously to consider, *that if you will sin with the multitude, all the angels in heaven and men on earth cannot keep you from suffering with the multitude.* If you will be wicked with them, you must unavoidably be miserable with them.[1] Say to thy soul, O my soul! if thou wilt sin with the multitude, thou must be shut out of heaven with the multitude, thou must be cast down to hell with the multitude: 'And I heard a voice from heaven saying, Come out of her, my people, that ye be not partakers of her sins, and that ye receive not of her plagues' (Rev. 18:4). Come out in affection, in action, and in habitation, for else the infection of sin will bring upon you the infliction of punishment. So saith the wise man, 'He that walketh with wise men shall be wise, but a companion of fools shall be destroyed,' or as the Hebrew hath it, 'shall be broken in pieces' (Prov. 13:20). Multitudes may help thee into sin, yea, one may draw thee into sin, but it is not multitudes that can help thee to escape punishments; as you may see in Moses and Aaron, that were provoked to sin by the multitude, but were shut out of the pleasant land, and fell by a hand of justice as well as others.

Remedy (3). The third remedy against this device of Satan is, solemnly to consider, *the worth and excellency of thy immortal*

---

for ever is to do as the most do. The multitude is the weakest and worst argument, saith Seneca.

[1] Sin and punishment are linked together with chains of adamant. Of sin we may say, as Isidore doth of the serpent, *Tot dolores, quot colores.* So many colours, so many colours.

soul. Thy soul is a jewel more worth than heaven and earth. The loss of thy soul is incomparable, irreparable, and irrecoverable; if that be lost, all is lost, and thou art undone for ever. Is it madness and folly in a man to kill himself for company, and is it not greater madness or folly to break the neck of thy soul, and to damn it for company? Suspect that way wherein thou seest multitudes to walk; the multitude being a stream that thou must row hard against, or thou wilt be carried into that gulf out of which angels cannot deliver thee. Is it not better to walk in a straight way alone, than to wander into crooked ways with company? Sure it is better to go to heaven alone than to hell with company.

I might add other things, but these may suffice for the present; and I am afraid, if these arguments do not stir you, other arguments will work but little upon you.[1]

DEVICE 7. *By casting in a multitude of vain thoughts, whilst the soul is in seeking of God, or in waiting on God*; and by this device he hath cooled some men's spirits in heavenly services, and taken off, at least for a time, many precious souls from religious performances. I have no heart to hear, nor no heart to pray, nor no delight in reading, nor in the society of the saints. Satan doth so dog and follow my soul, and is still a-casting in such a multitude of vain thoughts concerning God, the world, and my own soul, that I even tremble to think of waiting upon God in any religious service. Oh! the vain thoughts that Satan casts in do so distaste my soul, and so grieve, vex, perplex, and distract my soul, that they even make me weary of holy duties,

[1] What wise man would fetch gold out of a fiery crucible, hazard his immortal soul, to gain the world, by following a multitude in those steps that lead to the chambers of death and darkness?

yea, of my very life. Oh! I cannot be so raised and ravished, so heated and melted, so quickened and enlarged, so comforted and refreshed, as I should be, as I might be, and as I would be in religious services, by reason of that multitude of vain thoughts, that Satan is injecting or casting into my soul.[1]

Remedy (1). The first remedy against this device of Satan is, *to have your hearts strongly affected with the greatness, holiness, majesty, and glory of that God before whom you stand, and with whom your souls do converse in religious services.* Oh! let your souls be greatly affected with the presence, purity, and majesty of that God before whom thou standest. A man would be afraid of playing with a feather, when he is speaking with a king. Ah! when men have poor, low, light, slight thoughts of God, in their drawing near to God, they tempt the devil to bestir himself, and to cast in a multitude of vain thoughts to disturb and distract the soul in its waiting on God. There is nothing that will contribute so much to the keeping out of vain thoughts, as to look upon God as an omniscient God, an omnipresent God, an omnipotent God, a God full of all glorious perfections, a God whose majesty, purity, and glory will not suffer him to behold the least iniquity.[2] The not so much as one vain thought is, because they are greatly affected with the greatness, holiness, majesty, purity, and glory of God.

Remedy (2). The second remedy against this device of Satan

---

[1] Lord, now how fain would I serve thee, and vain thoughts will not suffer me!

[2] When Pompey could not keep his soldiers in the camp by persuasion, he cast himself all along in the narrow passage that led out of it, and bade them go if they would, but they must first trample upon their general; and the thoughts of this overcame them. You are wise, and know how to apply it to the point in hand.

is, *to be peremptory in religious services, notwithstanding all those wandering thoughts the soul is troubled with.* This will be a sweet help against them: for the soul to be resolute in waiting on God, whether it be troubled with vain thoughts or not;[1] to say, Well I will pray still, and hear still, and meditate still, and keep fellowship with the saints still. Many precious souls can say from experience, that when their souls have been peremptory in their waiting on God, that Satan hath left them, and hath not been so busy in vexing their souls with vain thoughts. When Satan perceives that all those trifling vain thoughts that he casts into the soul do but vex the soul into greater diligence, carefulness, watchfulness, and peremptoriness in holy and heavenly services, and that the soul loses nothing of his zeal, piety, and devotion, but doubles his care, diligence, and earnestness, he often ceases to interpose his trifles and vain thoughts, as he ceased to tempt Christ, when Christ was peremptory in resisting his temptations.

Remedy (3). The third remedy against this device of Satan is, to consider this, *that those vain and trifling thoughts that are cast into our souls, when we are waiting upon God in this or that religious service, if they be not cherished and indulged, but abhorred, resisted, and disclaimed, they are not sins upon our souls, though they may be troubles to our minds; they shall not be put upon our accounts, nor keep mercies and blessings from being enjoyed by us.* When a soul in uprightness can look God in the face, and say. Lord, when I approach near unto thee, there be a world of vain thoughts crowd in upon me, that do disturb my soul, and weaken my faith, and lessen my comfort

---

[1] It is a rule in the civil law that nothing seems to be done, if there remains aught to be done. If once thou sayest. 'It is enough,' thou art undone, saith Augustine.

and spiritual strength. Oh, these are my clog, my burden, my torment, my hell! Oh, do justice upon these, free me from these, that I may serve thee with more freeness, singleness, spiritualness, and sweetness of spirit.[1] These thoughts may vex that soul, but they shall not harm that soul, nor keep a blessing from that soul. If vain thoughts resisted and lamented could stop the current of mercy, and render a soul unhappy, there would be none on earth that should ever taste of mercy, or be everlastingly happy.

Remedy (4). The fourth remedy against this device of Satan is, solemnly to consider, *that watching against sinful thoughts, resisting of sinful thoughts, lamenting and weeping over sinful thoughts, carries with it the sweetest and strongest evidence of the truth and power of grace, and of the sincerity of your hearts, and is the readiest and the surest way to be rid of them* (Psa. 139:23). Many low and carnal considerations may work men to watch their words, their lives, their actions; as hope of gain, or to please friends, or to get a name in the world, and many other such like considerations. Oh! but to watch our thoughts, to weep and lament over them, this must needs be from some noble, spiritual, and internal principle, as love to God, a holy fear of God, a holy care and delight to please the Lord.[2] The schools do well observe, that outward sins are of greater infamy, but inward heart sins are of greater guilt, as we

---

[1] It is not Satan casting in of vain thoughts that can keep mercy from the soul, or undo the soul, but the lodging and cherishing of vain thoughts: 'O Jerusalem, how long shall vain thoughts lodge within thee?' (Jer. 4:14) (Heb. 'in the midst of thee'). They pass through the best hearts, they are lodged and cherished only in the worst hearts.

[2] Thoughts are the first-born, the blossoms of the soul, the beginning of our strength, whether for good or evil, and they are the greatest evidences for or against a man that can be.

see in the devil's. There is nothing that so speaks out a man
to be thoroughly and kindly wrought upon, as his having his
thoughts to be 'brought into obedience,' as the apostle speaks,
2 Cor. 10:4, 5. Grace is grown up to a very great height in that
soul where it prevails, to the subduing of those vain thoughts
that walk up and down in the soul.[1] Well! though you cannot
be rid of them, yet make resistance and opposition against
the first risings of them. When sinful thoughts arise, then
think thus, The Lord takes notice of these thoughts; 'he knows
them afar off,' as the Psalmist speaks (Psa. 138:6). He knew
Herod's bloody thoughts, and Judas's betraying thoughts, and
the Pharisees' cruel and blasphemous thoughts afar off.[2] Oh!
think thus: All these sinful thoughts, they defile and pollute
the soul, they deface and spoil much of the inward beauty and
glory of the soul. If I commit this or that sin, to which my
thoughts incline me, then either I must repent or not repent;
if I repent, it will cost me more grief, sorrow, shame, heart
breaking, and soul-bleeding, before my conscience will be qui-
eted, divine justice pacified, my comfort and joy restored, my
evidences cleared, and my pardon in the court of conscience
sealed, than the imagined profit or seeming sensual pleasure
can be worth: 'What fruit had you in those things whereof you
are now ashamed?' (Rom. 6:21).[3]

If I never repent, oh! then my sinful thoughts will be scorpi-
ons that will eternally vex me, the rods that will eternally lash

---

[1] Psa. 139:23; Isa. 59:7; 66:18; Matt. 9:4; 12:25.

[2] Zeno, a wise heathen, affirmed God even beheld the thoughts
(Matt. 15:15-18).

[3] Tears instead of gems were the ornaments of David's bed when he
had sinned; and so they must be thine, or else thou must lie down in the
bed of sorrow for ever.

me, the thorns that will everlastingly prick me, the dagger that will be eternally a-stabbing me, the worm that will be for ever a-gnawing me! Oh! therefore, watch against them, be constant in resisting them, and in lamenting and weeping over them, and then they shall not hurt thee, though they may for a time trouble thee. And remember this, he that doth this doth more than the most glistering and blustering hypocrite in the world doth.[1]

Remedy (5). The fifth remedy against this device of Satan is, *to labour more and more to be filled with the fullness of God, and to be enriched with all spiritual and heavenly things.* What is the reason that the angels in heaven have not so much as an idle thought? It is because they are filled with the fullness of God (Eph. 3:19).[2] Take it for an experienced truth, the more the soul is filled with the fullness of God and enriched with spiritual and heavenly things, the less room there is in that soul for vain thoughts. The fuller the vessel is of wine, the less room there is for water. Oh, then, lay up much of God, of Christ, of precious promises, and choice experiences in your hearts, and then you will be less troubled with vain thoughts. 'A good man, out of the good treasure of his heart, bringeth forth good things' (Matt. 12:35).

Remedy (6). The sixth remedy against this device of Satan is, *to keep up holy and spiritual affections; for such as your affections*

---

[1] Inward bleeding kills many a man; so will sinful thoughts, if not repented of.

[2] The words are an Hebraism. The Hebrews, when they would set out many excellent things, they add the name of God to it: city of God, cedars of God, wrestlings of God. So here, 'That ye may be filled with the fullness of God.'

are, such will be your thoughts. 'Oh how I love thy law! it is my meditation all the day' (Psa. 119:97). What we love most, we most muse upon. 'When I awake, I am still with thee' (Psa. 139:18). That which we much like, we shall much mind. They that are frequent in their love to God and his law, will be frequent in thinking of God and his law: a child will not forget his mother.

Remedy (7). The seventh remedy against this device of Satan is, *to avoid multiplicity of worldly business.* Oh let not the world take up your hearts and thoughts at other times. Souls that are torn in pieces with the cares of the world will be always vexed and tormented with vain thoughts in all their approaches to God.[1] Vain thoughts will be still crowding in upon him that lives in a crowd of business. The stars which have least circuit are nearest the pole; and men that are least perplexed with business are commonly nearest to God.

DEVICE 8. *By working them to rest in their performances; to rest in prayer, and to rest in hearing, reading, and the communion of saints.* And when Satan hath drawn the soul to rest upon the service done, then he will help the soul to reason thus; Why, thou wert as good never pray, as to pray and rest in prayer; as good never hear, as to hear and rest in hearing; as good never be in the communion of saints, as to rest in the communion of saints. And by this device he stops many souls in their heavenly race, and takes off poor souls from those

---

[1] 2 Tim. 2:4. 'No man that warreth entangleth himself'; it is a comparison which St Paul borroweth from the custom of the Roman empire, wherein soldiers were forbidden to be proctors (managers in court) of other men's causes, to undertake husbandry or merchandise.

services that should be their joy and crown (Isa. 58:1,2; Zech. 7:4-6; Matt. 6:2; Rom. 11:7).

Remedy (1). The first remedy against this device of Satan is, *to dwell much upon the imperfections and weaknesses that do attend your choicest services.* Oh the spots, the blots, the blemishes that are to be seen on the face of our fairest duties![1] When thou hast done all thou canst, thou hast need to close up all with this, 'Oh enter not into judgment with thy servant, O Lord' (Psa. 143:2), for the weaknesses that cleave to my best services. We may all say with the church, 'All our righteousnesses are as a menstruous cloth' (Isa. 64:6). If God should be strict to mark what is done amiss in our best actions, we are undone. Oh the water that is mingled with our wine, the dross that cleaves unto our gold!

Remedy (2). The second remedy against this device of Satan is, *to consider the impotence and inability of any of your best services, divinely to comfort, refresh, and bear your souls up from fainting, and sinking in the days of trouble, when darkness is round about you, when God shall say to you, as he did once to the Israelites,* 'Go and cry unto the gods that you have chosen; let them save you in the time of your tribulation' (Judg. 10:14). So, when God shall say in the day of your troubles. Go to your prayers, to your hearing, and to your fasting, and see if they can help you, if they can support you, if they can deliver you.[2] If God in that day doth but withhold the influence of his grace, thy former services will be but poor cordials to comfort thee; and then thou must and will cry out. Oh, 'none but

[1] Pride and high confidence is most apt to creep in upon duties well done, saith one.
[2] All good is in the chiefest good.

Christ, none but Christ.' Oh my prayers are not Christ, my hearing is not Christ, my fasting is not Christ. Oh! one smile of Christ, one glimpse of Christ, one good word from Christ, one nod of love from Christ in the day of trouble and darkness, will more revive and refresh the soul than all your former services, in which your souls rested, as if they were the bosom of Christ, which should be the only centre of our souls. Christ is the crown of crowns, the glory of glories, and the heaven of heavens.

Remedy (3). The third remedy against this device of Satan is, solemnly to consider, *that good things rested upon will as certainly undo us, and everlastingly destroy us, as the greatest enormities that can be committed by us.* Those souls that after they have done all, do not look up so high as Christ, and rest, and centre alone in Christ, laying down their services at the footstool of Christ, must lie down in sorrow; their bread is prepared for them in hell. 'Behold, all ye that kindle a fire, compass yourselves with the sparks: and walk in the light of your fire, and in the sparks ye have kindled. This shall ye have at mine hands; ye shall lie down in sorrow' (Isa. 50:11). Is it good to dwell with everlasting burnings, with a devouring fire? If it be, why then rest in your duties still; if otherwise, then see that you centre only in the bosom of Christ.

Remedy (4). The fourth remedy against this device of Satan is, *to dwell much upon the necessity and excellency of that resting-place that God hath provided for you.* Above all other resting-places, himself is your resting-place; his free mercy and love is your resting-place; the pure, glorious, matchless, and spotless righteousness of Christ is your resting-place. Ah! it is sad to think, that most men have forgotten their resting-place, as the Lord complains: 'My people have been as lost sheep, their shepherds have caused them to go astray, and have turned them away to the mountains: they are gone from mountain to hill, and forgotten their resting-place' (Jer. 50:6). So poor souls that see not the excellency of that resting-place that God hath appointed for their souls to lie down in, they wander from mountain to hill, from one duty to another, and here they will rest and there they will rest; but souls that see the excellency of that resting-place that God hath provided for them, they will say, Farewell prayer, farewell hearing, farewell fasting. I will rest no more in you, but now I will rest only in the bosom of Christ, the love of Christ, the righteousness of Christ.

IV.

SATAN'S DEVICES TO KEEP SAINTS IN A SAD, DOUBTING, QUESTIONING AND UNCOMFORTABLE CONDITION

———

THE third thing to be showed is: *the several devices that Satan hath to keep souls in a sad, doubting, questioning, and uncomfortable condition.*

Though he can never rob a believer of his crown, yet such is his malice and envy, that he will leave no stone unturned, no means unattempted, to rob them of their comfort and peace, to make their life a burden and a hell unto them, to cause them to spend their days in sorrow and mourning, in sighing and complaining, in doubting and questioning. Surely we have no interest in Christ; our graces are not true, our hopes are the hopes of hypocrites; our confidence is our presumption, our enjoyments are our delusions.[1]

I shall show you this in some particulars:

DEVICE 1. The first device that Satan hath to keep souls in a sad, doubting, and questioning condition, and so making

[1] Blessed John Bradford (the martyr), in one of his epistles, saith thus, 'O Lord, sometime methinks I feel it so with me, as if there were no difference between my heart and the wicked. I have a blind mind as they, a stout, stubborn, rebellious hard heart as they' and so he goes on.

their life a hell, is, *by causing them to be still poring and musing upon sin, to mind their sins more than their Saviour; yea, so to mind their sins as to forget, yea, to neglect their Saviour*; that, as the Psalmist speaks, 'The Lord is not in all their thoughts' (Psa. 10:4). Their eyes are so fixed upon their disease, that they cannot see the remedy, though it be near; and they do so muse upon their debts, that they have neither mind nor heart to think of their Surety.[1]

Remedy (1). The first remedy is for weak believers to consider, *that though Jesus Christ hath not freed them from the presence of sin, yet he hath freed them from the damnatory power of sin*. It is most true that sin and grace were never born together, neither shall sin and grace die together; yet while a believer breathes in this world, they must live together, they must keep house together. Christ in this life will not free any believer from the presence of any one sin, though he doth free every believer from the damning power of every sin. 'There is no condemnation to them that are in Christ Jesus, who walk not after the flesh, but after the Spirit' (Rom. 8:1). The law cannot condemn a believer, for Christ hath fulfilled it for him; divine justice cannot condemn him, for that Christ hath satisfied; his sins cannot condemn him, for they in the blood of Christ are pardoned; and his own conscience, upon righteous grounds, cannot condemn him, because Christ, that is greater than his conscience, hath acquitted him.[2]

---

[1] A Christian should wear Christ in his bosom as a flower of delight, for he is a whole paradise of delight. He that minds not Christ more than his sin, can never be thankful and fruitful as he should.

[2] My sins hurt me not, if they like me not. Sin is like that wild fig-tree, or ivy in the wall; cut off stump, body, bough, and branches, yet some strings or other will sprout out again, till the wall be plucked down.

Remedy (2). The second remedy against this device of Satan is, to consider, *that though Jesus Christ hath not freed you from the molesting and vexing power of sin, yet he hath freed you from the reign and dominion of sin. Thou sayest that sin doth so molest and vex thee, that thou canst not think of God, nor go to God, nor speak with God.*[1] Oh! but remember it is one thing for sin to molest and vex thee, and another thing for sin to reign and have dominion over thee. 'For sin shall not have dominion over you, for ye are not under the law, but under grace' (Rom. 6:14). Sin may rebel, but it shall never reign in a saint. It fareth with sin in the regenerate as with those beasts that Daniel speaks of, 'that had their dominion taken away, yet their lives were prolonged for a season and a time' (Dan. 7:12).

Now sin reigns in the soul when the soul willingly and readily obeys it, and submits to its commands, as subjects do actively obey and embrace the commands of their prince. The commands of a king are readily embraced and obeyed by his subjects, but the commands of a tyrant are embraced and obeyed unwillingly. All the service that is done to a tyrant is out of violence, and not out of obedience. A free and willing subjection to the commands of sin speaks out the soul to be under the reign and dominion of sin; but from this plague, this hell, Christ frees all believers.[2] Sin cannot say of a believer as the centurion said of his servants, 'I bid one. Go,

---

[1] The primitive Christians chose rather to be thrown to lions without than left to lusts within.

[2] It is a sign that sin hath not gained your consents but committed a rape upon your souls, when you cry out to God. If the ravished virgin under the law cried out, she was guiltless (Deut. 22:27); so when sin plays the tyrant over the soul, and the soul cries out, it is guiltless; those sins shall not be charged upon the soul.

and he goeth; and to another, Come, and he cometh; and to another. Do this, and he doeth it' (Matt. 8:9). No! the heart of a saint riseth against the commands of sin; and when sin would carry his soul to the devil, he hales his sin before the Lord, and cries out for justice. Lord! saith the believing soul, sin plays the tyrant, the devil in me; it would have me to do that which makes against thy holiness as well as against my happiness; against thy honour and glory, as my comfort and peace; therefore do me justice, thou righteous judge of heaven and earth, and let this tyrant sin die for it.

Remedy (3). The third remedy against this device of Satan is, *constantly to keep one eye upon the promises of remission of sin, as well as the other eye upon the inward operations of sin*. This is the most certain truth, that God would graciously pardon those sins to his people that he will not in this life fully subdue in his people. Paul prays thrice (*i.e.* often), to be delivered from the thorn in the flesh. All he can get is 'My grace is sufficient for thee' (2 Cor. 12:9); I will graciously pardon that to thee that I will not conquer in thee, saith God. 'And I will cleanse them from all their iniquity, whereby they have sinned against me, and whereby they have transgressed against me. I, even I, am he that blotteth out thy transgressions for mine own sake, and will not remember thy sins'[1] (Jer. 33:8, Isa. 43:25). Ah! you lamenting souls, that spend your days in sighing and groaning under the sense and burden of your sins, why do

---

[1] Isa. 44:22; Mic. 7:18, 19; Col. 2:13, 14. The promises of God are a precious book; every leaf drops myrrh and mercy. Though the weak Christian cannot open, read, and apply them, Christ can and will apply them to their souls. 'I, I am he, blotting out thy transgressions' today and tomorrow (the Hebrew denotes a continued act of God).

you deal so unkindly with God, and so injuriously with your own souls, as not to cast an eye upon those precious promises of remission of sin which may bear up and refresh your spirits in the darkest night, and under the heaviest burden of sin?

Remedy (4). The fourth remedy against this device of Satan is, *to look upon all your sins as charged upon the account of Christ, as debts which the Lord Jesus hath fully satisfied; and indeed, were there but one farthing of that debt unpaid that Christ was engaged to satisfy, it would not have stood with the unspotted justice of God to have let him come into heaven and sit down at his own right hand.* But all our debts, by his death, being discharged, we are freed, and he is exalted to sit down at the right hand of his Father, which is the top of his glory, and the greatest pledge of our felicity: 'For he hath made him to be sin for us that knew no sin, that we might be made the righteousness of God in him,' said the apostle (2 Cor. 5:21).[1] All our sins were made to meet upon Christ, as that evangelical prophet hath it: 'He was wounded for our transgressions, he was bruised for our iniquities, the chastisement of our peace was upon him, and with his stripes we are healed. All we like sheep have gone astray, we have turned every one to his own way, and the Lord hath laid on him the iniquity of us all'; or as the Hebrew hath it, 'He hath made the iniquity of us all to meet in him' (Isa. 53: 6). In law, we know that all the debts of the wife are charged upon the husband. Saith the wife to one and to another, If I owe you anything, go to my husband. So may a believer say to the law, and to the justice of God, If I owe you anything, go to my Christ, who hath undertaken for me. I must not sit down discouraged, under the apprehension

---

[1] Christ was the greatest of sinners by imputation and reputation.

of those debts, that Christ, to the utmost farthing, hath fully satisfied. Would it not argue much weakness, I had almost said much madness, for a debtor to sit down discouraged upon his looking over those debts that his surety hath readily, freely, and fully satisfied? The sense of his great love should engage a man for ever to love and honour his surety, and to bless that hand that hath paid the debt, and crossed the books. But to sit down discouraged when the debt is satisfied, is a sin that bespeaks repentance.[1]

Christ hath cleared all reckoning betwixt God and us. You remember the scapegoat. Upon his head all the iniquities of the children of Israel, and all their transgressions in all their sins, were confessed and put, and the goat did bear upon him all their iniquities (Lev. 16:21). Why! the Lord Jesus is that blessed scapegoat, upon whom all our sins were laid, and who alone hath carried 'our sins away into the land of forgetfulness, where they shall never be remembered more.'[2] A believer, under the guilt of his sin, may look the Lord in the face, and sweetly plead thus with him: It is true. Lord, I owed thee much, but thy Son was my ransom, my redemption. His blood was the price; he was my surety and undertook to answer for my sins; I know thou must be satisfied, and Christ hath satisfied thee to the utmost farthing: not for himself, for what sins had he of his own? but for me; they were my debts that he satisfied for; be pleased to look over the book, and thou shalt

[1] Christ hath the greatest worth and wealth in him. As the worth and value of many pieces of silver is in one piece of gold, so all the excellencies scattered abroad in the creatures are united in Christ. All the whole volume of perfections which are spread through heaven and earth are epitomised in him.

[2] Christ is the channel of grace from God.

find that it is crossed by thy own hand upon this very account, that Christ hath suffered and satisfied for them.[1]

Remedy (5). The fifth remedy against this device of Satan is, solemnly to consider, *of the reasons why the Lord is pleased to have his people exercised, troubled, and vexed with the operations of sinful corruptions*; and they are these: partly to keep them humble and low in their own eyes;[2] and partly to put them upon the use of all divine helps, whereby sin may be subdued and mortified; and partly, that they may live upon Christ for the perfecting the work of sanctification; and partly, to wean them from things below, and to make them heartsick of their absence from Christ, and to maintain in them bowels of compassion towards others that are subject to the same infirmities with them; and that they may distinguish between a state of grace and a state of glory, and that heaven may be more sweet to them in the close. Now doth the Lord upon these weighty reasons suffer his people to be exercised and molested with the operations of sinful corruptions? Oh then, let no believer speak, write, or conclude bitter things against his own soul and comforts, because that sin troubles and vexes his righteous soul; but lay his hand upon his mouth and be silent, because the Lord will have it so, upon such weighty grounds as the soul is not able to withstand.[3]

[1] The bloods of Abel, for so the Hebrew hath it, as if the blood of one Abel had so many tongues as drops, cried for vengeance against sin; but the blood of Christ cries louder for the pardon of sin.

[2] Augustine saith, that the first, second, and third virtue of a Christian is humility.

[3] We therefore learn, that we may teach, is a proverb among the Rabbins, After the Trojans had been wandering and tossing up and down the Mediterranean sea, as soon as they espied Italy, they cried out with exulting joy, 'Italy, Italy!' So will saints when they come to heaven.

Remedy (6). The sixth remedy against this device of Satan is, solemnly to consider, *that believers must repent for their being discouraged by their sins.* Their being discouraged by their sins will cost them many a prayer, many a tear, and many a groan; and that because their discouragements under sin flow from ignorance and unbelief. It springs from their ignorance of the richness, freeness, fullness, and everlastingness of God's love; and from their ignorance of the power, glory, sufficiency, and efficacy of the death and sufferings of the Lord Jesus Christ; and from their ignorance of the worth, glory, fullness, largeness, and completeness of the righteousness of Jesus Christ; and from their ignorance of that real, close, spiritual, glorious, and inseparable union that is between Christ and their precious souls. Ah! did precious souls know and believe the truth of these things as they should, they would not sit down dejected and overwhelmed under the sense and operation of sin.[1]

DEVICE 2. *By working them to make false definitions of their graces,* Satan knows, that as false definitions of sin wrong the soul one way, so false definitions of grace wrong the soul another way.

I will instance only in faith: Oh how doth Satan labour with might and main to work men to make false definitions of faith! Some he works to define faith too high, as that it is a full assurance of the love of God to a man's soul in particular, or a full persuasion of the pardon and remission of a man's own sins in particular. Saith Satan, What dost thou talk of faith?

---

[1] God never gave a believer a new heart that it should always lie a-bleeding, and that it should always be rent and torn in pieces with discouragements.

Faith is an assurance of the love of God, and of the pardon of sin; and this thou hast not; thou knowest thou art far off from this; therefore thou hast no faith. And by drawing men to make such a false definition of faith, he keeps them in a sad, doubting, and questioning condition, and makes them spend their days in sorrow and sighing, so that tears are their drink, and sorrow is their meat, and sighing is their work all the day long.

The philosophers say there are eight degrees of heat; we discern three. Now, if a man should define heat only by the highest degree, then all other degrees will be cast out from being heat. So if men shall define faith only by the highest degrees, by assurance of the love of God, and of the pardon of his sins in particular, what will become of lesser degrees of faith?

If a man should define a man to be a living man, only by the highest and strongest demonstrations of life, as laughing, leaping, running, working, and walking, would not many thousands that groan under internal and external weaknesses, and that cannot laugh, nor leap, nor run, nor work, nor walk, be found dead men by such a definition, that yet we know to be alive? It is so here, and you know how to apply it.

Remedy (1). The first remedy against this device of Satan is, solemnly to consider, *that there may be true faith, yea, great measures of faith, where there is no assurance.* The Canaanite woman in the Gospel had strong faith, yet no assurance that we read of. 'These things have I written unto you,' saith John, 'that believe on the name of the Son of God, that ye may know that ye have eternal life, and that ye may believe on the name of the Son of God' (1 John 5:13). In these words you see that they did believe, and had eternal life, in respect of the purpose and promise of God, and in respect of the seeds and beginnings of it in their souls, and in respect of Christ their head, who sits in heaven as a public person, representing all his chosen ones, 'Who hath raised us up together, and made us sit together in heavenly places in Christ Jesus' (Eph. 2:6); and yet they did not know that they had eternal life. It is one thing to have a right to heaven, and another thing to know it; it is one thing to be beloved, and another thing for a man to know that he is beloved. It is one thing for God to write a man's name in the book of life, and another thing for God to tell a man that his name is written in the book of life; and to say to him (Luke 10:20), 'Rejoice, because thy name is written in heaven.' So Paul: 'In whom ye also trusted, after ye heard the word of truth, the gospel of your salvation: in whom also, after ye believed, ye were sealed with that Holy Spirit of promise' (Eph. 1:13). So Micah: 'Rejoice not against me, O my enemy: for when I shall fall, I shall rise; when I shall sit in darkness, the Lord shall be a light unto me. I will bear the indignation of the Lord, because I have sinned' (or 'the sad countenance of God,' as the Hebrew hath it) (Mic. 7:8, 9). This soul had no assurance, for he sits in darkness, and was under the sad countenance of God; and yet had strong faith, as appears in those words, 'When I fall, I shall rise; when I sit in darkness, the Lord shall be a light unto me.' He will bring me forth to the light, and I shall behold his righteousness. And let this suffice for the first answer.[1]

Remedy (2). The second remedy against this device of Satan is, solemnly to consider, *that God in the Scripture doth define*

---

[1] So those in Isa. 50:10 had faith, though they had no assurance.

faith otherwise. God defines faith to be a receiving of Christ—
'As many as received him, to them he gave this privilege, to
be the sons of God' (John 1:12). To as many as believed on
his name'—to be a cleaving of the soul unto God, though no
joy, but afflictions, attend the soul (Acts 11:23). Yea, the Lord
defines faith to be a coming to God in Christ, and often to a
resting and staying, rolling of the soul upon Christ. It is safest
and sweetest to define as God defines, both vices and graces.
This is the only way to settle the soul, and to secure it against
the wiles of men and devils, who labour, by false definitions
of grace, to keep precious souls in a doubting, staggering, and
languishing condition, and so make their lives a burden, a
hell, unto them.[1]

Remedy (3). The third remedy against this device of Satan
is, seriously to consider this, *that there may be true faith where
there is much doubtings.* Witness those frequent sayings of
Christ to his disciples, 'Why are ye afraid, O ye of little faith?'[2]
Persons may be truly believing who nevertheless are some-
times doubting. In the same persons that the fore-mentioned
scriptures speak of, you may see their faith commended and
their doubts condemned, which doth necessarily suppose a
presence of both.

Remedy (4). The fourth remedy against this device of Satan
is, solemnly to consider, *that assurance is an effect of faith; there-
fore it cannot be faith.* The cause cannot be the effect, nor the
root the fruit. As the effect flows from the cause, the fruit from
the root, the stream from the fountain, so doth assurance flow
from faith. This truth I shall make good thus:

[1] Matt 11:28; John 6:37; Heb. 7:25, 26.
[2] Matt. 6:30; 14:31; 16:8; Luke 12:28.

The assurance of our salvation and pardon of sin doth primarily arise from the witness of the Spirit of God that we are the children of God (Eph. 1:13); and the Spirit never witnesseth this till we are believers: 'For we are sons by faith in Christ Jesus' (Gal. 4:6). Therefore assurance is not faith, but follows it, as the effect follows the cause.

Again, no man can be assured and persuaded of his salvation till he be united to Christ, till he be ingrafted into Christ; and a man cannot be ingrafted into Christ till he hath faith. He must first be ingrafted into Christ by faith before he can have assurance of his salvation; which doth clearly evidence, that assurance is not faith, but an effect and fruit of faith.

Again, faith cannot be lost, but assurance may; therefore assurance is not faith.[1] Though assurance be a precious flower in the garden of a saint, and is more infinitely sweet and delightful to the soul than all outward comforts and contents; yet it is but a flower that is subject to fade, and to lose its freshness and beauty, as saints by sad experience find.

Again, a man must first have faith before he can have assurance, therefore assurance is not faith. And that a man must first have faith before he can have assurance, is clear by this, a man must first be saved before he can be assured of his salvation; for he cannot be assured of that which is not. And a man must first have a saving faith before he can be saved by faith, for he cannot be saved by that which he hath not; therefore a man must first have faith before he can have assurance, and so it roundly follows that assurance is not faith.[2]

[1] Psa. 51:12; 30:6, 7; Songs of Sol. 5:6; Isa. 8:17.
[2] There are many thousand precious souls, of whom this world is not worthy, that have the faith of reliance, and yet lack assurance and the effects of it; as high joy, glorious peace, and vehement longings after the coming of Christ.

DEVICE 3. *By working the soul to make false inferences from the cross actings of Providence.* Saith Satan, Dost thou not see how Providence crosses thy prayers, and crosses thy desires, thy tears, thy hopes, thy endeavours?[1] Surely if his love were towards thee, if his soul did delight and take pleasure in thee, he would not deal thus with thee.

Remedy (1). The first remedy against this device of Satan is, solemnly to consider, *that many things may be cross to our desires that are not cross to our good.* Abraham, Jacob, David, Job, Moses, Jeremiah, Jonah, and Paul, met with many things that were contrary to their desires and endeavours, that were not contrary to their good; as all know that have wisely compared their desires and endeavours and God's actings together. Physic often works contrary to the patients' desires, when it doth not work contrary to their good.

I remember a story of a godly man, who had a great desire to go to France, and as he was going to take shipping he broke his leg; and it pleased Providence so to order it, that the ship that he should have gone in at that very same time was cast away, and not a man saved; and so by breaking a bone his life was saved. Though Providence did work cross to his desire, yet it did not work cross to his good.[2]

Remedy (2). The second remedy against this device of Satan is, solemnly to consider, *that the hand of God may be against a man, when the love and heart of God is much set upon a man.*

---

[1] Psa. 77:7, etc.; 31:1; 73: 2, 13.

[2] The Circumcellians being not able to withstand the preaching and writing of Augustine, sought his destruction, having beset the way he was to go to his visitation, but by God's providence he, missing his way, escaped the danger.

No man can conclude how the heart of God stands by his hand. The hand of God was against Ephraim, and yet his love, his heart, was dearly set upon Ephraim: 'I have surely heard Ephraim bemoaning himself thus: Thou hast chastised me, and I was chastised, as a bullock unaccustomed to the yoke. Turn thou me, and I shall be turned; for thou art the Lord my God. Surely, after that I was returned, I repented; and after that I was instructed, I smote upon my thigh; I was ashamed, yea, even confounded, because I did bear the reproach of my youth. Is Ephraim my dear son? is he a pleasant child? for since I spake against him, I do earnestly remember him still. Therefore my bowels are troubled for him; I will surely have mercy upon him, saith the Lord' (Jer. 31:18-20).[1]

God can look sourly, and chide bitterly, and strike heavily, even where and when he loves dearly. The hand of God was very much against Job, and yet his love, his heart, was very much set upon Job, as you may see by comparing chaps, 1 and 2, with 41 and 42. The hand of God was sore against David and Jonah, when his heart was much set upon them. He that shall conclude that the heart of God is against those that his hand is against, will condemn the generation of the just, whom God unjustly would not have condemned.

Remedy (3). The third remedy against this device of Satan, is, to consider, *that all the cross providences that befall the saints are but in order to some noble good that God doth intend to prefer[2] upon them.* Providence wrought cross to David's desire in taking

---

[1] God's providential hand may be with persons when his heart is set against them. God's providential hand was for a time with Saul, Haman, Asshur, and Jehu, and yet his heart was set against him. No man knoweth love or hatred by all that is before him (Eccles. 9:1, 2).

[2] = confer.

away the child sinfully begotten, but yet not cross to more noble good; for was it not far better for David to have such a legitimate heir as Solomon was, than that a bastard should wear the crown, and sway the sceptre?

Joseph, you know, was sold into a far country by the envy and malice of his brethren, and afterwards imprisoned because he would not be a prisoner to his mistress's lusts; yet all these providences did wonderfully conduce to his advancement, and the preservation of his father's family, which was then the visible church of Christ. It was so handled by a noble hand of providence, that what they sought to decline,[1] they did promote. Joseph was therefore sold by his brethren that he might not be worshipped, and yet he was therefore worshipped because he was sold.[2]

David was designed to a kingdom, but oh! the straits, troubles, and deaths that he runs through before he feels the weight of his crown! And all this was but in order to the sweetening of his crown, and to the settling of it more firmly and gloriously upon his head. God did so contrive it that Jonah's offence, and those cross actings of his that did attend it, should advantage that end which they seemed most directly to oppose. Jonah—he flies to Tarshish, then cast into the sea, then saved by a miracle. Then the mariners, as it is very probable, who cast Jonah into the sea, declared to the Ninevites what had happened; therefore he must be a man sent of God, and that his threatenings must be believed and hearkened to, and therefore they must repent and humble themselves, that the wrath threatened might not be executed.[3]

---

[1] = injure.

[2] Cf. Gen. 37:7, etc.

[3] The motions of divine providence are so dark, so deep, so changeable,

Remedy (4). The fourth remedy against this device of Satan is, seriously to consider, *that all the strange, dark, deep, and change-able providences that believers meet with, shall further them in their way to heaven, in their journey to happiness.* Divine wisdom and love will so order all things here below, that they shall work for the real, internal, and eternal good of them that love him. All the rugged providences that David met with did contrib-ute to the bringing of him to the throne; and all the rugged providences that Daniel and the 'three children' met with did contribute to their great advancement. So all the rugged provi-dences that believers meet with, they shall all contribute to the lifting up of their souls above all things, below God. As the waters lifted up Noah's ark nearer heaven, and as all the stones that were about Stephen's ears did but knock him the closer to Christ, the corner-stone, so all the strange rugged provi-dences that we meet with, they shall raise us nearer heaven, and knock us nearer to Christ, that precious corner-stone.[1]

DEVICE 4. *By suggesting to them that their graces are not true, but counterfeit.* Saith Satan, all is not gold that glitters, all is not free grace that you count grace, that you call grace. That which you call faith is but a fancy, and that which you call zeal is but a natural heat and passion; and that light you have, it is but common, it is short, to what many have attained to that are now in hell. Satan doth not labour more mightily to persuade hypocrites that their graces are true when they are counterfeit, than he doth to persuade precious souls

---

that the wisest and noblest souls cannot tell what conclusions to make.

[1] Orosius, speaking of Valentinian, saith: He that for Christ's name's sake had lost a tribuneship, within a while after succeeded his persecutor in the empire.

that their graces are counterfeit, when indeed they are true, and such as will abide the touchstone of Christ.[1]

Remedy (1). The first remedy against this device of Satan is, seriously to consider, *that grace is taken two ways.*

[1.] It is taken for the gracious *good-will and favour of God*, whereby he is pleased of his own free love to accept of some in Christ for his own. This, some call the first grace, because it is the fountain of all other graces, and the spring from whence they flow, and it is therefore called grace, because it makes a man gracious with God, but this is only in God.

[2.] Grace is taken for the *gifts of grace*, and they are of two sorts, common or special. Some are common to believers and hypocrites, as a gift of knowledge, a gift of prayer, etc. Some are special graces, and they are proper and peculiar to the saints, as faith, humility, meekness, love, patience, etc. (Gal. 5:22, 23).

Remedy (2). The second remedy against this device of Satan is, wisely to consider, *the differences betwixt renewing grace and restraining grace, betwixt sanctifying and temporary grace*; and this I will show you in these ten particulars.

[1.] True grace *makes all glorious within and without*: 'The King's daughter is all glorious within; her raiment is of wrought gold' (Psa. 45:13). True grace makes the understanding glorious, the affections glorious. It casts a general glory upon all the noble parts of the soul: 'The King's daughter is all glorious within.' And as it makes the inside glorious, so it makes the outside glorious: 'Her clothing is of wrought

---

[1] Yet it must be granted that many a fair flower may grow out of a stinking roots and many sweet dispositions and fair actions may be where there is only the corrupt root of nature.

gold.' It makes men look gloriously, and speak gloriously, and walk and act gloriously, so that vain souls shall be forced to say that these are they that have seen Jesus.[1] As grace is a fire to burn up and consume the dross and filth of the soul, so it is an ornament to beautify and adorn the soul. True grace makes all new, the inside new and the outside new: 'If any man be in Christ, he is a new creature' (2 Cor. 5:17),[2] but temporary grace doth not this. True grace changes the very nature of a man. Moral virtue doth only restrain or chain up the outward man, it doth not change the whole man. A lion in a grate is a lion still; he is restrained, but not changed, for he retains his lion-like nature still. So temporary graces restrain many men from this and that wickedness, but it doth not change and turn their hearts from wickedness. But now true grace, that turns a lion into a lamb, as you may see in Paul (Acts 9), and a notorious strumpet into a blessed and glorious penitent, as you may see in Mary Magdalene (Luke 7).[3]

[2.] *The objects* of true grace are *supernatural.* True grace is conversant about the choicest and the highest objects, about the most soul-ennobling and soul-greatening objects, as God, Christ, precious promises that are more worth than a world, and a kingdom that shakes not, a crown of glory that withers not, and heavenly treasures that rust not. The objects

---

[1] God brings not a pair of scales to weigh our graces, but a touchstone to try our graces. Purity, preciousness, and holiness is stamped upon all saving graces. Acts 15: 9; 2 Pet. 1:1; Jude 20.

[2] The Greek signifies 'a new creation': new Adam, new covenant, new paradise, new Lord, new law, new hearts, and new creatures go together.

[3] [It seems right to question this admittedly common mode of speaking of Mary of Magdala. It is not certain that the two were identical.]

of temporary grace are low and poor, and always within the compass of reason's reach.[1]

[3.] True grace enables a Christian, *when he is himself, to do spiritual actions with real pleasure and delight.* To souls truly gracious, Christ's yoke 'is easy, and his burden is light'; 'his commandments are not grievous, but joyous.' 'I delight in the law of God after the inward man,' saith Paul.[2] The blessed man is described by this, that he 'delights in the law of the Lord' (Psa. 1:2). 'It is joy to the just to do judgment,' saith Solomon (Prov. 21:15). To a gracious soul, 'Ah the ways of the Lord are pleasantness, and his paths are peace' (Prov. 3:17); but to souls that have but temporary grace, but moral virtues, religious services are a toil, not a pleasure; a burden, and not a delight. 'Wherefore have we fasted,' say they, 'and thou seest not? Wherefore have we afflicted our souls, and thou takest no knowledge?' (Isa. 58:3). 'Ye have said,' say those in Malachi, 'It is vain to serve God; and what profit is it that we have kept his ordinances, and that we have walked mournfully before the Lord of hosts?' (Mal. 3:14). 'When will the new moon be gone,' say those in Amos, 'that we may sell corn, and the Sabbath, that we may set forth wheat, making the ephah small, and the shekel great, and falsifying the balances by deceit' (Amos 8:5).

[4.] True grace makes *a man most careful, and most fearful of his own heart.*[3] It makes him most studious about his own heart, informing that, examining that, and watching over that; but temporary grace, moral virtues, make men more mindful and careful of others, to instruct them and counsel

[1] 2 Cor. 10:18; Prov. 14. A saint hath his feet where other men's heads are (Matt. 6).

[2] Matt. 11:30; I John 5:3; Rom. 7:22.

[3] Psa. 51:10; 119:36, 80; 139:23; 86:11.

them, and stir up them, and watch over them. Which doth with open mouth demonstrate that their graces are not saving and peculiar to saints, but that they are temporary, and no more than Judas, Demas, and the Pharisees had.

[5.] Grace will *work a man's heart to love and cleave to the strictest and holiest ways and things of God, for their purity and sanctity, in the face of all dangers and hardships.* 'Thy word is very pure, therefore thy servant loveth it' (Psa. 119:140). Others love it, and like it, and follow it, for the credit, the honour, the advantage that they get by it; but I love it for the spiritual beauty and purity of it. So the psalmist, 'All this is come upon us; yet have we not forgotten thee, neither have we dealt falsely in thy covenant. Our heart is not turned back, neither have our steps declined from thy way: though thou hast sore broken us in the place of dragons, and covered us with the shadow of death' (Psa. 44:17-19). But temporary grace will not bear up the soul against all oppositions and discouragements in the ways of God, as is clear by their apostasy in John 6:60, 66, and by the stony ground hearers falling away (Matt. 13:20, 21).[1]

[6.] True grace will *enable a man to step over the world's crown, to take up Christ's cross; to prefer the cross of Christ above the glory of this world.* It enabled Abraham, and Moses, and Daniel, with those other worthies in Heb. 11, to do so. Godfrey of Bullen [Bouillon], crusader king of Jerusalem, refused to be crowned with a crown of gold, saying, 'That it became not a Christian there to wear a crown of gold, where Christ had worn a crown of thorns.' Oh! but temporary grace cannot work the soul to prefer Christ's cross above the world's crown; but when these two meet, a temporary Christian steps over

---

[1] Grace is a panoply against all trouble, and a paradise of all pleasures.

Christ's cross to take up, and keep up, the world's crown. 'Demas hath forsaken us to embrace this present world' (2 Tim. 4:10). So the young man in the Gospel had many good things in him; he bid fair for heaven, and came near to heaven; but when Christ set his cross before him, he steps over that to enjoy the world's crown (Matt. 19:19-22). When Christ bid him, 'go and sell all that he had, and give to the poor,' 'he went away sorrowful, for he had great possessions.' If heaven be had upon no other terms, Christ may keep his heaven to himself, he will have none.[1]

[7.] Sanctifying grace, renewing grace, *puts the soul upon spiritual duties, from spiritual and intrinsical motives*, as from the sense of divine love, that doth constrain the soul to wait on God, and to act for God;[2] and the sense of the excellency and sweetness of communion with God, and the choice and precious discoveries that the soul hath formerly had of the beauty and glory of God, whilst it hath been in the service of God. The good looks, the good words, the blessed love-letters, the glorious kisses, and the sweet embraces that gracious souls have had from Christ in his service, do provoke and move them to wait upon him in holy duties. Ah! but restraining grace, temporary grace, puts men upon religious duties only from external motives, as the care of the creature, the eye of the creature, the rewards of the creature, and the keeping up

---

[1] Few are of Jerome's mind, that had rather have Paul's coat with his heavenly graces, than the purple of kings with their kingdoms. The king of Navarre told Beza, that in the cause of religion he would launch no further into their sea, than he might be sure to return safe to the haven. [Henry IV, afterwards the Apostate from Protestantism].

[2] As what I have, if offered to thee, pleaseth not thee, O Lord, without myself, so the good things we have from thee, though they may refresh us, yet they satisfy us not without thyself. (*Bernard*)

of a name among the creatures, and a thousand such like con-
siderations, as you may see in Saul, Jehu, Judas, Demas, and
the scribes and Pharisees.[1] The abbot in Melanchthon lived
strictly, and walked demurely, and looked humbly, so long as
he was but a monk, but when, by his seeming extraordinary
sanctity, he got to be abbot, he grew intolerably proud and
insolent; and being asked the reason of it, confessed, 'That his
former lowly look was but to see if he could find the keys of
the abbey.' Such poor, low, vain motives work temporary souls
to all the service they do perform.

[8.] Saving grace, renewing grace, will cause a man to follow
the Lord fully in the desertion of all sin, and in the obser-
vation of all God's precepts. Joshua and Caleb followed the
Lord fully[2] (Num. 14:24). Zacharias and Elizabeth were right-
eous before God, and walked in all the commandments and
ordinances of the Lord blameless (Luke 1:5, 6). The saints in
the Revelation are described by this, that 'they follow the
Lamb whithersoever he goes' (Rev. 14:4); but restraining grace,
temporary grace, cannot enable a man to follow the Lord
fully. All that temporary grace can enable a man to do, is
to follow the Lord partially, unevenly, and haltingly, as you
may see in Jehu, Herod, Judas, and the scribes and Pharisees,
who paid tithe of 'mint, and anise, and cummin, but omitted
the weightier matters of the law, judgment, mercy, and faith'
(Matt. 23:23). True grace works the heart to the hatred of all
sin, and to the love of all truth; it works a man to the hatred of

[1] It is an excellent speech of Bernard: Good art thou, O Lord, to the
soul that seeks thee, what art thou then to the soul that finds thee?

[2] 'Hath fulfilled after me' (Heb.). A metaphor taken from a ship
under sail, that is strongly carried with the wind, as fearing neither
rocks nor sands.

those sins that for his blood he cannot conquer, and to loathe those sins that he would give all the world to overcome (Psa. 119:104, 128).[1] So that a soul truly gracious can say, Though there be no one sin mortified and subdued in me, as it should, and as I would, yet every sin is hated and loathed by me. So a soul truly gracious can say, Though I do not obey any one command as I should, and as I would, yet every word is sweet, every command of God is precious (Psa. 119:6, 119, 127, 167). I dearly prize and greatly love those commands that I cannot obey; though there be many commands that I cannot in a strict sense fulfil, yet there is no command I would not fulfil, that I do not exceedingly love. 'I love thy commandments above gold, above fine gold:' 'My soul hath kept thy testimonies, and I love them exceedingly' (Psa. 119:127, 167).

[9.] *True grace leads the soul to rest in Christ, as in his 'summum bonum,' chiefest good.* It works the soul to centre in Christ, as in his highest and ultimate end. 'Whither should we go? thou hast the words of eternal life' (John 6:68). 'My beloved is white and ruddy, the chiefest of ten thousand; I found him whom my soul loved, I held him and would not let him go' (Songs of Sol. 5:10; 3:4). That wisdom a believer hath from Christ, it leads him to centre in the wisdom of Christ (1 Cor. 1:30); and that love the soul hath from Christ, it leads the soul to centre in the love of Christ; and that righteousness the soul hath from Christ, it leads the soul to rest and centre in the righteousness of Christ (Phil. 3:9).[2] True grace is a beam of Christ, and where it is, it

---

[1] I had rather go to hell pure from sin, than to heaven polluted with that filth (*Anselm*). Give what thou commandest, and command what thou wilt. (*Augustine*)

[2] Grace is that star that leads to Christ; it is that cloud and pillar of fire that leads the soul to the heavenly Canaan, where Christ sits chief.

will naturally lead the soul to rest in Christ. The stream doth not more naturally lead to the fountain, nor the effect to the cause, than true grace leads the soul to Christ. But restraining grace, temporary grace, works the soul to centre and rest in things below Christ. Sometimes it works the soul to centre in the praises of the creature; sometimes to rest in the rewards of the creature: 'Verily they have their reward,' said Christ (Matt. 6:1, 2): and so in an hundred other things (Zech. 7:3, 6).

[10.] True grace will *enable a soul to sit down satisfied and contented with the naked enjoyments of Christ*. The enjoyment of Christ without honour will satisfy the soul; the enjoyment of Christ without riches, the enjoyment of Christ without pleasures, and without the smiles of creatures, will content and satisfy the soul. 'It is enough; Joseph is alive' (Gen. 45:28). So saith a gracious soul, though honour is not, and riches are not, and health is not, and friends are not, it is enough that Christ is, that he reigns, conquers, and triumphs. Christ is the pot of manna, the cruse of oil, a bottomless ocean of all comfort, content, and satisfaction. He that hath him wants nothing; he that wants him enjoys nothing.[1] 'Having nothing,' saith Paul, 'and yet possessing all things' (2 Cor. 6:10). Oh! but a man that hath but temporary grace, that hath but restraining grace, cannot sit down satisfied and contented, under the want of outward comforts.[2] Christ is good with honours, saith such a soul; and Christ is good with riches, and Christ is good

[1] Saith Seneca: a contented man cannot be a poor man.

[2] Charles the Great's motto is also the motto of the saints; *Christus regnat, vincit, triumphat*: Christ reigns, conquers, triumphs. Augustine upon Psalm 12 brings in God rebuking a discontented Christian thus: What is thy faith? have I promised thee these things? What! wert thou made a Christian that thou shouldst flourish here in this world?

with pleasures, and he is good with such and such outward contents. I must have Christ and the world, or else with the young man in the Gospel, in spite of my soul, I shall forsake Christ to follow the world. Ah! how many shining professors be there in the world, that cannot sit down satisfied and contented, under the want of this or that outward comfort and content, but are like bedlams, fretting and vexing, raging and madding,[1] as if there were no God, no heaven, no hell, nor no Christ to make up all such outward wants to souls. But a soul truly gracious can say; In having nothing I have all things, because I have Christ; having therefore all things in him, I seek no other reward, for he is the universal reward. Such a soul can say: Nothing is sweet to me without the enjoyment of Christ in it; honours, nor riches, nor the smiles of creatures, are not sweet to me no farther than I see Christ, and taste Christ in them.[2] The confluence of all outward good cannot make a heaven of glory in my soul, if Christ, who is the top of my glory, be absent; as Absalom said, 'What is all this to me so long as I cannot see the king's face?' (2 Sam. 14:32). So saith the soul: Why do you tell me of this and that outward comfort, when I cannot see his face whom my soul loves? Why, my honour is not my Christ, nor riches is not Christ, nor the favour of the creature is not Christ; let me have him, and let the men of this world take the world, and divide it amongst themselves; I prize my Christ above all, I would enjoy my Christ above all other

[1] Going about as 'mad.'
[2] Content is the deputy of outward felicity, and supplies the place where it is absent. As the Jews throw the book of Esther to the ground before they read it, because the name of God is not in it, as the Rabbins have observed; so do saints in some sense those mercies wherein they do not read Christ's name, and see Christ's heart.

things in the world; his presence will make up the absence of all other comforts, and his absence will darken and embitter all my comforts; so that my comforts will neither taste like comforts, nor look like comforts, nor warm like comforts, when he that should comfort my soul stands afar off (Lam. 1:16). Christ is all and in all to souls truly gracious (Col. 3:11). We have all things in Christ, and Christ is all things to a Christian. If we be sick, he is a physician; if we thirst, he is a fountain; if our sins trouble us, he is righteousness; if we stand in need of help, he is mighty to save; if we fear death, he is life; if we be in darkness, he is light; if we be weak, he is strength; if we be in poverty, he is plenty; if we desire heaven, he is the way. The soul cannot say, this I would have, and that I would have; but saith Christ, it is in me, it is in me eminently, perfectly, eternally.[1]

DEVICE 5. By suggesting to them, *that conflict that is in them, is not a conflict that is only in saints, but such a conflict that is to be found in hypocrites and profane souls*; when the truth is, there is as much difference betwixt the conflict that is in them, and that which is in wicked men, as there is betwixt light and darkness, betwixt heaven and hell.[2] And the truth of this I shall evidence to you in the following particulars:

[1.] *The whole frame of a believer's soul is against sin*. Understanding, will, and affection, all the powers and faculties of the soul are in arms against sin. A covetous man may condemn covetousness, and yet the frame and bent of his heart may be

[1] Luther said, he had rather be in hell with Christ, than in heaven without him. None but Christ, none but Christ, said Lambert the martyr, lifting up his hands and his fingers' end flaming.

[2] John 8:44: the devil is a liar, and the father of it. The devil's breasts (saith Luther) are very fruitful with lies.

to it; a proud person may condemn pride, and yet the frame of his spirit may be to it; and the drunkard may condemn drunkenness, and yet the frame of his spirit may be to it;[1] a man may condemn stealing and lying, and yet the frame of his heart may be to it. 'Thou that preachest a man should not steal, dost thou steal? Thou that sayest a man should not commit adultery, dost thou commit adultery? Thou that abhorrest idols, dost thou commit sacrilege? Thou that makest thy boast of the law, through breaking the law dishonourest thou God?' (Rom. 2:21-23). But a saint's will is against it. 'The evil that I would not do, that I do'; and his affections are against it, 'What I hate, I do' (Rom. 7:19, 20).

[2.] A saint *conflicts against sin universally, the least as well as the greatest*; the most profitable and the most pleasing sin, as well as against those that are less pleasing and profitable. He will combat with all, though he cannot conquer one as he should, and as he would. He knows that all sin strikes at God's holiness, as well as his own happiness; at God's glory, as well as at his soul's comfort and peace.[2] He knows that all sin is hateful to God, and that all sinners are traitors to the

---

[1] It was a good saying of Augustine, *Domine, libera me a malo homine, me ipso*, Lord, deliver me from an evil man, myself. He complains that men do not tame their beasts in their own bosoms.

[2] Psa. 119:104, I hate every false way; the Hebrew signifies to hate with a deadly and irreconcilable hatred. He knows that all the parts of the old man hath, and doth play the part of a treacherous friend and a friendly traitor; therefore he strikes at all. The greater the combat is, the greater shall be the following rewards, saith Tertullian. True hatred is against the whole kind. Plutarch reports of one who would not be resolved of his doubts, because he would not lose the pleasure in seeking for resolution. So wicked men will not be rid of some sins, because they would not lose the seeming pleasure of sinning.

crown and dignity of the Lord Jesus. He looks upon one sin, and sees that that threw down Noah, the most righteous man in the world, and he looks upon another sin, and sees that that cast down Abraham, the greatest believer in the world, and he looks upon another sin, and sees that that threw down David, the best king in the world, and he looks upon another sin, and sees that that cast down Paul, the greatest apostle in the world. He sees that one sin threw down Samson, the strongest man in the world; another cast down Solomon, the wisest man in the world; and another Moses, the meekest man in the world; and another sin cast down Job, the patientest man in the world; and this raiseth a holy indignation against all, so that nothing can satisfy and content his soul but a destruction of all those lusts and vermin that vex and rack his righteous soul. It will not suffice a gracious soul to see justice done upon one sin, but he cries out for justice upon all. He would not have some crucified and others spared, but cries out. Lord, crucify them all, crucify them all. Oh! but now the conflict that is in wicked men is partial; they frown upon one sin and smile upon another; they strike at some sins yet stroke others; they thrust some out of doors but keep others close in their bosoms; as you may see in Jehu, Herod, Judas, Simon Magus, and Demas. Wicked men strike at gross sins, such as are not only against the law of God, but against the laws of nature and nations, but make nothing of less sins; as vain thoughts, idle words, sinful motions, and petty oaths. They fight against those sins that fight against their honour, profits, and pleasures, but make truce with those that are as right hands and as right eyes to them.

[3.] *The conflict that is in a saint, against sin, is maintained by several arguments*: by arguments drawn from the love of God, the honour of God, the sweetness and communion with God, and from the spiritual and heavenly blessings and privileges that are conferred upon them by God, and from arguments drawn from the blood of Christ, the glory of Christ, the eye of Christ, the kisses of Christ, and the intercession of Christ, and from arguments drawn from the earnest of the Spirit, the seal of the Spirit, the witness of the Spirit, the comforts of the Spirit. Oh! but the conflict that is in wicked men is from low, carnal, and legal arguments, drawn from the eye, ear, or hand of the creature, or drawn from shame, hell, and curses of the law (2 Cor. 12:7-9).[1]

[4.] The conflict that is in saints is a *constant conflict*. Though sin and grace were not born in the heart of a saint together, and though they shall not die together, yet, whilst a believer lives, they must conflict together. Paul had been fourteen years converted, when he cried out, 'I have a law in my members rebelling against the law of my mind, and leading me captive to the law of sin' (Rom. 7:2, 3). Pietro Candiano, one of the dukes of Venice, died fighting against the Nauratines with the weapons in his hands. So a saint lives fighting and dies fighting, he stands fighting and falls fighting, with his spiritual weapons in his hands.[2] But the conflict that is in wicked men is inconstant; now they fall out with sin, and anon they fall in with sin; now it is bitter, anon it is sweet; now the sinner turns from his sin, and anon he turns to the wallowing in sin, as the

---

[1] Though to be kept from sin brings comfort to us, yet for us to oppose sin from spiritual and heavenly arguments, and God to pardon sin, that brings most glory to God.

[2] It was an excellent saying of Eusebius Emesenus, Our fathers overcame the torrents of the flames, let us overcome the fiery darts of vices. Consider that the pleasure and sweetness that follows victory over sin, is a thousand times beyond that seeming sweetness that is in sin.

swine doth to the wallowing in the mire (2 Pet. 2:19, 20). One hour you shall have him praying against sin, as if he feared it more than hell, and the next hour you shall have him pursuing after sin, as if there were no God to punish him, no justice to damn him, no hell to torment him.

[5.] The conflict that is in the saints, is in the *same faculties*; there is the judgment against the judgment, the mind against the mind, the will against the will, the affections against the affections, that is, the regenerate part against the unregenerate part, in all the parts of the soul; but now, in wicked men, the conflict is not in the same faculties, but between the conscience and the will. The will of a sinner is bent strongly to such and such sins, but conscience puts in and tells the sinner, God hath made me his deputy, he hath given me a power to hang and draw, to examine, scourge, judge, and condemn, and if thou doest such and such wickedness, I shall be thy jailor and tormenter. I do not bear the rod nor the sword in vain, saith conscience; if thou sinnest, I shall do my office, and then thy life will be a hell: and this raises a tumult in the soul.[1]

[6.] The conflict that is in the saints, *is a more blessed, successful, and prevailing conflict.* A saint, by his conflict with sin, gains ground upon his sin: 'They that are Christ's,' saith the apostle, 'have crucified the world with the affections and lusts' (Gal. 5:24). Christ puts to his hand and helps them to lead captivity captive, and to set their feet upon the necks of those lusts that have formerly trampled upon their souls and their comforts. As the house of Saul grew weaker and weaker, and the house of David stronger and stronger, so the Lord, by the discoveries of his love, and by the influences of his Spirit,

---

[1] A heathen could say, their soul is in a mutiny; a wicked man is not friends with himself, he and his conscience are at difference. (*Aristotle*)

he causeth grace, the nobler part of a saint, to grow stronger and stronger, and corruption, like the house of Saul, to grow weaker and weaker. But sin in a wicked heart gets ground, and grows stronger and stronger, notwithstanding all his conflicts. His heart is more encouraged, emboldened, and hardened in a way of sin, as you may see in the Israelites, Pharaoh, Jehu, and Judas, who doubtless found many strange conflicts, tumults, and mutinies in their souls, when God spake such bitter things against them, and did such justice upon them (2 Tim. 3:13).[1] But remember this by way of caution: Though Christ hath given sin its death-wound, by his power, Spirit, death, and resurrection, yet it will die but a lingering death.[2] As a man that is mortally wounded dies by little and little, so doth sin in the heart of a saint. The death of Christ on the cross was a lingering death, so the death of sin in the soul is a lingering death; now it dies a little, and anon it dies a little, as the psalmist speaks, 'Slay them not, lest my people forget: scatter them by thy power; and bring them down, O Lord our shield' (Psa. 59:11). He would not have them utterly destroyed, but some relics preserved as a memorial. So God dealeth in respect of sin; it is wounded and brought down, but not wholly slain; something is still left as a monument of

[1] These two, grace and sin, are like two buckets of a well, when one is up, the other is down. They are like the two laurels at Rome, when one flourishes the other withers. The more grace thrives in the soul, the more sin dies in the soul. From naught they grow to be very naught, and from very naught to be stark naught. Lactantius said of Lucian, he spared neither God nor man.

[2] Mortification is a continued act, it is a daily dying to sin, 'I die daily.' A crucified man will strive and struggle, yet, in the eyes of the law, and in the account of all that see him, he is dead. It is just so with sin.

divine grace, and to keep us humble, wakeful, and watchful, and that our armour may be still kept on, and our weapons always in our hands. The best men's souls in this life hang between the flesh and the spirit, as it were like Mahomet's tomb at Mecca, between two loadstones; like Erasmus, as the papists paint him, betwixt heaven and hell; like the tribe of Manasseh, half on this side of Jordan, in the land of the Amorities, and half on that side, in the Holy Land; yet, in the issue, they shall overcome the flesh, and trample upon the necks of their spiritual enemies.[1]

DEVICE 6. *By suggesting to the soul, that surely his estate is not good, because he cannot joy and rejoice in Christ as once he could;* because he *hath lost that comfort and joy that once was in his spirit.* Saith Satan, Thou knowest the time was when thy heart was much carried out to joying and rejoicing in Christ; thou dost not forget the time when thy heart used to be full of joy and comfort; but now, how art thou fallen in thy joys and comforts! Therefore, thy estate is not good; thou dost but deceive thyself to think that ever it was good, for surely if it had, thy joy and comfort would have continued. And hereupon the soul is apt to take part with Satan, and say, It is even so; I see all is naught, and I have but deceived my own soul.

Remedy (1). The first remedy against this device of Satan is, to consider, *that the loss of comfort is a separable adjunct from grace.* The soul may be full of holy affections when it is empty

---

[1] There is no such pleasure, saith Cyprian, as to have overcome an offered pleasure; neither is there any greater conquest than that that is gotten over a man's corruptions. The Romans lost many a battle, and yet in the issue were conquerors in all their wars; it is just so with the saints.

of divine consolations.¹ There may be, and often is, true grace, yea, much grace, where there is not a drop of comfort, nor dram of joy. Comfort is not of the being, but of the well-being, of a Christian. God hath not so linked these two choice lovers together, but that they may be put asunder. That wisdom that is from above will never work a man to reason thus: I have no comfort, therefore I have no grace; I have lost that joy that once I had, therefore my condition is not good, was never good. But it will enable a man to reason thus: Though my comfort is gone, yet the God of my comfort abides; though my joy is lost, yet the seeds of grace remain. The best men's joys are as glass, bright and brittle, and evermore in danger of breaking.²

Remedy (2). The second remedy against this device of Satan is, solemnly to consider, *that the precious things that thou still enjoyest are far better than the joys and comforts that thou hast lost*. Thy union with Christ, thy communion with Christ, thy sonship, thy saintship, thy heirship, thou still enjoyest by Christ, are far better than the comforts thou hast lost by sin. What though thy comforts be gone, yet thy union and communion with Christ remains (Jer. 31:18-20). Though thy comforts be gone, yet thou art a son, though a comfortless son; an heir, though a comfortless heir; a saint, though a comfortless saint. Though the bag of silver, thy comforts, be lost, yet the box of jewels, thy union with Christ, thy communion with Christ, thy sonship, thy saintship, thy heirship, which thou still enjoyest, is far better than the bag of silver

¹ Psa. 63:1, 2, 8; Isa. 50:10; Mic. 7:8, 9; Psa. 42:5; Lam. 5:15.
² Spiritual joy is a sun that is often clouded; though it be as precious a flower as most paradise affords, yet it is subject to fade and wither.

thou hast lost; yea, the least of those precious jewels is more worth than all the comforts in the world. Well! let this be a cordial to comfort thee, a star to lead thee, and a staff to support thee, that thy box of jewels are safe, though thy bag of silver be lost.[1]

Remedy (3). The third remedy against this device of Satan is, to consider, *that thy condition is no other than what hath been the condition of those precious souls whose names were written upon the heart of Christ, and who are now at rest in the bosom of Christ.* One day you shall have them praising and rejoicing, the next day a-mourning and weeping. One day you shall have them a-singing, 'The Lord is our portion'; the next day a-sighing and expostulating with themselves, 'Why are ye cast down, O our souls?' 'Why is our harp turned to mourning? and our organ into the voice of them that weep?'[2]

Remedy (4). The fourth remedy against this device of Satan is, solemnly to consider, *that the causes of joy and comfort are not always the same.* Happily, thy former joy and comfort did spring from the witness of the Spirit, he bearing witness to thy soul, that thy nature was changed, thy sins pardoned, thy soul reconciled.[3] Now, the Spirit may, upon some special occasion, bear witness to the soul, that the heart of God is dearly set upon him, that he loves him with an everlasting love, and yet the soul may never enjoy such a testimony all the days of his

---

[1] When one objected to Faninus's cheerfulness to Christ's agony and sadness, he answered, Christ was sad, that I might be merry; he had my sins, and I have his righteousness.

[2] Psa. 51:12; 30:6, 7; Job 23:6, 8, 9, 30, 31; Lam. 1:16; Matt. 27:46; Psa. 42:5; Lam. 5:15.

[3] The Spirit doth not every day make a feast in the soul; he doth not make every day to be a day of weaving the wedding robes.

life again. Though the Spirit be a witnessing Spirit, it is not his office every day to witness to believers their interest in God, Christ, heaven.

Or, happily, thy former joy and comfort did spring from the newness and suddenness of the change of thy condition. For a man in one hour to have his night turned into day, his darkness turned into light, his bitter into sweet, God's frowns into smiles, his hatred into love, his hell into a heaven, must greatly joy and comfort him.[1] It cannot but make his heart to leap and dance in him, who, in one hour, shall see Satan accusing him, his own heart condemning him, the eternal God frowning upon him, the gates of heaven barred against him, all the creation standing armed, at the least beck of God, to execute vengeance on him, and the mouth of the infernal pit open to receive him. Now, in this hour, for Christ to come to the amazed soul, and to say to it, I have trod the wine-press of my Father's wrath for thee; I have laid down my life a ransom for thee; by my blood I have satisfied my Father's justice, and pacified his anger, and procured his love for thee; by my blood I have purchased the pardon of thy sins, thy freedom from hell, and thy right to heaven; oh! how wonderfully will this cause the soul to leap for joy!

Remedy (5). The fifth remedy against this device of Satan is, to consider, *that God will restore and make up the comforts of*

---

[1] A pardon given unexpectedly into the hand of a malefactor, when he is on the last step of the ladder, ready to be turned off, will cause much joy and rejoicing. The newness and suddenness of the change of his condition will cause his heart to leap and rejoice; yet, in process of time, much of his joy will be abated, though his life be as dear to him still as ever it was.

his people.[1] Though thy candle be put out, yet God will light it again, and make it burn more light than ever. Though thy sun for the present be clouded, yet he that rides upon the clouds shall scatter those clouds, and cause the sun to shine and warm thy heart as in former days, as the psalmist speaks: 'Thou which hast showed me great and sore troubles, shalt quicken me again, and shalt bring me up again from the depths of the earth. Thou shalt increase my greatness, and comfort me on every side' (Psa. 71:20, 21). God takes away a little comfort, that he may make room in the soul for a greater degree of comfort. This the prophet Isaiah sweetly shows: 'I have seen his ways, and will heal him; I will lead him also, and restore comforts unto him, and to his mourners' (Isa. 57:18). Bear up sweetly, O precious soul! thy storm shall end in a calm, and thy dark night in a sunshine day; thy mourning shall be turned into rejoicing, and the waters of consolation shall be sweeter and higher in thy soul than ever;[2] the mercy is surely thine, but the time of giving it is the Lord's. Wait but a little, and thou shalt find the Lord comforting thee on every side.

DEVICE 7. *By suggesting to the soul his often relapses into the same sin which formerly he hath pursued with particular sorrow, grief, shame, and tears, and prayed, complained, and resolved against.* Saith Satan, Thy heart is not right with God; surely

---

[1] Thomas Hudson the martyr, deserted at the stake, went from under his chain, and having prayed earnestly, was comforted immediately, and suffered valiantly. So Robert Glover, when he was within sight of the stake, cried out to his friend, He is come, He is come, meaning the Comforter the Christ promised to send.

[2] See Psa. 126:6 and 42:7, 8.

thy estate is not good; thou dost not flatter thyself to think that ever God will eternally own and embrace such a one as thou art, who complainest against sin, and yet relapsest into the same sin; who with tears and groans confessest thy sin, and yet ever and anon art fallen into the same sin.

I confess this is a very sad condition for a soul after he hath obtained mercy and pity from the Lord, after God hath spoken peace and pardon to him, and wiped the tears from his eyes, and set him upon his legs, to return to folly.[3] Ah! how do relapses lay men open to the greatest afflictions and worst temptations! How do they make the wound to bleed afresh! How do they darken and cloud former assurances and evidences for heaven! How do they put a sword into the hand of conscience to cut and slash the soul! They raise such fears, terrors, horrors, and doubts in the soul, that the soul cannot be so frequent in duty as formerly, nor so fervent in duty as formerly, nor so confident in duty as formerly, nor so bold, familiar, and delightful with God in duty as formerly, nor so constant in duty as formerly. They give Satan an advantage to triumph over Christ; they make the work of repentance more difficult; they make a man's life a burden, and they render death to be very terrible unto the soul.

Remedy (1). The first remedy against this device of Satan is, solemnly to consider, *that there are many scriptures that do clearly evidence a possibility of the saints falling into the same sins whereof they have formerly repented.* 'I will heal their backslidings, I will love them freely: for mine anger is turned away from them,' saith the Lord by the prophet Hosea (chap. 14:4). So the prophet Jeremiah speaks: 'Go and proclaim these words toward the

---

[3] A backslider may say, All my pains and charge is lost.

north, and say. Return, thou backsliding Israel, saith the Lord,
and I will not cause mine anger to fall upon you: for I am mer-
ciful, saith the Lord, and I will not keep mine anger for ever.
Turn, O backsliding Israel, saith the Lord; for I am married
unto you: and I will take you one of a city and two of a family,
and I will bring you to Zion' (chap. 3:12, 14). So the psalmist:
'They turned back, and dealt unfaithfully with their fathers;
they were turned aside like a deceitful bow.' And no wonder,
for though their repentance be never so sincere and sound, yet
their graces are but weak, and their mortification imperfect in
this life. Though by grace they are freed from the dominion of
sin, and from the damnatory power of every sin, and from the
love of all sin, yet grace doth not free them from the seed of any
one sin; and therefore it is possible for a soul to fall again and
again into the same sin. If the fire be not wholly put out, who
would think it impossible that it should catch and burn again
and again?[1]

Remedy (2). The second remedy against this device of Satan
is, seriously to consider, *that God hath nowhere engaged him-
self by any particular promise, that souls converted and united
to Christ shall not fall again and again into the same sin after
conversion.* I cannot find in the whole book of God where he
hath promised any such strength or power against this or
that particular sin, as that the soul should be for ever, in this
life, put out of a possibility of falling again and again into
the same sins; and where God hath not a mouth to speak, I

---

[1] The sin of backsliding is a soul-wounding sin, 'I will heal their
backsliding.' You read of no arms for the back, though you do for the
breast. When a soldier bragged too much of a great scar in his forehead,
Augustus Caesar (in whose time Christ was born) asked him if he did
not get it as he looked back when he fled.

must not have a heart to believe. God will graciously pardon those sins to his people that he will not in this life effectually subdue in his people. I would go far to speak with that soul that can show me a promise, that when our sorrow and grief hath been so great, or so much, for this or that sin, that then God will preserve us from ever falling into the same sin. The sight of such a promise would be as life from the dead to many a precious soul, who desires nothing more than to keep close to Christ, and fears nothing more than backsliding from Christ.[1]

Remedy (3). The third remedy against this device of Satan is, seriously to consider, *that the most renowned and now crowned saints have, in the days of their being on earth, relapsed into one and the same sin.*[2] Lot was twice overcome with wine; John twice worshipped the angel; Abraham did often dissemble, and lay his wife open to adultery to save his own life, which some heathens would not have done: 'And it came to pass, when God caused me to wander from my father's house, that I said unto her. This is thy kindness which thou shalt show unto me; at every place whither we shall come, say of me, He is my brother' (Gen. 20:13). David in his wrath was resolved, if ever man was, that he would be the death of Nabal, and all his innocent family; and after this he fell into the foul murder of Uriah. Though Christ told his disciples that his 'kingdom was not of this world,' yet again, and again, and again, three

[1] In some cases the saints have found God better than his word. He promised the children of Israel only the land of Canaan, but besides that he gave them two other kingdoms which he never promised. And to Zacharias he promised to give him his speech at the birth of the child, but besides that he gave him the gift of prophecy.

[2] A sheep may often slip into a slough, as well as a swine.

several times they would needs be on horseback; they would fain be high, great, and glorious in this world. Their pride and ambitious humour put them, that were but as so many beggars, upon striving for pre-eminence and greatness in the world, when their Lord and Master told them three several times of his sufferings in the world, and of his going out of the world. Jehoshaphat, though a godly man, yet joins affinity with Ahab (2 Chron. 18:1-3, 30, 31); and though he was saved by a miracle, yet soon after, he falls into the same sin, and 'joins himself with Ahaziah king of Israel, who did very wickedly' (2 Chron. 20:35-37). Samson is by the Spirit of the Lord numbered among the faithful worthies, yet he fell often into one gross sin, as is evident (Heb. 11:32). Peter, you know, relapsed often, and so did Jonah; and this comes to pass that they may see their own inability to stand, to resist or overcome any temptation or corruptions (Jude 14-16);[1] and that they may be taken off from all false confidences, and rest wholly upon God, and only upon God, and always upon God; and for the praise and honour of the power, wisdom, skill, mercy; and goodness of the physician of our souls, that can heal, help, and cure when the disease is most dangerous, when the soul is relapsed, and grows worse and worse, and when others say, 'There is no help for him in his God,' and when his own heart and hopes are dying.[2]

Remedy (4). The fourth remedy against this device of Satan is, to consider, *that there are relapses into enormities, and there*

---

[1] Perhaps the prodigal sets out unto us a Christian relapse, for he was a son before, and with his father, and then went away from him, and spent all; and yet he was not quite undone, but returned again.

[2] The prodigal saw the compassion of his father the greater, in receiving him after he had run away from him.

are relapses into infirmities. Now it is not usual with God to leave his people frequently to relapse into enormities; for by his Spirit and grace, by his smiles and frowns, by his word and rod, he doth usually preserve his people from a frequent relapsing into enormities; yet he doth leave his choicest ones frequently to relapse into infirmities (and of his grace he pardons them in course), as idle words, passion, and vain thoughts.[1] Though gracious souls strive against these, and complain of these, and weep over these, yet the Lord, to keep them humble, leaves them frequently to relapse into these; and the frequent relapses into infirmities shall never be their bane, because they be their burden.

Remedy (5). The fifth remedy against this device of Satan is, to consider, *that there are involuntary relapses, and there are voluntary relapses.* Involuntary relapses are, when the resolution and full bent of the heart is against sin, when the soul strives with all its might against sin, by sighs and groans, by prayers and tears, and yet out of weakness is forced to fall back into sin, because there is not spiritual strength enough to overcome. Now, though involuntary relapses must humble us, yet they must never discourage nor defeat us; for God will freely and readily pardon those, in course. Voluntary relapses are, when the soul longs and loves to 'return to the flesh-pots of Egypt' (Exod. 16:3); when it is a pleasure and a pastime to a man to return to his old courses, such voluntary relapses speak out the man blinded, hardened, and ripened for ruin.[2]

---

[1] Relapses into enormities are wounding and wasting sins; therefore the Lord is graciously pleased to put under his everlasting arms, and stay his chosen ones from frequent failing into them.

[2] There is a great difference between a sheep that by weakness falls into the mire, and a swine that delights to wallow in the mire; between

Remedy (6). The sixth remedy against this device of Satan is, to consider, *that there is no such power, or infinite virtue, in the greatest horror or sorrow the soul can be under for sin, nor in the sweetest or choicest discoveries of God's grace and love to the soul, as for ever to fence and secure the soul from relapsing into the same sin.* Grace is but a created habit, that may be prevailed against by the secret, subtle, and strong workings of sin in our hearts; and those discoveries that God makes of his love, beauty and glory to the soul, do not always abide in their freshness and power upon the heart; but by degrees they fade and wear off and then the soul may return again to folly, as we see in Peter, who, after he had a glorious testimony from Christ's own mouth of his blessedness and happiness, labours to prevent Christ from going up to Jerusalem to suffer, out of bare slavish fears that he and his fellows could not be secure, if his Master should be brought to suffer (Matt. 16:13-19, 22-24). And again, after this, Christ had him up into the mount, and there showed him his beauty and his glory, to strengthen him against the hour of temptation that was coming upon him; and yet, soon after he had the honour and happiness of seeing the glory of the Lord (which most of his disciples had not), he basely and most shamefully denies the Lord of glory, thinking by that means to provide for his own safety;[1] and yet again, after Christ had broke his heart with a look of love for his most unlovely dealings, and bade them that were first acquainted with his resurrection to 'go and tell Peter that he

---

a woman that is forced, though she strives and cries out, and an alluring adulteress.

[1] Christ upbraided his disciples for their unbelief and hardness of heart, who had seen his glory, 'as the glory of the only begotten of the Father, full of grace and truth.'

was risen' (Mark 16:7); I say, after all this, slavish fears prevail upon him, and he basely dissembles, and plays the Jew with the Jews, and the Gentile with the Gentiles, to the seducing of Barnabas (Gal. 2:11-13).

Yet, by way of caution, know, it is very rare that God doth leave his beloved ones frequently to relapse into one and the same gross sin; for the law of nature is in arms against gross sins, as well as the law of grace, so that a gracious soul cannot, dares not, will not, frequently return to gross folly. And God hath made even his dearest ones dearly smart for their relapses, as may be seen by his dealings with Samson, Jehoshaphat, and Peter. Ah, Lord! what a hard heart hath that man, that can see thee stripping and whipping thy dearest ones for their relapses, and yet making nothing of returning to folly.

DEVICE 8. By *persuading them that their estate is not good, their hearts are not upright, their graces are not sound, because they are so followed, vexed, and tormented with temptations*. It is his method, first to weary and vex thy soul with temptations, and then to tempt the soul, that surely it is not beloved, because it is so much tempted. And by this stratagem he keeps many precious souls in a sad, doubting, and mourning temper many years, as many of the precious sons of Sion have found by woeful experience.[1]

Remedy (1). The first remedy against this device of Satan is, solemnly to consider, *that those that have been best and most beloved, have been most tempted by Satan*. Though Satan can never rob a Christian of his crown, yet such is his malice,

---

[1] He may so tempt as to make a saint weary of his life (Job 10:1): 'My soul is weary of my life.'

that he will therefore tempt, that he may spoil them of their comforts. Such is his enmity to the Father, that the nearer and dearer any child is to him, the more will Satan trouble him, and vex him with temptations. Christ himself was most near and most dear, most innocent and most excellent, and yet none so much tempted as Christ. David was dearly beloved, and yet by Satan tempted to number the people.[1] Job was highly praised by God himself, and yet much tempted; witness those sad things that fell from his mouth, when he was wet to the skin. Peter was much prized by Christ; witness that choice testimony that Christ gave of his faith and happiness, and his showing him his glory in the mount, and that eye of pity that he cast upon him after his fearful fall, and yet tempted by Satan. 'And the Lord said, Simon, Simon, behold, Satan hath desired to have you, that he may sift you as wheat: but I have prayed for thee, that thy faith fail thee not' (Luke 22:31, 32).

Paul had the honour of being exalted as high as heaven, and of seeing that glory that could not be expressed; and yet he was no sooner stepped out of heaven, but he is buffeted by Satan, 'lest he should be exalted above measure' (2 Cor. 12:2, 7). If these, that were so really, so gloriously, so eminently beloved of God, if these, that have lived in heaven, and set their feet upon the stars, have been tempted, let no saints judge themselves not to be beloved, because they are tempted. It is as natural for saints to be tempted, that are dearly beloved, as it is for the sun to shine, or a bird to sing. The eagle complains not of her wings, nor the peacock of his train, nor the nightingale of her

---

[1] Pirates do not use to set upon poor empty vessels; and beggars need not fear the thief. Those that have most of God, and are most rich in grace, shall be most set upon by Satan, who is the greatest and wisest pirate in the world.

voice, because these are natural to them; no more should saints of their temptations, because they are natural to them. 'For we wrestle not against flesh and blood, but against principalities, against powers, against the rulers of the darkness of this world, against spiritual wickedness in high places' (Eph. 6:12).

Remedy (2). The second remedy against this device of Satan is, to consider, *that all the temptations that befall the saints shall be sanctified to them by a hand of love*. Ah! the choice experiences that the saints get of the power of God supporting them, of the wisdom of God directing them (so to handle their spiritual weapons, their graces, as not only to resist, but to overcome), of the mercy and goodness of the Lord pardoning and succouring of them. And therefore, saith Paul, 'I received the messenger of Satan for to buffet me, lest I should be exalted, lest I should be exalted above measure' (2 Cor. 12:7). Twice in that verse; he begins with it, and ends with it. If he had not been buffeted, who knows how his heart would have swelled; he might have been carried higher in conceit, than before he was in his ecstasy. Temptation is God's school, wherein he gives his people the clearest and sweetest discoveries of his love;[1] a school wherein God teaches his people to be more frequent and fervent in duty. When Paul was buffeted, then he prayed thrice, *i.e.* frequently and fervently; a school wherein God teaches his people to be more tender, meek, and compassionate to other poor, tempted souls than ever; a school wherein God teaches his people to see a greater evil in sin than ever, and a greater emptiness in the creature than ever, and a greater need of Christ and free grace than ever; a school wherein God will

---

[1] Luther said, there were three things that made a preacher—meditation, prayer and temptation.

teach his people that all temptations are but his goldsmiths, by which he will try and refine, and make his people more bright and glorious. The issue of all temptations shall be to the good of the saints, as you may see by the temptations that Adam and Eve, and Christ and David, and Job and Peter and Paul met with. Those hands of power and love, that bring light out of darkness, good out of evil, sweet out of bitter, life out of death, heaven out of hell, will bring much sweet and good to his people, out of all the temptations that come upon them.

Remedy (3). The third remedy against this device of Satan is, wisely to consider, *that no temptations do hurt or harm the saints, so long as they are resisted by them, and prove the greatest afflictions that can befall them*. It is not Satan's tempting, but your assenting; not his enticing, but your yielding, that makes temptations hurtful to your soul. If the soul when it is tempted, resists temptation, and saith with Christ, 'Get thee behind me, Satan' (Matt. 16:23); and with that young convert, 'I am not the man I was,' or as Luther counsels all men to answer all temptations with these words, *Christianus sum*, I am a Christian—if a man's temptation be his greatest affliction, then is the temptation no sin upon his soul, though it be a trouble upon his mind. When a soul can look the Lord in the face, and say, 'Ah, Lord! I have many outward troubles upon me, I have lost such and such a near mercy, and such and such desirable mercies; and yet thou that knowest the heart, thou knowest that all my crosses and losses do not make so many wounds in my soul, nor fetch so many sighs from my heart, or tears from my eyes, as those temptations do that Satan follows my soul with!' When it is thus with the soul, then temptations are only the soul's trouble, they are not the soul's sin.

Satan is a malicious and envious enemy. As his names are, so is he. His names are all names of enmity—the accuser, the tempter, the destroyer, the devourer, the envious one. And this malice and envy of his he shows sometimes by tempting men to such sins as are quite contrary to the temperature of their bodies, as he did Vespasian and Julian, men of sweet and excellent natures, to be most bloody murderers.[1] And sometimes he shows his malice by tempting men to such things as will bring them no honour nor profit. 'Fall down and worship me' (Matt. 4:9). He tempts to blasphemy, and atheism, the thoughts and first motions whereof cause the heart and flesh to tremble. And sometimes he shows his malice by tempting them to those sins which they have not found their natures prone to, and which they abhor in others. Now, if the soul resists these, and complains of these, and groans and mourns under these, and looks up to the Lord Jesus to be delivered from these, then shall they not be put down to the soul's account, but to Satan's, who shall be so much the more tormented, by how much the more the saints have been by him maliciously tempted.

Make present and peremptory resistance against Satan's temptations, bid defiance to the temptation at first sight. It is safe to resist, it is dangerous to dispute. Eve lost herself and her posterity by falling into lists[2] of dispute, when she should have resisted, and stood upon terms of defiance with

[1] Sometimes he shows his malice by letting those things abide by the soul as may most vex and plague the soul, as Gregory observes in his leaving of Job s wife, which was not out of his forgetfulness, carelessness, or any love or pity to Job, but to vex and torment him, and to work him to blaspheme God, despair, and die.

[2] 'Artifices.'

Satan. He that would stand in the hour of temptation must plead with Christ, 'It is written.' He that would triumph over temptations must plead still, 'It is written.'[1] Satan is bold and impudent, and if you are not peremptory in your resistance, he will give you fresh onsets. It is your greatest honour, and your highest wisdom, peremptorily to withstand the beginnings of a temptation, for an after-remedy comes often too late.

Mrs Catherine Bretterege once, after a great conflict with Satan, said, 'Reason not with me, I am but a weak woman; if thou hast anything to say, say it to my Christ; he is my advocate, my strength, and my redeemer, and he shall plead for me.'

Men must not seek to resist Satan's craft with craft, but by open defiance. He shoots with Satan in his own bow, who thinks by disputing and reasoning to put him off. As soon as a temptation shows its face, say to the temptation, as Ephraim to his idols, 'Get you hence, what have I any more to do with you?' (Hos. 14:8). Oh! say to the temptation, as David said to the sons of Zeruiah, 'What have I to do with you?' (2 Sam. 16:10). You will be too hard for me. He that doth thus resist temptations, shall never be undone by temptations.[2]

Make strong and constant resistance against Satan's temptations. Make resistance against temptations by arguments

---

[1] When Constantine the emperor was told that there was no means to core his leprosy but by bathing his body in the blood of infants, he immediately answered, I had rather not be cured than use such a remedy.

[2] I have read of one, who, being tempted with offers of money to desert Christ, gave this excellent answer: Let not any man think that he will embrace other men's goods to forsake Christ, who hath forsaken his own proper goods to follow Christ.

drawn from the honour of God, the love of God, your union and communion with God; and from the blood of Christ, the death of Christ, the kindness of Christ, the intercession of Christ, and the glory of Christ; and from the voice of the Spirit, the counsel of the Spirit, the comforts of the Spirit, the presence of the Spirit, the seal of the Spirit, the whisperings of the Spirit, the commands of the Spirit, the assistance of the Spirit, the witness of the Spirit; and from the glory of heaven, the excellency of grace, the beauty of holiness, the worth of the soul, and the vileness or bitterness and evil of sin, the least sin being a greater evil than the greatest temptation in the world. And look that you make constant resistance, as well as strong resistance; be constant in arms. Satan will come on with new temptations when old ones are too weak.[1] In a calm prepare for a storm. The tempter is restless, impudent, and subtle; he will suit his temptations to your constitutions and inclinations. Satan loves to sail with the wind. If your knowledge be weak, he will tempt you to error; if your conscience be tender, he will tempt you to scrupulosity and too much preciseness, as to do nothing but hear, pray, and read; if your consciences be wide and large, he will tempt you to carnal security; if you are bold-spirited, he will tempt you to presumption; if timorous, to desperation; if flexible, to inconstancy; if proud and stiff, to gross folly; therefore still fit for fresh assaults, make one victory a step to another. When you have overcome a temptation, take heed of unbending your bow, and look well to it, that your bow be always bent, and that it remains in strength. When you have overcome one temptation, you

---

[1] Luke 4:13, 'And when the devil had ended all the temptation, he departed from him for a season.' Christ had no rest until he was exactly tried with all sorts of temptations.

must be ready to enter the list[1] with another. As distrust in some sense is the mother of safety, so security is the gate of danger. A man had need to fear this most of all, that he fears not at all. If Satan be always roaring, we should be always a-watching and resisting of him. And certainly he that makes strong and constant resistance of Satan's temptations, shall in the end get above his temptations, and for the present is secure enough from being ruined by his temptations.

For a close of this, remember, that it is dangerous to yield to the least sin to be rid of the greatest temptation. To take this course were as if a man should think to wash himself clean in ink, or as if a man should exchange a light cross, made of paper, for an iron cross, which is heavy, toilsome, and bloody. The least sin set home upon the conscience, will more wound, vex, and oppress the soul, than all the temptations in the world can; therefore never yield to the least sin to be rid of the greatest temptation.[2] Sidonius Apollinarius relateth how a certain man named Maximus, arriving at the top of honour by indirect means, was the first day very much wearied, and fetching a deep sigh, said, 'Oh, Damocles! how happy do I esteem of thee, for having been a king but the space of a dinner! I have been one whole day, and can bear it no longer.' I will leave you to make the application.

---

[1] 'Course.'

[2] He that will yield to sin to be rid of temptation, will be so much the more tempted, and the less able to withstand temptations.

V.

SATAN'S DEVICES TO AND ENSNARE ALL SORTS AND RANKS OF MEN IN THE WORLD

———

I. DEVICES AGAINST THE GREAT AND HONOURABLE OF THE EARTH

DEVICE 1. His first device to destroy the great and honourable of the earth is, *by working them to make it their business to seek themselves, to seek how to greaten themselves, to raise themselves*, to enrich themselves, to secure themselves, as you may see in Pharaoh, Ahab, Rehoboam, Jeroboam, Absalom, Joab, Haman, and others. But were the Scripture silent, our own experiences do abundantly evidence this way and method of Satan to destroy the great and the honourable; to bury their names in the dust, and their souls in hell, by drawing them wholly to mind themselves, and only to mind themselves, and in all things to mind themselves, and always to mind themselves. 'All,' said the apostle 'mind themselves' (Phil. 2:21). All comparatively, in respect of the paucity of others that let fall their private interests, and drown all self-respects in the glory of God and the public good.

Remedy (1). The first remedy against this device of Satan

is, solemnly to consider, *that self-seeking is a sin that will put men upon a world of sins, upon sins not only against the law of God, the rules of the gospel, but that are against the very laws of nature, that are so much darkened by the fall of man.*[1] It puts the Pharisees upon opposing Christ, and Judas upon betraying Christ, and Pilate upon condemning Christ. It puts Gehazi upon lying, and Balaam upon cursing, and Saul and Absalom upon plotting David's ruin. It puts Pharaoh and Haman upon contriving ways to destroy those Jews that God did purpose to save by his mighty arm. It puts men upon using wicked balances, and the bag of deceitful weights. It puts men upon ways of oppression and 'selling the righteous for silver, and the poor for a pair of shoes' (Amos 2:6). I know not any sin in the world but this sin of self-seeking will put men upon it, though it be their eternal loss.

Remedy (2.) The second remedy against this device of Satan is, seriously to consider, *that self-peeking doth exceedingly abase a man.* It strips him of all his royalty and glory. Of a lord it makes a man become a servant to the creature, ay, often to the worst of creatures; yea, a slave to slaves, as you may see in Judas, Demas, Balaam, and the scribes and Pharisees.[2] Self-seekers bow down to the creatures, as Gideon's many thousands bowed down to the waters. Self-seeking will make a man say anything, do anything, and be anything, to please the lusts of others, and to get advantages upon others. Self-seeking transforms a man into

[1] Self-love is the root of the hatred of others, 2 Tim. 3:2. First, lovers of themselves, and then fierce, etc. The naturalists observe, that those beasts which are most cruel to others are most loving to their own.

[2] A self-seeker is a Cato without, but a Nero within. Domitian would seem to love them best whom he willed least should live, and that is the very temper of self-seekers.

all shapes and forms; now it makes a man appear as an angel of light, anon as an angel of darkness.[1] Now self-seekers are seemingly for God, anon they are openly against God; now you shall have them crying, 'Hosanna in the highest,' and anon, 'Crucify him, crucify him'; now you shall have them build with the saints, and anon you shall have them plotting the overthrow of the saints, as those self-seekers did in Ezra and Nehemiah's time. Self-seekers are the basest of all persons. There is no service so base, so poor, so low, but they will bow to it. They cannot look neither above, nor beyond their own lusts, and the enjoyment of the creature (Rom. 1:25). These are the prime and ultimate objects of their intendments.

Remedy (3). The third remedy against this device of Satan is, solemnly *to dwell upon those dreadful curses and woes that are from heaven denounced against self-seekers from heaven denounced against self-seekers.* 'Woe unto them that join house to house, that lay field to field, till there be no place, that they may be placed alone in the midst of the earth' (Isa. 5:8). So Habakkuk 2:6, 9-12: 'Woe to him that increaseth that which is not his, and to him that ladeth himself with thick clay!' 'Woe to him that coveteth an evil covetousness to his house, that he may set his nest on high, that he may be delivered from the power of evil! Thou hast consulted shame to thy house by cutting off many people, and hast sinned against thy soul. For the stone shall cry out of the wall, and the beam out of the timber shall answer it. Woe to him that buildeth a town with blood, and establisheth a city by iniquity!' The materials

---

[1] It was death in Moses' rites to counterfeit that ceremonial and figurative ointment, Exod. 30:33. What shall it then be to counterfeit the Spirit of life and holiness!

of the house built up by oppression shall come as joint witnesses. The stones of the wall shall cry, 'Lord, we were built up by blood and violence'; and the beam shall answer, 'True, Lord, even so it is.' The stones shall cry, Vengeance, Lord! upon these self-seekers! and the beam shall answer, 'Woe to him, because he built his house with blood!'[1] So Isaiah: 'Woe unto them that decree unrighteous decrees, and that write grievousness which they have prescribed; to turn aside the needy from judgment, and to take away the right from the poor of my people, that widows may be their prey, and that they may rob the fatherless' (Isa. 10:1, 2). So Amos: 'Woe unto them that are at ease in Zion, and trust in the mountain of Samaria, which are named chief of the nations, to whom the house of Israel came; that put far away the evil day, and cause the seat of violence to come near; that lie upon beds of ivory, and stretch themselves upon their couches, and eat the lambs out of the flock, and the calves out of the middle of the stall; that drink wine in bowls, and anoint themselves with the chief ointments: but they are not grieved for the afflictions of Joseph' (Amos 6:1, 3-6). So Micah: 'Woe to them that devise iniquity, and work evil upon their beds! when the morning is light, they practise it, because it is in the power of their hand. And they covet fields, and take them by violence, and houses, and take them away. So they oppress a man and his house, even a man and his heritage' (Mic. 2:1, 2).

[1] Crassus, a very rich Roman, and a great self-seeker, for greedy desire of gold he managed war against the Parthians, by whom both he and thirty thousand Romans were slain. And because the barbarians conjectured that he made his assault upon them for their gold, therefore they melted gold, and poured it into his dead body, saying, Satisfy thyself with gold.

By these scriptures, you see that self-seekers labour like a woman in travail, but their birth proves their death, their pleasure their pain, their comforts their torment, their glory their shame, their exaltation their desolation. Loss, disgrace, trouble and shame, vexation and confusion, will be the certain portion of self-seekers.

When the Tartarians had taken in battle the Duke of Muscovia, they made a cup of his skull, with this inscription, 'All covet, all lose.'[1]

Remedy (4). The fourth remedy against this device of Satan is, solemnly to consider, *that self-seekers are self-losers and self-destroyers.* Absalom and Judas seek themselves, and hang themselves. Saul seeks himself, and kills himself. Ahab seeks himself, and loses himself, his crown and kingdom. Pharaoh seeks himself, and overthrows himself and his mighty army in the Red Sea. Cain sought himself, and slew two at once, his brother and his own soul. Gehazi sought change of raiment, but God changed his raiment into a leprous skin. Haman sought himself, and lost himself. The princes and residents sought themselves, in the ruin of Daniel, but ruined themselves, their wives and children. That which self-seekers think should be a staff to support them, becomes by the hand of justice an iron rod to break them; that which they would have as springs to refresh them, becomes a gulf utterly to consume them. The crosses of self-seekers shall always exceed their mercies: their pain their pleasure; their torments their comforts. Every self-seeker is a self-tormentor, a self-destroyer; he carries a hell, an executioner, in his own bosom.[2]

---

[1] Tacitus the Roman emperor's word was, He that is too much for himself, fails to be good to others.

[2] Adam seeks himself, and loses himself, paradise, and that blessed

Remedy (5). The fifth remedy against this device of Satan is, *to dwell much upon the famous examples of those worthy saints that have denied themselves and preferred the public good before their own particular advantage.*[1] As Moses: 'And the Lord said unto Moses, Let me alone, that I may destroy them, and blot out their name from under heaven: and I will make of thee a nation mightier and greater than they' (Deut. 9:14). Oh! but this offer would not take with Moses, he being a man of brave public spirit. He is hot in his desires and prayers that the people might be spared and pardoned; saith he, 'Pardon, I beseech thee, the iniquity of this people, according unto the greatness of thy mercy, and as thou hast forgiven this people from Egypt until now. And the Lord said, I have pardoned according to thy word' (Num. 14:19, 20). Ah! should God make such an offer to many that write themselves Moses, and are called by many, Moses, I am afraid they would prefer their own advantage above the public good; they would not care what became of the people, so they and theirs might be made great and glorious in the world; they would not care so they might have a Babel built for them, though it was upon the ashes and ruin of the people. Baser spirits than these are not in hell; no, not in hell; and I am sure there are no such spirits in heaven. Such men's hearts and principles must be changed, or they will be

image that God had stamped upon him. Lot seeks himself (Gen. 13:10, 11) and loses himself and his goods. Peter seeks to save himself, and miserably loses himself. Hezekiah, in the business of the ambassadors, seeks himself, and lost himself and his life too, had not God saved him by a miracle.

[1] It is good to be of his opinion and mind, who was rather willing to beautify Italy than his own house. The ancients were wont to place the statues of their princes by their fountains, intimating they were (or at least should be) fountains of the public good.

undone for ever. Nehemiah was a choice soul, a man of a brave public spirit, a man that spent his time, his strength, and his estate, for the good and ease of his people. 'Moreover,' saith he, 'from the time that I was appointed to be their governor in the land of Judah, from the twentieth year even unto the two and thirtieth year of Artaxerxes the king, that is, twelve years, I and my brethren have not eaten the bread of the governor. Yea, also I continued in the work of this wall: and all my servants were gathered hither unto the work. Moreover, there were at my table an hundred and fifty of the Jews and rulers, besides those that came unto us from among the heathen that are about us. Now, that which was prepared for me daily was one ox, and six choice sheep; also fowls were prepared for me, and once in ten days store of all sorts of wine: yet for all this required I not the bread of the governor, because the bondage was heavy upon the people. Think upon me, O my God, for good, according to all that I have done for this people' (Neh. 5:14-19). So Daniel was a man of a brave public spirit: 'Then the presidents and princes sought to find occasion against Daniel concerning the kingdom; but they could find no occasion nor fault; forasmuch as he was faithful, neither was there any error or fault found in him. Then said these men. We shall not find any occasion against this Daniel, except we find it against him concerning the law of his God' (Dan. 6:4, 5).[1]

Christ had a public spirit; he laid out himself, and laid down himself for a public good. Oh! never leave looking

---

[1] A certain great emperor coming into Egypt, to show the zeal he had for the public good, saith to the Egyptians, Draw from me as from your river Nilus. The Counsellor saith, a statesman should be thus tripartited: his will to God, his love to his master, his heart to his country, his secret to his friend, his time to business.

and meditating upon these precious and sweet examples till your souls are quickened and raised up, to act for the public good, more than for your own particular advantage. Many heathens have been excellent at this.[1]

Macrobius writes of Augustus Caesar, in whose time Christ was born, that he carried such an entire and fatherly affection to the commonwealth, that he called it *filiam suam*, his own daughter; and therefore refused to be called *Dominus,* the lord or master of his country, and would only be called *Pater patriae*, father of his country, because he governed it not by fear but by love; the senate and the people of Rome jointly saluting him by the name of *Pater patriae*, father of his country. The people very much lamented his death, using that speech, 'Would he had never been born, or never died.'

So Marcus Regulus, to save his country from ruin, exposed himself to the greatest sufferings that the malice and rage of his enemies could inflict. So Titus and Aristides, and many others, have been famous for their preferring the public good above their own advantage. My prayer is, and shall be, that all our rulers may be so spirited by God, that they may be willing to be anything, to be nothing, to deny themselves, and to trample their sinful selves under feet, in order to the honour of God, and a public good; that so neither saints nor heathens may be witnesses against them in that day, wherein the hearts and practices of all the rulers in the world shall be open and bare before him that judges the world in righteousness and judgment.

Remedy (6). The sixth remedy against this device of Satan

[1] Solomon's tribunal was underpropped with lions, to show what spirit and metal a magistrate should be made of.

is, seriously to consider, *that self is a great let¹ to divine things; therefore the prophets and apostles were usually carried out of themselves, when they had the clearest, choicest, highest, and most glorious visions.* Self-seeking blinds the soul that it cannot see a beauty in Christ, nor an excellency in holiness; it distempers the palate, that a man cannot taste sweetness in the word of God, nor in the ways of God, nor in the society of the people of God. It shuts the hand against all the soul-enriching offers of Christ; it hardens the heart against all the knocks and entreaties of Christ; it makes the soul as an empty vine, and as a barren wilderness: 'Israel is an empty vine, he bringeth forth fruit to himself' (Hos. 10:1). There is nothing that speaks a man to be more empty and void of God, Christ, and grace, than self-seeking. The Pharisees were great self-seekers, and great undervaluers of Christ, his word and Spirit. There is not a greater hindrance to all the duties of piety than self-seeking. Oh! this is that that keeps many a soul from looking after God and the precious things of eternity. They cannot wait on God, nor act for God, nor abide in those ways wherein they might meet with God, by reason of self. Self-seeking is that which puts many a man upon neglecting and slighting the things of his peace. Self-seekers will neither go into heaven themselves, nor suffer others to enter, that are ready to take the kingdom by violence, as you may see in the scribes and Pharisees. Oh! but a gracious spirit is acted quite other ways, as you may see in that sweet scripture (Song of Sol. 7:13), 'At our gates are all manner of pleasant fruits, new and old, which I have laid up for thee, O beloved.' All the church hath and is, is only for him. Let others bear fruit to themselves, and lay up for themselves, gracious spirits will hide for Christ and lay

¹ Hindrance.

up for Christ.[1] All the divine endeavours and productions of saints fall into God's bosom, and empty themselves into his lap. As Christ lays up his merits for them, his graces for them, his comforts for them, his crown for them, so they lay up all their fruits, and all their loves, all their graces, and all their experiences, and all their services, only for him who is the soul of their comforts, and the crown and top of all their royalty and glory.

DEVICE 2. *By engaging them against the people of the Most High, against those that are his jewels, his pleasant portion, the delight of his eye and the joy of his heart.* Thus he drew Pharaoh to engage against the children of Israel, and that was his overthrow (Exod. 14). So he engaged Haman against the Jews, and so brought him to hang upon that gallows that he had made for Mordecai (Esther 7). So he engaged those princes and presidents against Daniel, which was the utter ruin of them and their relations (Dan. 6). So in Rev. 20:7-9, 'And when the thousand years are expired, Satan shall be loosed out of his prison. And he shall go out to deceive the nations which are in the four quarters of the earth, Gog and Magog, to gather them together to battle, whose number is as the sand of the sea. And they went up upon the breadth of the earth, and compassed the camp of the saints about, and the beloved city; and fire came down from heaven and consumed them.'

Remedy (1). The first remedy against this device of Satan

---

[1] Self-seekers, with Esau, prefer a mess of pottage above their birth-right, and with the men of Shechem, esteem the bramble above the vine, the olive, and the fig-tree, yea, empty things above a full Christ, and base things above a glorious Christ. The saints' motto is, 'For thee, Lord, for thee; not unto us, O Lord.'

is, solemnly to consider, *that none have engaged against the saints, but have been ruined by the God of saints.* Divine justice hath been too hard for all that have opposed and engaged against the saints, as is evident in Saul, Pharaoh, and Haman; 'He reproved kings for their sakes, saying. Touch not mine anointed, and do my prophets no harm' (Psa. 105:15). When men of Balaam's spirits and principles have been engaged against the saints, how hath the angel of the Lord met them in the way, and jostled their bones against the wall! How hath he broke their backs and necks, and by his drawn sword cut them off in the prime of their days, and in the height of their sins![1] Ah! what a harvest hath hell had in our days, of those who have engaged against the Lamb, and those that are called, chosen and faithful! Ah! how hath divine justice poured out their blood as water upon the ground! how hath he laid their honour and glory in the dust, who, in the pride and madness of their hearts, said, as Pharaoh, 'We will pursue, we will over-take, we will divide the spoil, our lusts shall be satisfied upon them. We will draw our sword, our hand shall destroy them' (Exod. 15:9). In the things wherein they have spoken and done proudly, justice hath been above them. History abounds in nothing more than in instances of this kind.

Remedy (2). The second remedy against this device of Satan is, *to dwell some time every morning upon the following scriptures, wherein God hath engaged himself to stand by his people and for his people, and to make them victorious over the greatest and wisest of their enemies.* 'Associate yourselves,' saith the Lord by the

[1] As they said once of the Grecians in the epigram, whom they thought invulnerable, We shoot at them, but they fall not down; we wound them, and not kill them. The number of opposers makes the Christian's conquest the more illustrious, said Pedarelus in Erasmus.

prophet, 'O ye people, and ye shall be broken in pieces; and give ear, all ye of far countries: gird yourselves, and ye shall be broken in pieces. Take counsel together, and it shall come to nought; speak the word, and it shall not stand: for God is with us.' 'Fear not, thou worm Jacob, and ye men of Israel: I will help thee, saith the Lord, and thy Redeemer, the Holy One of Israel. Behold, I will make thee a new sharp threshing instrument having teeth: thou shalt thresh the mountains, and beat them small, and shalt make the hills as chaff. Thou shalt fan them, and the wind shall carry them away, and the whirlwind shall scatter them, and thou shalt rejoice in the Lord, and shalt glory in the Holy One of Israel.' 'No weapon that is formed against thee shall prosper, and every tongue that shall rise against thee in judgment thou shalt condemn. This is the heritage of the servants of the Lord, and their righteousness is of me, saith the Lord.' 'Now also many nations are gathered together against thee that say. Let her be defiled, and let our eye look upon Sion. But they know not the thoughts of the Lord, neither understand they his counsel; for he shall gather them as sheaves into the floor. Arise and thresh, O daughter of Sion: I will make thy horn iron, and I will make thy hoof brass, and thou shalt beat in pieces many people, and I will consecrate their gain unto the Lord, and their substance unto the Lord of the whole earth.' 'Behold, I will make Jerusalem a cup of trembling unto all the people round about, when they shall be in the siege, both against Judah and against Jerusalem. And in that day will I make Jerusalem a burdensome stone for all people: all that burden themselves with it shall be cut in pieces, though all the people of the earth be gathered together against it.'[1]

---

[1] Isa. 8:9, 10; 41:14, 15, and 54:17; Mic. 4:11-13; Zech. 12:2, 3.

Remedy (3). The third remedy against this device of Satan is, to consider, *that you cannot engage against the saints, but you must engage against God himself, by reason of that near and blessed union that is between God and them.* You cannot be fighters against the saints, but you will be found in the casting up of the account to be fighters against God himself.[1] And what greater madness than for weakness itself to engage against an almighty strength! The near union that is between the Lord and believers, is set forth by that near union that is betwixt a husband and his wife. 'They two shall be one flesh. This is a great mystery: but I speak concerning Christ and the church; we are members of his body, of his flesh, and of his bones,' saith the apostle (Eph. 5:32). This near union is set forth by that union that is between the head and the members, which make up one body, and by that union that is betwixt the graff and the stock, which are made one by insition.[2] The union between the Lord and a believer is so near, that you cannot strike a believer, but the Lord is sensible of it, and takes it as done to himself.[3] 'Saul, Saul, why persecutest thou me?' (Acts 9:4); and 'in all their afflictions he was afflicted' (Isa. 63:9). Ah, souls! who ever engaged against God and prospered? who ever took up the sword against him but perished by it? God can speak you to hell and nod you to hell at pleasure. It is your greatest concernment to lay down your weapons at his feet, and to 'Kiss the Son, lest he be angry, and you perish in the midway' (Psa. 2:12).

[1] Acts 5:39. It seems to be drawn from the fable of the giants, which were said to make war with the gods.

[2] = grafting.

[3] The soul's happiness consists not in anything, but in its union with God; nor its misery lies not so much in anything, as in its disunion from God.

Remedy (4). The fourth remedy against this device of Satan is, solemnly to consider, *that you are much engaged to the saints, as instruments for the mercies that you do enjoy, and for the preventing and removing of many a judgment that otherwise might have been your ruin before this day.* Were it not for the saints' sake, God would quickly make the heavens to be as brass and the earth as iron; God would quickly strip thee of thy robes and glory, and set thee upon the dunghill with Job. They are the props that bear the world from falling about thy ears, and that keep the iron rod from breaking of thy bones. 'Therefore he said that he would destroy them, had not Moses his chosen stood before him in the breach, to turn away his wrath, lest he should destroy them' (Psa. 106:23).

Ah! had not the saints many a time cast themselves into the breach betwixt God's wrath and you, you had been cut off from the land of the living, and had had your portion with those whose names are written in the dust.[1] Many a nation, many a family, is surrounded with blessings for the Joseph's sakes that live therein, and are preserved from many calamities and miseries for the Moses', the Daniels', the Noahs', and the Jobs', sakes, that dwell amongst them. That is a sweet word (Prov. 10:25), 'As the whirlwind passeth, so is the wicked no more: but the righteous is an everlasting foundation, or is the foundation of the world.' The righteous is the foundation of the world, which but for their sakes would soon shatter and fall to ruin. So the psalmist (Psa. 75:3), 'The earth and all the inhabitants thereof are dissolved: I bear up the pillars of it. Selah.'

---

[1] He could have what he would of God, said one concerning Luther. Prayer is the gate of heaven, a key to let us into paradise. When the danger is over, the saint is forgotten, is a French proverb, and that which many saints in England have found by experience.

The emperor Marcus Aurelius being in Almany[1] with his army, was enclosed in a dry country by his enemies, who so stopped all the passages that he and his army were like to perish for want of water. The emperor's lieutenant seeing him so distressed, told him that he had heard that the Christians could obtain any thing of their God by their prayers, whereupon the emperor, having a legion of Christians in his army, desired them to pray to their God for his and the army's delivery out of that danger, which they presently did, and presently a great thunder fell amongst the enemies, and abundance of water upon the Romans, whereby their thirst was quenched, and the enemies overthrown without any fight.[2] [3]I shall close up this last remedy with those sweet words of the psalmist: 'In Judah is God known; his name is great in Israel. In Salem also is his tabernacle, and his dwelling-place in Zion. There brake he the arrows of the bow, the shield, and the sword, and the battle. Selah' (Psa. 76:1-3).

II. DEVICE AGAINST
THE LEARNED AND THE WISE

Secondly, Satan hath his devices to ensnare and destroy the learned and the wise: and that, sometimes *by working them to pride themselves in their parts and abilities; and sometimes by drawing them to rest upon their parts and abilities; and sometimes by causing them to make light and slight of those that want their parts and abilities, though they excel them in grace and*

[1] Germany.
[2] The famous 'Thundering Legion.'
[3] Mary, Queen of Scots, that was mother to King James I, was wont to say, That she feared Knox's prayers more than an army of ten thousand men.

holiness; and sometimes by drawing them to engage their parts and abilities in those ways and things that make against the honour of Christ, the joy of the Spirit, the advancement of the gospel, and the liberty of the saints.[1]

Remedy (1). The first remedy against this device of Satan is, seriously to consider, *that you have nothing but what you have received, Christ being as well the fountain of common gifts as of saving grace.* 'What hast thou,' saith the apostle, 'that thou hast not received? And if thou hast received it, why dost thou glory as though thou hadst not received it?' (1 Cor. 4:7).[2] There are those that would hammer out their own happiness, like the spider climbing up by the thread of her own weaving. Of all the parts and abilities that be in you, you may well say as the young man did of his hatchet, 'Alas, master! it was but borrowed' (2 Kings 6:5). Alas, Lord! all I have is but borrowed from that fountain that fills all the vessels in heaven and on earth, and it overflows. My gifts are not so much mine as thine: 'Of thine own have we offered unto thee,' said that princely prophet (1 Chron. 29:14).

Remedy (2). The second remedy against this device of Satan is, solemnly to consider, *that men's learning and trusting to their own wits, parts, and abilities, have been their utter overthrow and ruin;* as you may see in Ahithophel, and those presidents and princes that engaged against Daniel, and in the scribes and Pharisees. God loves to confute men in their confidences.[3]

---

[1] John 5:44; 1 Kings 22:22-25; 1 Cor. 1:18-29. The truth of this you may see in the learned scribes and Pharisees.

[2] Whatsoever thou art, thou owest to him that made thee; and whatsoever thou hast, thou owest to him that redeemed thee (*Bernard*).

[3] General councils were seldom successful, because men came with

He that stands upon his parts and abilities, doth but stand upon a quicksand that will certainly fail him. There is nothing in the world that provokes God more to withdraw from the soul than this; and how can the soul stand, when his strength is departed from him? Everything that a man leans upon but God, will be a dart that will certainly pierce his heart through and through. Ah! how many in these days have lost their estates, their friends, their lives, their souls, by leaning upon their admired parts and abilities! The saints are described by their leaning upon their beloved, the Lord Jesus (Song of Sol. 8:5). He that leans only upon the bosom of Christ, lives the highest, choicest, safest, and sweetest life. Miseries always lie at that man's door that leans upon anything below the precious bosom of Christ; such a man is most in danger, and this is none of his least plagues, that he thinks himself secure. It is the greatest wisdom in the world to take the wise man's counsel: 'Trust in the Lord with all thine heart, and lean not to thine own understanding' (Prov. 3:5).

Remedy (3). The third remedy against this device of Satan is, to consider, *that you do not transcend others more in parts and abilities, than they do you in grace and holiness.* There may be, and often is, great parts and abilities, where there is but little grace, yea, no grace; and there may be, and often is, a great deal of grace, where there is but weak parts and abilities.[1] You may be higher than others in gifts of knowledge, utterance, and learning, and those very souls may be higher than you in

---

confidence, leaning to their own understanding, and seeking for victory rather than verity, saith one.

[1] Judas and the scribes and Pharisees had great parts, but no grace. The disciples had grace, but weak parts.

their communion with God, in their delighting in God, in their dependence upon God, in their affections to God, and in their humble, holy, and unblameable walking before God.[1] Is it not folly and madness in a man, to make light and slight of another, because he is not so rich in lead or iron as he, when he is a thousand thousand times richer in silver and gold, in jewels and in pearls, than he? And is it not madness and folly with a witness, in those that have greater parts and abilities than others, to slight them upon that account, when that those very persons that they make light and slight of have a thousand times more grace than they? And yet, ah! how doth this evil spirit prevail in the world!

It was the sad complaint of Augustine in his time: 'The unlearned,' saith he, 'rise up and take heaven by violence, and we with all our learning are thrust down to hell.' It is sad to see how many of the rabbis of these times do make an idol of their parts and abilities, and with what an eye of pride, scorn, and contempt do they look upon those that want their parts, and that do not worship the idol that they have set up in their own hearts. Paul, who was the great doctor of the Gentiles, did wonderfully transcend in all parts and abilities the doctors and rabbis of our times, and yet, ah! how humbly, how tenderly, how sweetly, doth he carry himself towards the meanest and the weakest! 'To the weak I became as weak, that I might win the weak: I am made all things to all men, that I might by all means save some' (1 Cor. 9:22). 'Who is weak, and I am not weak? Who is offended, and I burn not? Wherefore, if meat make my brother to offend, I will eat no flesh while the world standeth, lest I make my brother to offend' (1 Cor. 8:13). But,

[1] Luke 11:1; 24:19-28.

ah how little of this sweet spirit is to be found in the doctors
of our age, who look sourly and speak bitterly against those
that do not see as they see, nor cannot speak as they speak.
Sirs! the Spirit of the Lord, even in despised saints, will be
too hard for you, and his appearance in them, in these latter
days, will be so full of spiritual beauty and glory, as that they
will darken that, that you are too apt to count and call your
glory. The Spirit of the Lord will not suffer his choicest jewel
grace to be always buried under the straw and stubble of
parts and gifts (Isa. 60:13-17).

Remedy (4). The fourth remedy against this device of Satan
is, to consider, *that there is no such way for men to have their
gifts and parts blasted and withered, as to pride themselves in
them, as to rest upon them, as to make light and slight of those
that want them, as to engage them against those persons, ways,
and things, that Jesus Christ hath set his heart upon.* Ah! how
hath God blasted and withered the parts and abilities of many
among us, that have once been famous shining lights![1] How is
their sun darkened, and their glory clouded!

'How is the sword of the Lord upon their arm, and upon
their right eye! how is their arm clean dried up, and their right
eye utterly darkened!' as the prophet speaks (Zech. 11:17). This
is matter of humiliation and lamentation. Many precious dis-
cerning saints do see this, and in secret mourn for it; and oh!
that they were kindly sensible of God's withdrawing from
them, that they may repent, keep humble, and carry it
sweetly towards God's jewels, and lean only upon the Lord,

---

[1] Becanus saith, that the tree of knowledge bears many leaves, and
little fruit. Ah! that it were not so with many in these days, who once
did outshine the stars.

and not upon their parts and understanding, that so the Lord may delight to visit them with his grace at such a rate as that their faces may shine more gloriously than ever, and that they may be more serviceable to the honour of Christ, and the faith of the saints, than formerly they have been.

III. DEVICE AGAINST THE SAINTS

Thirdly, Satan hath his devices to destroy the saints; and one great device that he hath to destroy the saints is, *by working them first to be strange, and then to divide, and then to be bitter and jealous, and then 'to bite and devour one another'* (Gal. 5:15). Our own woeful experience is too great a proof of this. The Israelites in Egypt did not more vex one another than Christians in these days have done, which occasioned a deadly consumption to fall upon some.[1]

Remedy (1). The first remedy against this device of Satan is, *to dwell more upon one another's graces than upon one another's weaknesses and infirmities, it is sad to consider that saints should have many eyes to behold one another's infirmities,* and not one eye to see each other's graces, that they should use spectacles to behold one another's weaknesses, rather than looking-glasses to behold one another's graces.[2]

Erasmus tells of one who collected all the lame and defective verses in Homer's works, but passed over all that was excellent. Ah! that this were not the practice of many that shall at last meet in heaven, that they were not careful and

---

[1] If we knock, we break. Dissolution is the daughter of dissension.

[2] Flavius Vespasian, the emperor, was more ready to conceal the vices of his friends than their virtues. Can you think seriously of this, Christians, that a heathen should excel you, and not blush?

skilful to collect all the weaknesses of others, and to pass over all those things that are excellent in them. The Corinthians did eye more the incestuous person's sin than his sorrow, which was like to have drowned him in sorrow.

Tell me, saints, is it not a more sweet, comfortable, and delightful thing to look more upon one another's graces than upon one another's infirmities? Tell me what pleasure, what delight, what comfort is there in looking upon the enemies, the wounds, the sores, the sickness, the diseases, the nakedness of our friends? Now sin, you know, is the soul's enemy, the soul's wound, the soul's sores, the soul's sickness, the soul's disease, the soul's nakedness; and ah! what a heart hath that man that loves thus to look! Grace is the choicest flower in all a Christian's garden; it is the richest jewel in all his crown; it is his princely robes; it is the top of royalty; and therefore must needs be the most pleasing, sweet, and delightful object for a gracious eye to be fixed upon. Sin is darkness, grace is light; sin is hell, grace is heaven; and what madness is it to look more at darkness than at light, more at hell than at heaven![1]

Tell me, saints, doth not God look more upon his people's graces than upon their weaknesses? Surely he doth. He looks more at David's and Asaph's uprightness than upon their infirmities, though they were great and many. He eyes more Job's patience than his passion. 'Remember the patience of Job,' not a word of his impatience (James 5:11). He that drew Alexander whilst he had a scar upon his face, drew him with his finger upon the scar. God puts his fingers upon his people's scars, that no blemish may appear. Ah! saints, that you would make it the top of your glory in this, to be like your

---

[1] Not race or place, but grace truly sets forth a man.

heavenly Father! By so doing, much sin would be prevented, the designs of wicked men frustrated, Satan outwitted, many wounds healed, many sad hearts cheered, and God more abundantly honoured.[1]

Remedy (2). The second remedy against this device of Satan is, solemnly to consider, *that love and union makes most for your own safety and security.* We shall be invincible if we be inseparable. The world may frown upon you, and plot against you, but they cannot hurt you. Unity is the best bond of safety in every church and commonwealth.[2]

And this did that Scythian king in Plutarch's book represent lively to his eighty sons, when, being ready to die, he commanded a bundle of arrows fast bound together to be given to his sons to break; they all tried to break them, but, being bound fast together, they could not; then he caused the band to be cut, and then they broke them with ease. He applied it thus: 'My sons, so long as you keep together, you will be invincible; but if the band of union be broke betwixt you, you will easily be broken in pieces.'[3]

Pliny writes of a stone in the island of Scyros, that if it be whole, though a large and heavy one, it swims above water, but being broken, it sinks.[4] So long as saints keep whole, nothing shall sink them; but if they break, they are in danger of sinking and drowning.

---

[1] Sin is Satan's work, grace is God's work; and is it not most meet that the child should eye most and mind most his father's work?

[2] There was a temple of Concord amongst the heathens; and shall it not be found among Christians, that are temples of the Holy Ghost?

[3] Pancirollus saith, that the most precious pearl among the Romans was called *unio*, union.

[4] No doubt a volcanic, porous product.

Remedy (3). The third remedy against this device of Satan is, *to dwell upon those commands of God that do require you to love one another*. Oh! when your hearts begin to rise against each other, charge the commands of God upon your hearts, and say to your souls, O our souls! hath not the eternal God commanded you to love them that love the Lord? And is it not life to obey, and death to rebel?[1] Therefore look that you fulfill the commands of the Lord, for his commands are not like those that are easily reversed; but they are like those of the Medes, that cannot be changed. Oh! be much in pondering upon these commands of God. 'A new commandment I give unto you, that ye love one another; as I have loved you, that ye also love one another' (John 13:34). It is called a new commandment, because it is renewed in the gospel, and set home by Christ's example, and because it is rare, choice, special, and remarkable above all others.[2] 'This is my commandment, That ye love one another, as I have loved you.' 'These things I command you, that ye love one another.' 'Owe no man any thing, but love one another: for he that loveth another, hath fulfilled the law.' 'Let brotherly love continue.' 'Love one another, for love is of God, and every one that loveth is born of God, and knoweth God.' 'See that ye love one another with a pure heart fervently.' 'Finally, be ye all of one mind, having compassion one of another. Love as brethren, be pitiful, be courteous.' 'For this is the message that ye heard from the beginning, that we should love one another.' 'And this

---

[1] To act, or run cross to God's express command, though under pretence of revelation from God, is as much as a man's life is worth, as you may see in that sad story (1 Kings 13:24).

[2] Some conceive it to be an Hebraism, in which language *new*, rare, and excellent, are synonyms.

is his commandment, that we should believe on the name of his Son Jesus Christ, and love one another, as he gave us commandment.' 'Beloved, if God so loved us, we ought also to love one another.'[1] Oh! dwell much upon these precious commands, that your love may be inflamed one to another.

In the primitive times, it was much taken notice of by the heathens, that in the depth of misery, when fathers and mothers forsook their children, Christians, otherwise strangers, stuck one to another, whose love of religion proved firmer than that of nature. Ah! that there were more of that spirit among the saints in these days! The world was once destroyed with water for the heat of lusts, and it is thought it will be again destroyed with fire for the coldness of love.[2]

Remedy (4). The fourth remedy against this device of Satan is, *to dwell more upon these choice and sweet things wherein you agree, than upon those things wherein you differ.* Ah! did you but thus, how would sinful heats be abated, and your love raised, and your spirits sweetened one to another! You agree in most, you differ but in a few; you agree in the greatest and weightiest, as concerning God, Christ, the Spirit, and the Scripture. You differ only in those points that have been long disputable amongst men of greatest piety and parts. You agree to own the Scripture, to hold to Christ the head, and to walk according to the law of the new creature.[3] Shall Herod and Pilate agree? Shall Turks and pagans

[1] John 15:12, 17; Rom. 13:8; Heb. 13:1; 1 John 4:7; 1 Pet. 1:22, and 3:8; 1 John 3:11, 23; 4:11.

[2] The ancients use to say commonly, that Alexander and Hephaestion had but one soul in two distinct bodies, because their joy and sorrow, glory and disgrace, was mutual to them both.

[3] What a sad thing was it that a heathen should say, No beasts are so mischievous to men as Christians are one to another.

agree? Shall bears and lions, tigers, and wolves, yea, shall a legion of devils, agree in one body? And shall not saints agree, who differ only in such things as have least of the heart of God in them, and that shall never hinder your meeting in heaven?

Remedy (5). The fifth remedy against this device of Satan is, solemnly to consider, *that God delights to be styled Deus pacis, the God of peace; and Christ to be styled Princeps pacis, the Prince of peace, and King of Salem, that is, King of peace; and the Spirit is a Spirit of peace.* 'The fruit of the Spirit is love, joy, peace' (Gal. 5:22). Oh! why then should not the saints be children of peace? Certainly, men of froward, unquiet, fiery spirits cannot have that sweet evidence of their interest in the God of peace, and in the Prince of peace, and in the Spirit of peace, as those precious souls have that follow after the things that make for love and peace. The very name of peace is sweet and comfortable; the fruit and effect thereof pleasant and profitable, more to be desired than innumerable triumphs; it is a blessing that ushers in a multitude of other blessings[1] (2 Cor. 13:11; Isa. 9:6).

The ancients were wont to paint peace in the form of a woman, with a horn of plenty in her hand.[2] Ah! peace and love among the saints, is that which will secure them and their mercies at home; yea, it will multiply their mercies; it will engage the God of mercy to crown them with the choicest mercies; and it is that that will render them most terrible, invincible, and successful abroad. Love and peace among the saints is that which puts the counsels of their enemies to a stand, and renders all their enterprises abortive; it is that which doth most weaken their hands, wound their hopes, and kill their hearts.

---

[1] Where peace is, there is Christ, because Christ is peace.

[2] The Grecians had the statue of Peace, with Pluto, the god of riches, in her arms.

Remedy (6). The sixth remedy against this device of Satan is, *to make more care and conscience of keeping up your peace with God.* Ah! Christians, I am afraid that your remissness herein is that which hath occasioned much of that sourness, bitterness, and divisions that be among you. Ah! you have not, as you should, kept up your peace with God, and therefore it is that you do so dreadfully break the peace among yourselves. The Lord hath promised. 'That when a man's ways please him, he will make his enemies to be at peace with him' (Prov. 16:7). Ah! how much more then would God make the children of peace to keep the peace among themselves, if their ways do but please him! All creatures are at his beck and check. Laban followed Jacob with one troop. Esau met him with another, both with hostile intentions; but Jacob's ways pleasing the Lord, God by his mighty power so works that Laban leaves him with a kiss, and Esau met him with a kiss; he hath an oath of one, tears of the other, peace with both. If we make it our business to keep up our league with God, God will make it his work and his glory to maintain our peace with men; but if men make light of keeping up their peace with God, it is just with God to leave them to a spirit of pride, envy, passion, contention, division, and confusion, to leave them 'to bite and devour one another, till they be consumed one of another.'[1]

Remedy (7). The seventh remedy against this device of Satan is, *to dwell much upon that near relation and union that is*

---

[1] Pharnaces sent a crown to Caesar at the same time he rebelled against him; but he returned the crown and this message back, *Faceret imperata prius*: Let him return to his obedience first. There is no sound peace to be had with God or man, but in a way of obedience.

between you. This consideration had a sweet influence upon Abraham's heart: 'And Abraham said unto Lot, Let there be no strife, I pray thee, between me and thee, and between my herdsmen and thy herdsmen; for we are brethren' (Gen. 13:8).[1] That is a sweet word in the psalmist, 'Behold, how good and how pleasant it is for brethren to live together in unity' (Psa. 133:1). It is not *good and not pleasant, or pleasant and not good, but good and pleasant.* There be some things that be good and not pleasant, as patience and discipline; and there be some things that are pleasant but not good, as carnal pleasures, and voluptuousness. And there are some things that are neither good nor pleasant, as malice, envy, and worldly sorrow; and there are some things that are both good and pleasant, as piety, charity, peace, and union among brethren; and oh! that we could see more of this among those that shall one day meet in their Father's kingdom and never part. And as they are brethren, so they are all fellow-members: 'Now ye are the body of Christ, and members in particular' (1 Cor. 12:27). And again: 'We are members of his body, of his flesh, and of his bones' (Eph. 5:30). Shall the members of the natural body be serviceable and useful to one another, and shall the members of this spiritual body cut and destroy one another? Is it against the law of nature for the natural members to cut and slash one another?[2] And is it not much more against the law of nature and of grace for the members of Christ's glorious body to do so? And as you are all fellow-members, so you are fellow-soldiers under the same Captain of salvation,

[1] The Hebrew signifies, Oh! let there be no bitterness between us, for we are brethren.

[2] The parti-coloured coats were characters of the king's children; so is following after peace now.

the Lord Jesus, fighting against the world, the flesh, and the devil. And as you are all fellow-soldiers, so you are all fellow-sufferers under the same enemies, the devil and the world. And as you are all fellow-sufferers, so are you fellow-travellers towards the land of Canaan, 'the new Jerusalem that is above.' 'Here we have no abiding city, but we look for one to come.' The heirs of heaven are strangers on earth. And as you are all fellow-travellers, so are you all fellow-heirs of the same crown and inheritance.[1]

Remedy (8). The eighth remedy against this device of Satan is, *to dwell upon the miseries of discord*. Dissolution is the daughter of dissension. Ah! how doth the name of Christ, and the way of Christ, suffer by the discord of saints! How are many that are entering upon the ways of God hindered and sadded, and the mouths of the wicked opened, and their hearts hardened against God and his ways, by the discord of his people! Remember this, the disagreement of Christians is the devil's triumph; and what a sad thing is this, that Christians should give Satan cause to triumph![2]

It was a notable saying of one, 'Take away strife, and call back peace, lest thou lose a man, thy friend; and the devil, an enemy, joy over you both.'

Remedy (9). The ninth remedy against this device of Satan is, seriously to consider, *that it is no disparagement to you to be first in seeking peace and reconcilement, but rather an honour to you, that you have begun to seek peace*. Abraham was the elder,

[1] Rev. 12:7, 8; Heb. 2:10; Rev. 2:10; John 15:19, 20; Heb. 12:14; 13:4; Rom. 8:15-17.
[2] Our dissensions are one of the Jews' greatest stumbling-blocks. Can you think of it, and your hearts not bleed?

and more worthy than Lot, both in respect of grace and nature also, for he was uncle unto Lot, and yet he first seeks peace of his inferior, which God hath recorded as his honour.[1] Ah! how doth the God of peace, by his Spirit and messengers, pursue after peace with poor creatures! God first makes offer of peace to us: 'Now then, we are ambassadors for Christ, as though God did beseech you by us: we pray you in Christ's stead, be ye reconciled to God' (2 Cor. 5:20). God's grace first kneels to us, and who can turn their backs upon such blessed and bleeding embracements, but souls in whom Satan the god of this world kings it? God is the party wronged, and yet he sues for peace with us at first: 'I said, Behold me, behold me, unto a nation that was not called by my name' (Isa. 65:1).[2] Ah! how doth the sweetness, the freeness, and the riches of his grace break forth and shine upon poor souls. When a man goes from the sun, yet the sunbeams follow him; so when we go from the Sun of righteousness, yet then the beams of his love and mercy follow us. Christ first sent to Peter that had denied him, and the rest that had forsaken him: 'Go your ways, and tell his disciples and Peter, that he goeth before you into Galilee: there shall ye see him, as he said unto you' (Mark 16:7). Ah! souls, it is not a base, low thing, but a God-like thing, though we are wronged by others, yet to be the first in seeking after peace. Such actings will speak out much of God with a man's spirit.

Christians, it is not matter of liberty whether you will or you will not pursue after peace, but it is matter of duty that lies upon

[1] They shall both have the name and the note, the comfort and the credit, of being most like unto God, who first begin to pursue after peace.

[2] 'Behold me! behold me!' It is geminated [doubled] to show God's exceeding forwardness to show favour and mercy to them.

you; you are bound by express precept to follow after peace; and though it may seem to fly from you, yet you must pursue after it: 'Follow peace with all men, and holiness, without which no man can see the Lord' (Heb. 12:14).[1] Peace and holiness are to be pursued after with the greatest eagerness that can be imagined. So the psalmist: 'Depart from evil, and do good; seek peace and pursue it' (Psa. 34:14). The Hebrew word that is here rendered *seek*, signifies to seek earnestly, vehemently, affectionately, studiously, industriously. 'And pursue it.' That Hebrew word signifies earnestly to pursue, being a metaphor taken from the eagerness of wild beasts or ravenous fowls, which will run or fly both fast and far rather than be disappointed of their prey. So the apostle presses the same duty upon the Romans: 'Let us follow after the things that make for peace, and things wherein one may edify another' (Rom. 14:19). Ah! you froward, sour, dogged Christians, can you look upon these commands of God without tears and blushing?

I have read a remarkable story of Aristippus, though but a heathen, who went of his own accord to Aeschines his enemy, and said, 'Shall we never be reconciled till we become a table-talk to all the country?' and when Aeschines answered he would most gladly be at peace with him, 'Remember, then, said Aristippus, that though I were the elder and better man, yet I sought first unto thee.' Thou art indeed, said Aeschines, a far better man than I, for I began the quarrel, but thou the reconcilement. My prayer shall be that this heathen may not rise in judgment against the flourishing professors of our times, 'Who whet their tongues like a sword, and bend their bows to shoot their arrows, even bitter words' (Psa. 64:3).

---

[1] The Greek signifies to follow after peace, as the persecutor doth him whom he persecuted.

Remedy (10). The tenth remedy against this device of Satan is, *for saints to join together and walk together in the ways of grace and holiness so far as they do agree, making the word their only touchstone and judge of their actions.* That is sweet advice that the apostle gives: 'I press toward the mark for the prize of the high calling of God in Christ Jesus' (Phil. 3:14-16). 'Let us therefore, as many as be perfect—comparatively or conceitedly[1] so—be thus minded. And if in anything ye be otherwise minded, God shall reveal even this unto you. Nevertheless, whereto we have already attained, let us walk by the same rule, let us mind the same thing.' Ah! Christians, God loses much, and you lose much, and Satan gains much by this, that you do not, that you will not, walk lovingly together so far as your ways lie together. It is your sin and shame that you do not, that you will not, pray together, and hear together, and confer together, and mourn together, because that in some far lesser things you are not agreed together. What folly and madness is it in those whose way of a hundred miles lies fourscore and nineteen together, yet will not walk so far together, because that they cannot go the other mile together; yet such is the folly and madness of many Christians in these days, who will not do many things they may do, because they cannot do everything they should do. I fear God will whip them into a better temper before he hath done with them. He will break their bones, and pierce their hearts, but he will cure them of this malady.

And be sure you make the word the only touchstone and judge of all persons and actions: 'To the law and to the testimony, if they speak not according to this word, it is because

---

[1] Those who have reason to *conceive* themselves 'perfect.'

there is no light in them' (Isa. 8:20). It is best and safest to make that to be the judge of all men and things now that all shall be judged by in the latter day: 'The word,' saith 'Christ, that I have spoken, the same shall judge him in the last day' (John 12:48). Make not your dim light, your notions, your fancies, your opinions, the judge of men's action, but still judge by rule, and plead, 'It is written.'

When a vain importunate soul cried out in contest with a holy man, 'Hear me, hear me,' the holy man answered, 'Neither hear me, nor I thee, but let us both hear the apostle.' Constantine, in all the disputes before him with the Arians, would still call for the word of God as the only way, if not to convert, yet to stop their mouths.

Remedy (11). The eleventh remedy against this device of Satan is, *to be much in self-judging:* 'Judge yourselves, and you shall not be judged of the Lord' (1 Cor. 11:31). Ah! were Christians' hearts more taken up in judging themselves and condemning themselves, they would not be so apt to judge and censure others, and to carry it sourly and bitterly towards others that differ from them.[1] There are no souls in the world that are so fearful to judge others as those that do most judge themselves, nor so careful to make a righteous judgment of men or things as those that are most careful to judge themselves. There are none in the world that tremble to think evil of others, to speak evil of others, or to do evil to others, as those that make it their business to judge themselves. There are none that make such sweet constructions and charitable interpretations of men and

---

[1] It is storied of Nero, himself being unchaste, he did think there was no man chaste.

things, as those that are best and most in judging themselves.[1] One request I have to you that are much in judging others and little in judging yourselves, to you that are so apt and prone to judge harshly, falsely, and unrighteously, and that is, that you will every morning dwell a little upon these scriptures: 'Judge not, that ye be not judged; for with what judgment ye judge, ye shall be judged; and with what measure ye mete, it shall be measured to you again' (Matt. 7:1, 2). 'Judge not according to appearance, but judge righteous judgment' (John 7:24). 'Let not him that eateth not judge him that eateth, for God hath received him. Why dost thou judge thy brother? or why dost thou set at nought thy brother?' (Rom. 14:3, 10, 13). 'We shall all stand before the judgment-seat of Christ. Let us not judge one another anymore, but judge this rather, that no man put a stumbling-block or an occasion to fall in his brother's way.' 'Judge nothing before the time, until the Lord come, who both will bring to light the hidden things of darkness, and will manifest the counsels of the heart, and then shall every man have praise of God' (1 Cor. 4:5), 'Speak not evil one of another, brethren; he that speaketh evil of his brother, and judgeth his brother, speaketh evil of the law, and judgeth the law; but if thou judgest the law, thou art not a doer of the law, but a judge. There is one lawgiver, who is able to save and to destroy' (James 4:11, 12). 'Who art thou that judgest another man's servant? to his own master he standeth or falleth; yea, he shall be holden up, for God is able to make him stand' (Rom. 14:4).

---

[1] In the Olympic games, the wrestlers did not put their crowns upon their own heads, but upon the heads of others. It is just so with souls that are good at self-judging.

One Delphidius accusing another before Julian about that which he could not prove, the party denying the fact, Delphidius answers, If it be sufficient to deny what is laid to one's charge, who shall be found guilty? Julian answers, And if it be sufficient to be accused, who can be innocent? You are wise, and know how to apply it.

Remedy (12). The twelfth remedy against this device of Satan is this, above all, *labour to be clothed with humility.* Humility makes a man peaceable among brethren, fruitful in well-doing, cheerful in suffering, and constant in holy walking (1 Pet. 5:5). Humility fits for the highest services we owe to Christ, and yet will not neglect the lowest service to the meanest saint (John 13:5). Humility can feed upon the meanest dish, and yet it is maintained by the choicest delicates, as God, Christ, and glory. Humility will make a man bless him that curses him, and pray for those that persecute him. An humble heart is an habitation for God, a scholar for Christ, a companion of angels, a preserver of grace, and a fitter for glory. Humility is the nurse of our graces, the preserver of our mercies, and the great promoter of holy duties. Humility cannot find three things on this side heaven: it cannot find fullness in the creature, nor sweetness in sin, nor life in an ordinance without Christ. An humble soul always finds three things on this side heaven: the soul to be empty, Christ to be full, and every mercy and duty to be sweet wherein God is enjoyed.[1] Humility can weep over other men's weaknesses, and joy and rejoice over their graces. Humility will make a man quiet and contented in the meanest condition, and it will preserve a man from envying other men's prosperous condition (1 Thess.

---

[1] Humility, said Bernard, is that which keeps all graces together.

1:2, 3). Humility honours those that are strong in grace, and puts two hands under those that are weak in grace (Eph. 3:8). Humility makes a man richer than other men, and it makes a man judge himself the poorest among men. Humility will see much good abroad, when it can see but little at home. Ah, Christian! though faith be the champion of grace, and love the nurse of grace, yet humility is the beautifier of grace; it casts a general glory upon all the graces in the soul. Ah! did Christians more abound in humility, they would be less bitter, froward, and sour, and they would be more gentle, meek, and sweet in their spirits and practices. Humility will make a man have high thoughts of others and low thoughts of a man's self; it will make a man see much glory and excellency in others, and much baseness and sinfulness in a man's self; it will make a man see others rich, and himself poor; others strong, and himself weak; others wise, and himself foolish.[1] Humility will make a man excellent at covering others' infirmities, and at recording their gracious services, and at delighting in their graces; it makes a man joy in every light that outshines his own, and every wind that blows others good. Humility is better at believing than it is at questioning other men's happiness. I judge, saith an humble soul, it is well with these Christians now, but it will be far better with them hereafter. They are now upon the borders of the New Jerusalem, and it will be but as a day before they slide into Jerusalem. An humble soul is more willing to say. Heaven is that man's, than mine; and Christ is that Christian's, than mine; and God is their God in

---

[1] The humble soul is like the violet, 'which grows low, hangs the head downwards, and hides itself with its own leaves' and were it not that the fragrant smell of his many virtues discovered him to the world, he would choose to live and die in his self-contenting secrecy.

covenant, than mine. Ah! were Christians more humble, there would be less fire and more love among them than now is.

IV. DEVICES AGAINST
POOR AND IGNORANT SOULS

Fourthly, As Satan hath his device to destroy gracious souls, so he hath his devices to destroy poor ignorant souls, and that sometimes *by drawing them to affect ignorance, and to neglect, slight, and despise the means of knowledge.* Ignorance is the mother of mistake, the cause of trouble, error, and of terror; it is the highway to hell, and it makes a man both a prisoner and a slave to the devil at once.[1] Ignorance unmans a man; it makes a man a beast, yea, makes him more miserable than the beast that perisheth.[2] There are none so easily nor so frequently taken in Satan's snares as ignorant souls. They are easily drawn to dance with the devil all day, and to dream of supping with Christ at night.

Remedy (1). The first remedy against this device of Satan is, seriously to consider, *that an ignorant heart is an evil heart.* 'Without knowledge the mind is not good' (Prov. 19:2). As an ignorant heart is a naughty heart, it is a heart in the dark; and no good can come into a dark heart, but it must pass through the understanding: 'And if the eye be dark, all the body is dark' (Matt. 6:23). A leprous head and a leprous heart are inseparable companions. Ignorant hearts are so evil that they let fly on all hands, and spare not to spit their venom in the very face of God, as Pharaoh did when thick darkness was upon him.

[1] Hos. 4:6; Matt. 22:29.
[2] Ignorant ones have this advantage, they have a cooler hell.

Remedy (2). The second remedy against this device of Satan is to consider, *that ignorance is the deformity of the soul. As blindness is the deformity of the face, so is ignorance the deformity of the soul.* As the want of fleshly eyes spoils the beauty of the face, so the want of spiritual eyes spoils the beauty of the soul. A man without knowledge is as a workman without his hands, as a painter without his eyes, as a traveller without his legs, or as a ship without sails, or a bird without wings, or like a body without a soul.

Remedy (3). The third remedy against this device of Satan is, solemnly to consider, *that ignorance makes men the objects of God's hatred and wrath.* 'It is a people that do err in their hearts, and have not known my ways. Wherefore I swear in my wrath, they should never enter into my rest' (Heb. 3:10, 11). 'My people are a people of no understanding; therefore he that made them will have no mercy on them' (Isa. 27:11). Christ hath said that he will come 'in flaming fire, to render vengeance on them that know not God' (2 Thess. 1:8). Ignorance will end in vengeance. When you see a poor blind man here, you do not loathe him, nor hate him, but you pity him. Oh! but soul-blindness makes you abominable in the sight of God. God hath sworn that ignorant persons shall never come into heaven. Heaven itself would be a hell to ignorant souls.[1]

'My people are destroyed for want of knowledge; because thou hast rejected knowledge, I will reject thee' (Hos. 4:6).

Chilo, one of the seven sages, being asked what God had done, answered, 'He exalted humble men, and suppressed proud ignorant fools.'[2]

[1] They must needs err that know not God's ways, yet cannot they wander so wide as to miss of hell.

[2] Rome saith that ignorance is the mother of devotion, but the Scripture saith, it is the mother of destruction.

Remedy (4). The fourth remedy against this device of Satan
is, to consider, *that ignorance is a sin that leads to all sins. All
sins are seminally in ignorance.* 'You do err, not knowing the
Scriptures' (Matt. 22:29). It puts men upon hating and perse-
cuting the saints. 'They shall hate you, and put you out of the
synagogues: yea, the time cometh, that whosoever killeth you
will think that he doeth God service. And these things will
they do unto you, because they have not known the Father,
nor me' (John 16:2, 3). Paul thanks his ignorance for all his
cruelties to Christians. 'I was a blasphemer, and a persecutor,
and injurious: but I obtained mercy, because I did it ignor-
antly' (1 Tim. 1:13).[1] It was ignorance that put the Jews upon
crucifying Christ: 'Father, forgive them,' saith Christ of his
murderers, 'for they know not what they do' (Luke 23:34). 'For
if the princes of this world had known, they would not have
crucified the Lord of glory' (1 Cor. 2:8).[2] Sin at first was the
cause of ignorance, but now ignorance is the cause of all sin.
'Swearing, and lying, and killing, and stealing, and whoring
abound,' saith the prophet, 'because there is no knowledge of
God in the land.' There are none so frequent, and so impudent
in the ways of sin, as ignorant souls; they care not, nor mind
not what they do, nor what they say against God, Christ,
heaven, holiness, and their own souls. 'Our tongues are our
own, who shall control us?' 'They are corrupt, and speak

---

[1] It seems right to note that the apostle does not allege his ignorance,
for which he was responsible, as the ground of the 'mercy' shown him,
but only as the source and explanation of his sin and violence. The
clause, 'but I obtained mercy,' is parenthetic, and it is of importance to
note this.

[2] Aristotle makes ignorance the mother of all the misrule in the
world.

wickedly concerning oppression: they speak loftily. They set their mouth against the heavens; and their tongue walketh through the earth. Have all the workers of iniquity no knowledge? who eat up my people as they eat bread, and call not upon the Lord?'[1]

[1] They did like Oedipus, who killed his father Laius, king of Thebes, and thought he killed his enemy.

APPENDIX

———

I. TOUCHING FIVE MORE OF SATAN'S DEVICES

DEVICE 1. *By suggesting to the soul the greatness and vileness of his sins.* What! saith Satan, dost thou think thou shalt ever obtain mercy by Christ, that hast sinned with so high a hand against Christ? that hast slighted the tenders of grace? that hast grieved the Spirit of grace? that hast despised the word of grace? that hast trampled under feet the blood of the covenant by which thou mightest have been pardoned, purged, justified, and saved? that hast spoken and done all the evil that thou couldest? No! no! saith Satan, he hath mercy for others, but not for thee; pardon for others, but not for thee; righteousness for others, but not for thee. Therefore it is in vain for thee to think of believing in Christ, or resting and leaning thy guilty soul upon Christ (Jer. 3:5).

Remedy (1). The first remedy against this device of Satan is, to consider, *that the greater your sins are, the more you stand in need of a Saviour.* The greater your burden is, the more you stand in need of one to help to bear it. The deeper the wound is, the more need there is of the chirurgeon;[1] the

———

[1] = Surgeon.

more dangerous the disease is, the more need there is of the physician. Who but madmen will argue thus: My burden is great, therefore I will not call out for help; my wound is deep, therefore I will not call out for balm; my disease is dangerous, therefore I will not go to the physician. Ah! it is spiritual madness, it is the devil's logic to argue thus; My sins are great, therefore I will not go to Christ, I dare not rest nor lean on Christ; whereas the soul should reason thus: The greater my sins are, the more I stand in need of mercy, of pardon, and therefore I will go to Christ, who delights in mercy, who pardons sin for his own name's sake, who is as able and as willing to forgive pounds as pence, thousands as hundreds (Mic. 7:18; Isa. 43:25).

Remedy (2). The second remedy against this device of Satan is, solemnly to consider, *that the promise of grace and mercy is to returning souls.* And, therefore, though thou art never so wicked, yet if thou wilt return, God will be thine, and mercy shall be thine, and pardon shall be thine (2 Chron. 30:9): 'For if you turn again unto the Lord, your brethren and your children shall find compassion before them that lead them captive, so that they shall come again into this land: for the Lord our God is gracious and merciful, and will not turn away his face from you, if ye return unto him.' So Jer. 3:12: 'Go and proclaim these words towards the north, and say, Return, thou backsliding Israel, saith the Lord, and I will not cause my anger to fall upon you: for I am merciful, saith the Lord, and I will not keep anger for ever.' So Joel 2:13: 'And rend your hearts, and not your garments, and turn unto the Lord your God: for he is gracious and merciful, slow to anger, and of great kindness, and repenteth him of the evil.' So Isa. 55:7:

'Let the wicked forsake his ways, and the unrighteous man his thoughts: and let him return unto the Lord, and he will have mercy upon him; and to our God, for he will abundantly pardon,' or, as the Hebrew reads it, 'He will multiply pardon.' So Ezek. 18.

Ah! sinner, it is not thy great transgressions that shall exclude thee from mercy, if thou wilt break off thy sins by repentance and return to the fountain of mercy. Christ's heart, Christ's arms, are wide open to embrace the returning prodigal. It is not simply the greatness of thy sins, but thy peremptory persisting in sin, that will be thy eternal overthrow.

Remedy (3). The third remedy against this device of Satan is, solemnly to consider, *that the greatest sinners have obtained mercy, and therefore all the angels in heaven, all the men on earth, and all the devils in hell cannot tell to the contrary, but that thou mayest obtain mercy.* Manasseh was a notorious sinner; he erected altars for Baal, he worshipped and served all the host of heaven; he caused his sons to pass through the fire; he gave himself to witchcraft and sorcery; he made Judah to sin more wickedly than the heathen did, whom the Lord destroyed before the children of Israel; he caused the streets of Jerusalem to run down with innocent blood (2 Kings 21). Ah! what a devil incarnate was he in his actings! Yet when he humbled himself, and sought the Lord, the Lord was entreated of him and heard his supplication, and brought him to Jerusalem, and made himself known unto him, and crowned him with mercy and loving-kindness, as you may see in 2 Chron.[1] So Paul was once a blasphemer, a persecutor and injurious, yet

---

[1] The Hebrew doctors writ that he slew Isaiah the prophet, who was his father-in-law.

he obtained mercy (1 Tim. 1:13). So Mary Magdalene was a notorious strumpet, a common whore, out of whom Christ cast seven devils, yet she is pardoned by Christ, and dearly beloved of Christ (Luke 7:37, 38). So Mark 16:9, 'Now, when Jesus was risen early the first day of the week, he appeared first to Mary Magdalene, out of whom he had cast seven devils.'[1]

Jansenius on the place saith, it is very observable that our Saviour after his resurrection first appeared to Mary Magdalene and Peter, that had been grievous sinners; that even the worst of sinners may be comforted and encouraged to come to Christ, to believe in Christ, to rest and stay their souls upon Christ, for mercy here and glory hereafter. That is a very precious word for the worst of sinners to hang upon (Psa. 68.) The psalmist speaking of Christ saith, 'Thou hast ascended on high, thou hast led captivity captive; thou hast received gifts for men; yea, for the rebellious also, that the Lord God might dwell amongst them.'

What though thou art a rebellious child, or a rebellious servant! What though thou art a rebellious swearer, a rebellious drunkard, a rebellious Sabbath breaker! Yet Christ hath received gifts for thee, 'even for the rebellious also.' He hath received the gift of pardon, the gift of righteousness, yea, all the gifts of the Spirit for thee, that thy heart may be made a delightful house for God to dwell in.

John Bodin hath a story concerning a great rebel that had made a strong party against a Roman emperor. The emperor makes proclamation, that whoever could bring the rebel dead or alive, he should have such a great sum of money. The rebel hearing of this, comes and presents himself before the

[1] See footnote on page 168.

emperor, and demands the sum of money. Now, saith the emperor, if I should put him to death, the world would say I did it to save my money. And so he pardons the rebel, and gives him the money.

Ah! sinners! Shall a heathen do this, that had but a drop of mercy and compassion in him; and will not Christ do much more, that hath all fullness of grace, mercy, and glory in himself? Surely his bowels do yearn towards the worst of rebels. Ah! if you still but come in, you will find him ready to pardon, yea, one made up of pardoning mercy. Oh! the readiness and willingness of Jesus Christ to receive to favour the greatest rebels! The father of mercies did meet, embrace, and kiss that prodigal mouth which came from feeding with swine and kissing of harlots (Col. 1:19; 2:3, 4).[1]

Ephraim had committed idolatry, and was backslidden from God; he was guilty of lukewarmness and unbelief, &c., yet saith God, 'Ephraim is my dear son, he is a pleasant child, my bowels are troubled for him, I will have mercy,' or rather as it is in the original, 'I will have mercy, mercy upon him, saith the Lord.'[2]

Well! saith God, though Ephraim be guilty of crimson sins, yet he is a son, a dear son, a precious son, a pleasant child; though he be black with filth, and red with guilt, yet my bowels are troubled for him; I will have mercy, mercy upon him. Ah sinners, if these bowels of mercy do not melt, win, and draw you, justice will be a swift witness against you, and make you lie down in eternal misery for kicking against the bowels of mercy.

---

[1] Neh. 9:17; Hebrew, 'But thou art a God of pardons.'
[2] Hos. 4:17; 5. 3; 6. 8, 11; 12:12, 14; 13:12. *Vide* Jer. 31:20.

Christ hangs out still, as once that warlike Scythian did, a white flag of grace and mercy to returning sinners that humble themselves at his feet for favour; but if sinners stand out, Christ will put forth his red flag, his bloody flag, and they shall die for ever by a hand of justice. Sinners! there is no way to avoid perishing by Christ's iron rod, but by kissing his golden sceptre.

Remedy (4). The fourth remedy against this device of Satan is, to consider, *that Jesus Christ hath nowhere in all the Scripture excepted against the worst of sinners that are willing to receive him, to believe in him, to rest upon him for happiness and blessedness.* Ah! sinners, why should you be more cruel and unmerciful to your own souls than Christ is? Christ hath not excluded you from mercy, why should you exclude your own souls from mercy? Oh that you would dwell often upon that choice Scripture (John 6:37): 'All that the Father giveth me shall come to me; and him that cometh to me I will in no wise cast out,' or as the original hath it, 'I will not cast out.' Well! saith Christ, if any man will come, or is coming to me, let him be more sinful or less; more unworthy or less; let him be never so guilty, never so filthy, never so rebellious, never so leprous, yet if he will but come, I will not cast him off. So much is held forth in 1 Cor. 6:9-11, 'Know ye not that the unrighteous shall not inherit the kingdom of God? Be not deceived: neither fornicators, nor idolaters, nor adulterers, nor effeminate, nor abusers of themselves with mankind, nor thieves, nor covetous, nor drunkards, nor revilers, nor extortioners, shall inherit the kingdom of God. And such were some of you: but ye are washed, but ye are sanctified, but ye are justified, in the name of the Lord Jesus, and by the Spirit of our God.'

Ah! sinners, do not think that he that hath received such notorious sinners to mercy will reject you. 'He is yesterday, and today, and the same for ever' (Heb. 13:8). Christ was born in an inn, to show that he receives all comers; his garments were divided into four parts, to show that out of what part of the world soever we come, we shall be received. If we be naked, Christ hath robes to clothe us; if we be harbourless, Christ hath room to lodge us. That is a choice scripture (Acts 10:34, 35) 'Then Peter opened his mouth and said, Of a truth I perceive that God is no respecter of persons. But in every nation, he that feareth him, and worketh righteousness, is accepted with him.'

The three tongues that were written upon the cross, Greek, Latin, and Hebrew (John 19:19, 20), to witness Christ to be the king of the Jews, do each of them in their several idioms avouch this singular axiom, that Christ is an all-sufficient Saviour; and 'a threefold cord is not easily broken.' The apostle puts this out of doubt; Heb. 7:25: 'Wherefore he is able also to save them to the uttermost that come unto God by him, seeing he ever liveth to make intercession for them.' Now, he were not an all-sufficient Saviour if he were not able to save the greatest, as well as the least of sinners. Ah! sinners, tell Jesus Christ that he hath not excluded you from mercy, and therefore you are resolved that you will sit, wait, weep, and knock at the door of mercy, till he shall say, Souls, be of good cheer, your sins are forgiven, your persons are justified, and your souls shall be saved.

Remedy (5). The fifth remedy against this device of Satan is, to consider, *that the greater sinner thou art, the dearer thou wilt be to Christ, when he shall behold thee as the travail of his soul* (Isa. 53:11): 'He shall see of the travail of his soul, and be satisfied.' The dearer we pay for anything, the dearer that thing is to us. Christ hath paid most, and prayed most, and sighed most, and wept most, and bled most for the greatest sinners, and therefore they are dearer to Christ than others that are less sinful. Rachel was dearer to Jacob than Leah, because she cost him more; he obeyed, endured, and suffered more by day and night for her than for Leah. Ah! sinners, the greatness of your sins does but set off the freeness and riches of Christ's grace, and the freeness of his love. This maketh heaven and earth to ring of his praise, that he loves those that are most unlovely, that he shows most favour to them that have sinned most highly against him, as might be showed by several instances in Scripture, as Paul, Mary Magdalene, and others. Who sinned more against Christ than these? And who had sweeter and choicer manifestations of divine love and favour than these?

Remedy (6). The sixth remedy against this device of Satan is, seriously to consider, *that the longer you keep off from Christ, the greater and stronger your sins will grow*. All divine power and strength against sin flows from the soul's union and communion with Christ (Rom. 8:10; 1 John 1:6, 7). While you keep off from Christ, you keep off from that strength and power which is alone able to make you trample down strength, lead captivity captive, and slay the Goliaths that bid defiance to Christ. It is only faith in Christ that makes a man triumph over sin, Satan, hell, and the world (1 John 5:4). It is only faith in Christ that binds the strong man's hand and foot, that stops the issue of blood, that makes a man strong in resisting, and happy in conquering (Matt. 5:15-35). Sin always dies most where faith lives most. The most believing soul is the most mortified soul. Ah! sinner, remember this, there is no way on earth effectually to be rid of the guilt, filth, and power of sin, but by believing in a Saviour. It is not resolving, it is not complaining, it is not mourning, but believing, that will make thee divinely victorious over that body of sin that to this day is too strong for thee, and that will certainly be thy ruin, if it be not ruined by a hand of faith.

Remedy (7). The seventh remedy against this device of Satan is, wisely to consider, *that as there is nothing in Christ to discourage the greatest sinners from believing in him, so there is everything in Christ that may encourage the greatest sinners to believe in him, to rest and lean upon him for all happiness and blessedness* (Song of Sol. 1:3). If you look upon his nature, his disposition, his names, his titles, his offices as king, priest, and prophet, you will find nothing to discourage the greatest sinners from believing in him, but many things to encourage the greatest sinners to receive him, to believe in him.[1] Christ is the greatest good, the choicest good, the chiefest good, the most suitable good, the most necessary good. He is a pure good, a real good, a total good, an eternal good, and a soul-satisfying good (Rev. 3:17, 18). Sinners, are you poor? Christ hath gold to enrich you. Are you naked? Christ hath royal robes, he hath white raiment to clothe you. Are you blind? Christ hath eye-salve to enlighten you. Are you hungry? Christ will be manna to feed you. Are you thirsty? He will be a well of living water to refresh you. Are you wounded? He hath a balm under his wings to heal you. Are you sick? He is a physician to cure you. Are you prisoners? He hath laid down a ransom for you. Ah,

[1] Col. 1:19; 2:3; Song of Sol. 5:10.

sinners! tell me, tell me, is there anything in Christ to keep you off from believing? No! Is there not everything in Christ that may encourage you to believe in him? Yes! Oh, then, believe in him, and then, 'Though your sins be as scarlet, they shall be as white as snow, though they be red like crimson, they shall be as wool' (Isa. 1:18). Nay, then, your iniquities shall be forgotten as well as forgiven, they shall be remembered no more. God will cast them behind his back, he will throw them into the bottom of the sea (Isa. 43:25; 38:17; Mic. 7:19).

Remedy (8). The eighth remedy against this device of Satan is, seriously to consider, *the absolute necessity of believing in Christ.* Heaven is too holy and too hot to hold unbelievers; their lodging is prepared in hell (Rev. 21:8): 'But the fearful and unbelieving etc. shall have their part in the lake which burneth with fire and brimstone, which is the second death.' 'If ye believe not that I am he,' saith Christ, 'you shall die in your sins' (John 8:24). And he that dies in his sins must go to judgment and to hell in his sins. Every unbeliever is a condemned man: 'He that believeth not' saith John, 'is condemned already, because he hath not believed in the name of the only begotten Son of God. And he that believeth not the Son, shall not see life, but the wrath of God abideth on him' (John 3:18, 36). Ah, sinners! the law, the gospel, and your own consciences, have passed the sentence of condemnation upon you, and there is no way to reverse the sentence but by believing in Christ. And therefore my counsel is this. Stir up yourselves to lay hold on the Lord Jesus, and look up to him, and wait on him, from whom every good and perfect gift comes, and give him no rest till he hath given thee that jewel faith, that is more worth than heaven and earth, and that will make thee happy in life, joyful in death, and glorious in the day of Christ (Isa. 64:7; James 1:17; Isa. 62:7).

And thus much for the remedies against this first device of Satan, whereby he keeps off thousands from believing in Christ.

DEVICE 2. *By suggesting to sinners their unworthiness.* Ah! saith Satan, as thou art worthy of the greatest misery, so thou art unworthy of the least crumb of mercy. What! dost thou think, saith Satan, that ever Christ will own, receive, or embrace such an unworthy wretch as thou art? No, no; if there were any worthiness in thee, then, indeed, Christ might be willing to be entertained by thee. Thou art unworthy to entertain Christ into thy house, how much more unworthy art thou to entertain Christ into thy heart.

Remedy (1). The first remedy against this device of Satan is, seriously to consider, *that God hath nowhere in the Scripture required any worthiness in the creature before believing in Christ.* If you make a diligent search through all the Scripture, you shall not find, from the first line in Genesis to the last line in the Revelation, one word that speaks out God's requiring any worthiness in the creature before the soul's believing in Christ, before the soul's leaning and resting upon Christ for happiness and blessedness; and why, then, should that be a bar and hindrance to thy faith, which God doth nowhere require of thee before thou comest to Christ, that thou mayest have life? (Matt. 19:8; John 5:39). Ah, sinners! remember Satan objects your unworthiness against you only out of a design to keep Christ and your souls asunder for ever; and therefore, in the face of all your unworthiness, rest upon Christ, come to Christ, believe in Christ, and you are happy for ever (John 6:40, 47).

Remedy (2). The second remedy against this device of Satan is, wisely to consider, *that none ever received Christ, embraced Christ, and obtained mercy and pardon from Christ, but unworthy souls.* Pray, what worthiness was in Matthew, Zacchaeus, Mary Magdalene, Manasseh, Paul, and Lydia, before their coming to Christ, before their faith in Christ? Surely none! Ah, sinners! you should reason thus: Christ hath bestowed the choicest mercies, the greatest favours, the highest dignities, the sweetest privileges, upon unworthy sinners, and therefore, O our souls, do not you faint, do not you despair, but patiently and quietly wait for the salvation of the Lord. Who can tell but that free grace and mercy may shine forth upon us, though we are unworthy, and give us a portion among those worthies that are now triumphing in heaven.

Remedy (3). The third remedy against this device of Satan is, *that if the soul will keep off from Christ till it be worthy, it will never close with Christ,* it will never embrace Christ. It will never be one with Christ, it must lie down in everlasting sorrow (Isa. 50:11).God hath laid up all worthiness in Christ, that the creature may know where to find it, and may make out after it. There is no way on earth to make unworthy souls worthy, but by believing in Christ (James 2:23). Believing in Christ, of slaves, it will make you worthy sons; of enemies, it will make you worthy friends. God will count none worthy, nor call none worthy, nor carry it towards none as worthy, but believers, who are made worthy by the worthiness of Christ's person, righteousness, satisfaction, and intercession (Rev. 3:4).

Remedy (4). The fourth remedy against this device of Satan is, solemnly to consider, *that if you make a diligent search into your own hearts, you shall find that it is the pride and folly of your own hearts that puts you upon bringing of a worthiness to Christ.* Oh! you would fain bring something to Christ that might render you acceptable to him; you are loath to come empty-handed. The Lord cries out, 'Ho, every one that thirsteth, come ye to the waters, and he that hath no money: come ye, buy and eat; yea, come, buy wine and milk without money, and without price. Wherefore do ye spend your money upon that which is not bread, and your labour for that which satisfieth not?' (Isa. 55:1, 2). Here the Lord calls upon moneyless, upon penniless souls, upon unworthy souls, to come and partake of his precious favours freely. But sinners are proud and foolish, and because they have no money, no worthiness to bring, they will not come, though he sweetly invites them. Ah, sinners! what is more just than that you should perish for ever, that prefer husks among swine before the milk and wine, the sweet and precious things of the gospel, that are freely and sweetly offered to you. Well, sinners! remember this, it is not so much the sense of your unworthiness, as your pride, that keeps you off from a blessed closing with the Lord Jesus.

DEVICE 3. *By suggesting to sinners the want of such and such preparations and qualifications.* Saith Satan, thou art not prepared to entertain Christ; thou art not thus and thus humbled and justified; thou art not heart-sick of sin; thou hast not been under horrors and terrors as such and such; thou must stay till thou art prepared and qualified to receive the Lord Jesus.

Remedy (1). The first remedy against this device of Satan is, solemnly to consider, *that such as have not been so and so prepared and qualified as Satan suggests, have received Christ, believed in Christ, and been saved by Christ.* Matthew was called, sitting at the receipt of custom, and there was such power went along with Christ's call, that made him to follow him (Matt. 9:9). We read not of any horrors or terrors that he was under before his being called by Christ. Pray, what preparations and qualifications were found in Zacchaeus, Paul, the jailor, and Lydia, before their conversion? (Luke 19:9; Acts 16:14, *seq*.). God brings in some by the sweet and still voice of the gospel, and usually such that are thus brought into Christ are the sweetest, humblest, choicest, and fruitfullest Christians. God is a free agent to work by law or gospel, by smiles or frowns, by presenting hell or heaven to sinners' souls. God thunders from mount Sinai upon some souls, and conquers them by thundering. God speaks to others in a still voice, and by that conquers them. You that are brought to Christ by the law, do not you judge and condemn them that are brought to Christ by the gospel; and you that are brought to Christ by the gospel, do not you despise those that are brought to Christ by the law. Some are brought to Christ by fire, storms, and tempests, others by more easy and gentle gales of the Spirit. The Spirit is free in the works of conversion, and, as the wind, it blows when, where, and how it pleases (John 3:8). Thrice happy are those souls that are brought to Christ, whether it be in a winter's night or in a summer's day.

Remedy (2). The second remedy against this device of Satan is, solemnly, *to dwell upon these following scriptures, which do clearly evidence that poor sinners which are not so and so prepared*

*and qualified to meet with Christ, to receive and embrace the Lord
Jesus Christ, may, notwithstanding that, believe in Christ; and rest
and lean upon him for happiness and blessedness, according to the
gospel.* Read Prov. 1:20-33 and chap 8:1-11 and chap. 9:1-6; Ezek.
16:1-14; John 3:14-18, 36; Rev. 3:15-20. Here the Lord Jesus Christ
stands knocking at the Laodiceans' door; he would fain have
them to sup with him, and that he might sup with them; that
is, that they might have intimate communion and fellowship
one with another.

Now, pray tell me, what preparations or qualifications had
these Laodiceans to entertain Christ? Surely none; for they
were lukewarm, they were 'neither hot nor cold,' they were
'wretched, and miserable, and poor, and blind, and naked'; and
yet Christ, to show his free grace and his condescending love,
invites the very worst of sinners to open to him, though they
were no ways so and so prepared or qualified to entertain him.

Remedy (3). The third remedy against this device of Satan
is, seriously to consider, *that the Lord does not in all the Scrip-
ture require such and such preparations and qualifications before
men come to Christ, before they believe in Christ, or entertain, or
embrace the Lord Jesus.* Believing in Christ is the great thing
that God presses upon sinners throughout the Scripture, as all
know that know anything of Scripture.

Obj. But does not Christ say, 'Come unto me all ye that
labour and are heavy laden, and I will give you rest'? (Matt.
11:28).

To this I shall give these three answers;

[1.] That though the invitation be to such that 'labour and
are heavy laden,' yet the promise of giving rest, it is made over
to 'coming,' to 'believing.'

[2.] That all this scripture proves and shows is, that such as labour under sin as under a heavy burden, and that are laden with the guilt of sin and sense of God's displeasure, ought to come to Christ for rest; but it doth not prove that only such must come to Christ, nor that all men must be thus burdened and laden with the sense of their sins and the wrath of God, before they come to Christ. Poor sinners, when they are under the sense of sin and wrath of God, are prone to run from creature to creature, and from duty to duty, and from ordinance to ordinance, to find rest; and if they could find it in any thing or creature, Christ should never hear of them; but here the Lord sweetly invites them: and to encourage them, he engages himself to give them rest: 'Come,' saith Christ, 'and I will give you rest.' I will not *show* you rest, nor barely *tell* you of rest, but 'I will *give* you rest.' I am faithfulness itself, and cannot lie, 'I *will* give you rest.' I that have the greatest power to give it, the greatest will to give it, the greatest right to give it, 'Come, *laden sinners*, and I will give you rest.' Rest is the most desirable good, the most suitable good, and to you the greatest good. 'Come,' saith Christ, that is, 'believe in me, and I will give you rest'; I will give you peace with God, and peace with conscience; I will turn your storm into an everlasting calm; I will give you such rest, that the world can neither give to you nor take from you.

[3.] No one scripture speaks out the whole mind of God; therefore do but compare this one scripture with those several scriptures that are laid down in the second remedy last mentioned, and it will clearly appear, that though men are thus and thus burdened and laden with their sins and filled with horror and terror, if they may come to Christ, they may receive and embrace the Lord Jesus Christ.

Remedy (4). The fourth remedy against this device of Satan is, to consider, *that all that trouble for sin, all that sorrow, shame, and mourning which is acceptable to God, and delightful to God, and prevalent with God, blows from faith in Christ, as the stream doth from the fountain, as the branch doth from the root, as the effect doth from the cause.* Zech. 12:10, 'They shall look on him whom they have pierced, and they shall mourn for him.' All gospel mourning flows from believing; they shall first look, and then mourn. 'All that know anything know this, that 'whatsoever is not of faith is sin' (Rom. 14:23). Till men have faith in Christ, their best services are but glorious sins.

DEVICE 4. *By suggesting to a sinner Christ's unwillingness to save.* It is true, saith Satan. Christ is able to save thee, but is he willing? Surely, though he is able, yet he is not willing to save such a wretch as thou art, that hast trampled his blood under thy feet, and that hast been in open rebellion against him all thy days.

Remedy (1). *First, the great journey that he hath taken, from heaven to earth, on purpose to save sinners, doth strongly demonstrate his willingness to save them.* Matt. 9:13: 'I came not to call the righteous, but sinners to repentance.' 1 Tim. 1:13: 'This is a faithful saying, and worthy of all acceptation, that Christ Jesus came into the world to save sinners, of whom I am chief.'

Remedy (2). *Secondly, his divesting himself of his glory in order to sinners' salvation, speaks out his willingness to save them.* He leaves his Father's bosom, he puts off his glorious robes, and lays aside his glorious crown, and bids adieu to his glistering courtiers the angels; and all this he doth, that he may accomplish sinners' salvation.[1]

---

[1] From the cradle to the cross, his whole life was a life of sufferings.

Remedy (3). *Thirdly, that sea of sin, that sea of wrath, that sea of trouble, that sea of blood that Jesus Christ waded through, that sinners might be pardoned, justified, reconciled, and saved, doth strongly evidence his willingness to save sinners* (2 Cor. 5:19, 20).

Remedy (4). *Fourthly, his sending his ambassadors, early and late, to woo and entreat sinners to be reconciled to him, doth with open mouth show his readiness and willingness to save sinners.*

Remedy (5). *Fifthly, his complaints against such as refuse him, and that turn their backs upon him, and that will not be saved by him, doth strongly declare his willingness to save them*: 'He came to his own, and his own received him not' (John 1:11). So in John 5:40: 'But ye will not come to me, that ye may have life.'

Remedy (6). *Sixthly, the joy and delight that he takes at the conversion of sinners doth demonstrate his willingness that they should be saved* (Luke 15:7): 'I say unto you, that likewise joy shall be in heaven over one sinner that repenteth, more than over ninety and nine just persons that need no repentance.' God the Father rejoiceth at the return of his prodigal son; Christ rejoices to see the travail of his soul; the Spirit rejoices that he hath another temple to dwell in; and the angels rejoice that they have another brother to delight in (Isa. 53:11).

DEVICE 5. *By working a sinner to mind more the secret decrees and counsels of God, than his own duty.* What needest thou to busy thyself about receiving, embracing, and entertaining of Christ? saith Satan; if thou art elected, thou shalt be saved; if not, all that thou canst do will do thee no good. Nay, he will work the soul not only to doubt of its election, but to conclude that he is not elected, and therefore, let him do what he can, he shall never be saved.

Remedy (1). The first remedy against this device of Satan is, seriously to consider, *that all the angels in heaven, nor all the men on earth, nor all the devils in hell, cannot tell to the contrary, but that thou mayest be an elect person, a chosen vessel.* Thou mayest be confident of this, that God never made Satan one of his privy council, God never acquainted him with the names or persons of such that he hath set his love upon to eternity.

Remedy (2). The second remedy against this device of Satan is, *to meddle with that which thou hast to do.* 'Secret things belong to the Lord, but revealed things belong to thee' (Deut. 29:29). Thy work, sinner, is, to be peremptory in believing, and in returning to the Lord; thy work is to cast thyself upon Christ, lie at his feet, to wait on him in his ways; and to give him no rest till he shall say, Sinner, I am thy portion, I am thy salvation, and nothing shall separate between thee and me.

II. SEVEN CHARACTERS OF FALSE TEACHERS

Satan labours might and main, by false teachers, which are his messengers and ambassadors, to deceive, delude, and for ever undo the precious souls of men[1] (Jer. 23:13): 'I have seen folly in the prophets of Samaria; they prophesied in Baal, and caused my people Israel to err'; Mic. 3:5: 'The prophets make my people to err.' They seduce them, and carry them out of the right way into by-paths and blind thickets of error, blasphemy, and wickedness, where they are lost for ever. 'Beware of false prophets, for they come to you in sheep's clothing, but inwardly they are ravening wolves' (Matt. 7:15).

---

[1] Acts 20:28-30; 2 Cor. 2:13-15; Eph. 4:14; 2 Tim. 3:4-6; Titus 1:11, 12; 2 Pet. 2:18, 19.

These lick and suck the blood of souls (Phil. 3:2), 'Beware of dogs, beware of evil workers, beware of the concision.' These kiss and kill; these cry. Peace, peace, till souls fall into everlasting flames (Prov. 7).

Now the best way to deliver poor souls from being deluded and destroyed by these messengers of Satan is, to discover them in their colours, that so, being known, poor souls may shun them, and fly from them as from hell itself.

Now you may know them by these characters following:

[1.] *The first character.* False teachers are *men-pleasers.*[1] They preach more to please the ear than to profit the heart (Isa. 30:10): 'Which say to the seers, See not; and to the prophets, Prophesy not unto us right things: speak to us smooth things; prophesy deceits.' Jer. 5:30, 31; 'A wonderful and horrible thing is committed in the land; the prophets prophesy falsely, and the priests bear rule by their means, and my people love to have it so. And what will you do in the end thereof?' They handle holy things rather with wit and dalliance than with fear and reverence. False teachers are soul-undoers. They are like evil chirurgeons, that skin over the wound, but never heal it. Flattery undid Ahab and Herod, Nero and Alexander. False teachers are hell's greatest enrichers. Not bitter, but flattering words do all the mischief, said Valerian, the Roman emperor. Such smooth teachers are sweet soul-poisoners (Jer. 23:16, 17).[2]

[2.] *The second character.* False teachers are *notable in casting dirt, scorn, and reproach upon the persons, names, and credits of Christ's most faithful ambassadors.* Thus Korah, Dathan,

---

[1] But so are not true teachers; Gal. 1:10; 1 Thess. 2:1-4.

[2] Whilst an ass is stroked under the belly, you may lay on his back what burden you please.

and Abiram charged Moses and Aaron that they took too much upon them, seeing all the congregation was holy (Num. 16:3). You take too much state, too much power, too much honour, too much holiness upon you; for what are you more than others, that you take so much upon you? And so Ahab's false prophets fell foul on good Micaiah, paying of him with blows for want of better reasons (1 Kings 22:10-26). Yea, Paul, that great apostle of the Gentiles, had his ministry undermined and his reputation blasted by false teachers: 'For his letters,' say they, 'are weighty and powerful, but his bodily presence is weak and his speech contemptible' (2 Cor. 10:10). They rather contemn him than admire him; they look upon him as a dunce rather than a doctor. And the same hard measure had our Lord Jesus from the scribes and Pharisees, who laboured as for life to build their own credit upon the ruins of his reputation.[1] And never did the devil drive a more full trade this way than he does in these days (Matt. 27:63). Oh! the dirt, the filth, the scorn that is thrown upon those of whom the world is not worthy! I suppose false teachers mind not that saying of Augustine: He that willingly takes from my good name, unwillingly adds to my reward.

[3.] *The third character.* False teachers are venters of the devices and visions of their own heads and hearts.[2] Jer. 14:14: 'Then the Lord said unto me. The prophets prophesy lies in my name: I sent them not, neither have I commanded them, neither spake unto them: they prophesy unto you a false vision and divination, and a thing of nought, and the deceit

---

[1] The proverb is, A man's eye and his good name can bear no jests. Yea, and Lucian, that blasphemous atheist, termeth him the crucified cozener.

[2] Matt. 24:4, 5; 2 Cor. 11:14; Titus 1:10; Rom. 16:18.

of their heart'; chap. 23:16: 'Thus saith the Lord of hosts, Hearken not unto the words of the prophets that prophesy unto you; they make you vain: they speak a vision of their own heart, and not out of the mouth of the Lord.' Are there not multitudes in this nation whose visions are but golden delusions, lying vanities, brain-sick fantasies? These are Satan's great benefactors, and such as divine justice will hang up in hell as the greatest malefactors, if the physician of souls do not prevent it.

[4.] *The fourth character.* False teachers easily pass over the great and weighty things both of law and gospel, and stand most upon those things that are of the least moment and concernment to the souls of men.[1] 1 Tim. 1:5-7: 'Now the end of the commandment is charity out of a pure heart, and of a good conscience, and of faith unfeigned; from which some having swerved, have turned aside unto vain jangling, desiring to be teachers of the law, and understand neither what they say nor whereof they affirm.' Matt. 23:23: 'Woe unto you, scribes and Pharisees, hypocrites; for ye pay tithe of mint, and anise and cummin, and have omitted the weightier matters of the law, judgment, mercy, and faith; these ought ye to have done, and not to leave the other undone.' False teachers are nice in the lesser things of the law, and as negligent in the greater. 1 Tim. 6:3-5: 'If any man teach otherwise, and consent not to wholesome words, even the words of our Lord Jesus Christ, and to the doctrine which is according to godliness, he is proud, knowing nothing, but doting about questions and strife of words, whereof cometh envy, strife, railings, evil surmisings,

---

[1] Luther complained of such in his time as would strain at a gnat, and swallow a camel. This age is full of such teachers, such monsters. The high priest's spirit (Matt. 23:24) lives and thrives in these days.

perverse disputings of men of corrupt minds, and destitute of the truth, supposing that gain is godliness: from such withdraw thyself.' If such teachers are not hypocrites in grain, I know nothing (Rom. 2:22). The earth groans to bear them, and hell is fitted for them (Matt. 23:32).

[5.] *The fifth character.* False teachers *cover and colour their dangerous principles and soul-impostures with very fair speeches and plausible pretences, with high notions and golden expressions.* Many in these days are bewitched and deceived by the magnificent words, lofty strains, and stately terms of deceivers, viz. illumination, revelation, deification, and fiery triplicity. As strumpets paint their faces, and deck and perfume their beds, the better to allure and deceive simple souls,[1] so false teachers will put a great deal of paint and garnish upon their most dangerous principles and blasphemies, that they may the better deceive and delude poor ignorant souls. They know sugared poison goes down sweetly; they wrap up their pernicious, soul-killing pills in gold. In the days of Hadrian the emperor, there was one Ben-Cosbi gathered a multitude of Jews together, and called himself *Ben-cocuba*, the son of a star, applying that promise to himself (Num. 24:17), but he proved *Bar-chosaba*, the son of a lie. And so will all false teachers, for all their flourishes prove at the last the sons of lies.

[6.] *The sixth character.* False teachers *strive more to win over men to their opinions, than to better them in their conversations.* Matt. 23:15: 'Woe unto you, scribes and Pharisees, hypocrites! for ye compass sea and land to make one proselyte, and when he is made, ye make him twofold more the child of hell than yourselves.' They busy themselves most about men's heads. Their

---

[1] Gal. 6:12; 2 Cor. 11:13-15; Rom. 16:17, 18; Matt. 16:6, 11; 12:7, 15.

work is not to better men's hearts, and mend their lives; and in this they are very much like their father the devil, who will spare no pains to gain proselytes.[1]

[7.] *The seventh character.* False teachers make merchandise of their followers (2 Pet. 2:1-3): 'But there were false prophets also among the people, even as there shall be false teachers among you, who privily shall bring in damnable heresies, even denying the Lord that bought them, and bring upon themselves swift destruction. And many shall follow their pernicious ways; by reason of whom the way of truth shall be evil spoken of. And through covetousness shall they with feigned words make merchandise of you: whose judgment now of a long time lingereth not, and their damnation slumbereth not.' They eye your goods more than your good; and mind more the serving of themselves, than the saving of your souls. So they may have your substance, they care not though Satan has your souls (Rev. 18:11-13). That they may the better pick your purse, they will hold forth such principles as are very indulgent to the flesh. False teachers are the great worshippers of the golden calf (Jer. 6:13).[2] Now, by these characters you may know them, and so shun them, and deliver your souls out of their dangerous snares; which that you may, my prayers shall meet yours at the throne of grace. And now, to prevent objections, I shall lay down some propositions or conclusions concerning Satan and his devices, and then give you the reasons of the point, and so come to make some use and application of the whole to ourselves.

---

[1] For shame! says Epictetus to his Stoics; either live as Stoics, or leave off the name *of* Stoics. The application is easy.

[2] Crates threw his money into the sea, resolving to drown it, lest it should drown him. But false teachers care not who they drown, so they may have their money.

III. SIX PROPOSITIONS CONCERNING
SATAN AND HIS DEVICES

Proposition (1). The proposition is this, *that though Satan hath his devices to draw souls to sin, yet we must be careful that we do not lay all our temptations upon Satan, that we do not wrong the devil, and father that upon him that is to be fathered upon our own base hearts.* I think that oftentimes men charge that upon the devil that is to be charged upon their own hearts, 'And the Lord said unto the woman, What is this that thou hast done? And the woman said, The serpent beguiled me, and I did eat' (Gen. 3:13). Sin and shifting came into the world together.[1] This is no small baseness of our hearts, that they will be naught, ay, very naught, and yet will father that naughtiness upon Satan. Man hath an evil root within him; that were there no devil to tempt him, nor no wicked men in the world to entice him, yet that root of bitterness, that cursed sinful nature that is in him, would draw him to sin, though he knows beforehand that 'the wages of sin is eternal death' (Rom. 6:23). 'For out of the heart proceed evil thoughts, murders, adulteries, fornications, thefts, false witness, blasphemies' (Matt. 15:19). The whole frame of man is out of frame. The understanding is dark, the will cross, the memory slippery, the affections crooked, the conscience corrupted, the tongue poisoned, and the heart wholly evil, only evil, and continually evil. Should God chain up Satan, and give him no liberty to tempt or entice the sons of men to vanity or folly, yet they would not, yet they could not but sin against him, by reason of that cursed nature that is in them, that will still be a-provoking them to those sins that will pro-

---

[1] We are no sooner born, than buried in a bog of wickedness. (*Cicero*)

voke and stir up the anger of God against them (Jude 15, 16). Satan hath only a persuading sleight, not an enforcing might. He may tempt us, but without ourselves he cannot conquer us; he may entice us, but without ourselves he cannot hurt us. Our hearts carry the greatest stroke in every sin. Satan can never undo a man without himself; but a man may easily undo himself without Satan. Satan can only present the golden cup, but he hath no power to force us to drink the poison that is in the cup; he can only present to us the glory of the world, he cannot force us to fall down and worship him, to enjoy the world; he can only spread his snares, he hath no power to force us to walk in the midst of his snares. Therefore do the devil so much right, as not to excuse yourselves, by your accusing him, and laying the load upon him, that you should lay upon your own hearts.[1]

Prop. (2). The second proposition is, *that Satan hath a great hand and stroke in most sins*. It was Satan that tempted our first parents to rebellion; it was Satan that provoked David to number the people; it was Satan that put Peter upon rebuking Christ; therefore saith Christ, 'Get thee behind me, Satan'; it was Satan that put Cain upon murdering of righteous Abel, therefore it is that he is called 'a murderer from the beginning'; it was Satan that put treason into the heart of Judas against Christ, 'And supper being ended, the devil having put into the heart of Judas Iscariot, Simon's son, to betray him'; it was Satan that put Ananias upon lying; Peter said, 'Ananias, why hath Satan filled thine heart to lie to the Holy Ghost?'[2] As the hand of Joab was in the tale of the woman of Tekoah,

---

[1] The fire is our wood, though it be the devil's flame. (*Nazianzen*)

[2] Gen. 3:1-5; 1 Chron. 21:1; Matt. 16:22, 23; John 8:44; 13:2; Acts 5:3.

so Satan's hand is usually in all the sins that men commit. Such is Satan's malice against God, and his envy against man, that he will have a hand one way or other in all the sins, though he knows that all the sins he provokes others to shall be charged upon him to his greater woe, and eternal torment.

Ambrose brings in the devil boasting against Christ and challenging Judas as his own: 'He is not thine, Lord Jesus, he is mine; his thoughts beat for me; he eats with thee, but is fed by me; he takes bread from thee, but money from me; he drinks wine with thee, and sells thy blood to me.' Such is his malice against Christ, and his wrath and rage against man, that he will take all advantages to draw men to that, that may give him advantage to triumph over Christ and men's souls for ever.

Prop. (3). The third proposition is. *That Satan must have a double leave before he can do anything against us.* He must have leave from God, and leave from ourselves, before he can act anything against our happiness. He must have his commission from God, as you may see in the example of Job (Job 1:11, 12; 2:3-6). Though the devil had malice enough to destroy him, yet he had not so much as power to touch him, till God gave him a commission.

They could not so much as enter into the swine without leave from Christ (Luke 8:32). Satan would fain have combated with Peter, but this he could not do without leave. 'Satan hath desired to have you, to winnow you' (Luke 22:31). So Satan could never have overthrown Ahab and Saul, but by a commission from God (1 Kings 22). Ah! what a cordial, what a comfort should this be to the saints, that their greatest, subtlest, and watchfullest enemy cannot hurt nor harm them, without leave from him who is their sweetest Saviour, their dearest husband, and their choicest friend.

And as Satan must have leave from God, so he must have leave of us. When he tempts, we must assent; when he makes offers, we must hearken; when he commands, we must obey, or else all his labour and temptations will be frustrated, and the evil that he tempts us to shall be put down only to his account. That is a remarkable passage in Acts 5:3, 'Why hath Satan filled thy heart to lie to the Holy Ghost?' He doth not expostulate the matter with Satan; he doth not say, Satan, 'Why hast thou filled Ananias's heart to make him lie to the Holy Ghost?' but he expostulates the case with Ananias; Peter said, 'Ananias, why hath Satan filled *thine* heart to lie to the Holy Ghost?' Why hast thou given him an advantage to fill thy heart with infidelity, hypocrisy, and obstinate audacity, to lie to the Holy Ghost? As if he had said, Satan could never have done this in thee, which will now for ever undo thee, unless thou hadst given him leave. If, when a temptation comes, a man cries out, and saith, Ah, Lord! here is a temptation that would force me, that would deflower my soul, and I have no strength to withstand it; oh! help! help! for thy honour's sake, for thy Son's sake, for thy promise's sake; it is a sign that Satan hath not gained your consent, but committed a rape upon your souls, which he shall dearly pay for.

Prop. (4). The fourth proposition is, *that no weapons but spiritual weapons will be useful and serviceable to the soul in fighting and combating with the devil.* This the apostle shows: 'Wherefore take unto you,' saith he, 'the whole armour of God, that ye may be able to stand in the evil day, and having done all, to stand' (Eph. 6:13). So the same apostle tells you. 'That the weapons of your warfare are not carnal, but mighty through God, to the casting down of strongholds' (2 Cor. 10:4). You have not to do with a weak, but with a mighty enemy, and therefore you had need to look to it, that your weapons are mighty, and that they cannot be, unless they are spiritual.

Carnal weapons have no might nor spirit in them towards the making of a conquest upon Satan.[1] It was not David's sling nor stone that gave him the honour and advantage of setting his feet upon Goliath, but his faith in the name of the Lord of hosts. 'Thou comest to me with a sword, with a spear, and with a shield, but I am come to thee in the name of the Lord of hosts, the God of the armies of Israel, whom thou hast defied' (1 Sam. 17:45). He that fights against Satan, in the strength of his own resolutions, constitution or education, will certainly fly and fall before him. Satan will be too hard for such a soul, and lead him captive at his pleasure. The only way to stand, conquer, and triumph, is still to plead, 'It is written,' as Christ did (Matt. 4:10). There is no sword but the two-edged sword of the Spirit, that will be found to be metal of proof when a soul comes to engage against Satan; therefore, when you are tempted to uncleanness, plead, 'It is written, be ye holy, as I am holy' (1 Pet. 1:16); and, 'Let us cleanse ourselves from all filthiness of the flesh and spirit, perfecting holiness in the fear of the Lord' (2 Cor. 7:1). If he tempts you to distrust God's providence and fatherly care of you, plead, It is written, 'They that fear the Lord shall want nothing that is good' (Psa. 34:9).

[1] We read of many that, out of greatness of spirit, could offer violence to nature, but were at a loss when they came to deal with a corruption or a temptation. Heraclitus's motto was, *A Deo victoria*, It is God that gives victory; and that should be every Christian's motto.

It is written, 'The Lord will give grace and glory, and no good thing will he withhold from them that purely live' (Psa. 84:11). If he tempt you to fear that you shall faint, and fall, and never be able to run to the end of the race that is set before you, plead. It is written, 'The righteous shall hold on his way, and he that hath clean hands shall be stronger and stronger' (Job 17:9).

It is written, 'I will make an everlasting covenant with them, that I will not turn away from them, to do them good, but I will put my fear in their hearts, that they may not depart from me' (Jer. 32:40).

It is written, 'They that wait upon the Lord shall renew their strength; they shall mount up with wings as eagles; they shall run, and not be weary; and they shall walk, and not faint' (Isa. 40:31). If Satan tempt you to think that because your sun for the present is set in a cloud, that therefore it will rise no more, and that the face of God will shine no more upon you; that your best days are now at an end, and that you must spend all your time in sorrow and sighing; plead, It is written, 'He will turn again, he will have compassion upon us, and cast all our sins into the depth of the sea' (Mic. 7:19).

It is written, 'For a small moment have I forsaken thee, but with great mercies will I gather thee. In a little wrath I hid my face from thee for a moment, but with everlasting kindness will I have mercy on thee, saith the Lord, thy Redeemer' (Isa. 54:7, 8, 10).

It is written, 'The mountains shall depart, and the hills be removed, but my kindness shall not depart from thee, neither shall the covenant of my peace be removed, saith the Lord that hath mercy on thee.'

It is written, 'Can a woman forget her sucking child, that she should not have compassion on the son of her womb? Yea, they may forget, yet will not I forget thee. Behold, I have graven thee upon the palms of my hands, thy walls are continually before me' (Isa. 49:15, 16).

If ever you would be too hard for Satan, and after all his assaults, have your bow abide in strength, then take to you the word of God, which is 'the two-edged sword of the Spirit, and the shield of faith, whereby you shall be able to quench all the fiery darts of the devil' (Eph. 6:16). It is not spitting at Satan's name, nor crossing yourselves, nor leaning to your own resolutions, that will get you the victory.

Luther reports of Staupitius, a German minister, that he acknowledged himself, that before he came to understand aright the free and powerful grace of God, he vowed and resolved an hundred times against some particular sin, and never could get power over it. At last he saw the reason to be his trusting to his own resolution. Therefore be skilful in the word of righteousness, and in the actings of faith upon Christ and his victory, and that crown of glory that is set before you, and Satan will certainly fly from you (James 4:7).

Prop. (5). The fifth proposition is, *that we may read much of Satan's nature and disposition by the divers names and epithets that are given him in the Scripture.* Sometimes he is called Behemoth, whereby the greatness and brutishness of the devil is figured (Job 40:15). Those evil spirits are sometimes called accusers, for their calumnies and slanders; and *evil ones*, for their malice. Satan is *Adversarius,* an adversary, that troubleth and molesteth (1 Pet. 5:8). Abaddon is a destroyer (Rev. 9:11). They are *tempters*, for their suggestion; *lions,* for their devouring; *dragons,* for their cruelty; and *serpents,* for their subtilty. As his names are, so is he; as face answers to face, so do Satan's names answer to his nature. He hath the worst names and the worst nature of all created creatures.

Prop. (6). The sixth proposition is, *that God will shortly tread down Satan under the saints' feet.* Christ, our champion, hath already won the field, and will shortly set our feet upon the necks of our spiritual enemies. Satan is a foiled adversary. Christ hath led him captive, and triumphed over him upon the cross. Christ hath already overcome him, and put weapons into your hands, that you may overcome him also, and set your feet upon his neck. Though Satan be a roaring lion, yet Christ, who is the lion of the tribe of Judah, will make Satan fly and fall before you. Let Satan do his worst, yet you shall have the honour and the happiness to triumph over him.[1] Cheer up, you precious sons of Sion, for the certainty and sweetness of victory will abundantly recompense you for all the pains you have taken in making resistance against Satan's temptations. The broken horns of Satan shall be trumpets of our triumph and the cornets of our joy.

FIVE REASONS OF THE POINT

Now I shall come to the reasons of the point, and so draw to a close *Reason* (1). The first reason is, *that their hearts may be kept in an humble, praying, watching frame.* Oh! hath Satan so many devices to ensnare and undo the souls of men! How should this awaken dull, drowsy souls, and make them stand upon their watch! A saint should be like the seraphim, beset

---

[1] Rom. 16:20. The Greek word signifies to break or crash a thing to pieces. Being applied to the feet, it noteth that breaking or crushing which is by stamping upon a thing.

all over with eyes and lights, that he may avoid Satan's snares, and stand fast in the hour of temptation.

The Lord hath in the Scripture discovered the several snares, plots, and devices that the devil hath to undo the souls of men, that so, being forewarned, they may be forearmed; that they may be always upon their watch-tower, and hold their weapons in their hands, as the Jews did in Nehemiah's time.[1]

Reason (2). The second reason is, *from that malice, envy, and enmity that is in Satan against the souls of men*. Satan is full of envy and enmity, and that makes him very studious to suit his snares and plots to the tempers, constitutions, fancies, and callings of men, that so he may make them as miserable as himself.[2]

The Russians are so malicious, that you shall have a man hide some of his own goods in the house of him whom he hateth, and then accuse him for the stealing of them.[3] So doth Satan, out of malice to the souls of men, hide his goods, his wares, as I may say, in the souls of men, and then go and accuse them before the Lord; and a thousand, thousand other ways Satan's malice, envy, and enmity puts him upon, eternally to undo the precious souls of men.

Reason (3). The third reason is drawn from that long experience that Satan hath had. *He is a spirit of mighty abilities; and his abilities to lay snares before us are mightily increased by that long standing of his*. He is a spirit of above five thousand years'

---

[1] The philosopher had a ball of brass in his hand; if he chanced to sleep it fell into a basin and awaked him to his studies. You are wise, and know how to apply it.

[2] Malice cares not what it saith or doth, so it may kill or gall.

[3] An envious heart and plotting head are inseparable companions.

standing. He hath had time enough to study all those ways and methods which tend most to ensnare and undo the souls of men. And as he hath time enough, so he hath made it his whole study, his only study, his constant study, to find out snares, depths, and stratagems, to entangle and overthrow the souls of men. When he was but a young serpent, he did easily deceive and outwit our first parents (Gen. 3); but now he is grown that 'old serpent,' as John speaks (Rev. 12:9), he is as old as the world, and is grown very cunning by experience.

Reason (4). The fourth reason is, *in judgment to the men of the world, that they may stumble and fall, and be ensnared for ever.* Wicked men that withstand the offers of mercy, and despise the Spirit of grace, that will not open, though God knocks never so hard by his word and rod, by his Spirit arid conscience, are given up by a hand of justice, to be hardened, deceived, and ensnared by Satan, to their everlasting ruin (1 Kings 22:23). And what can be more just than that they should be taken and charmed with Satan's wiles, who have frequently refused to be charmed by the Spirit of grace, though he hath charmed never so wisely, and never so sweetly?

Reason (5). The fifth reason is, *that the excellency and power of God's grace may be more illustrated and manifested, by making men able to grapple with this mighty adversary, and that notwithstanding all the plots, devices, and stratagems of Satan, yet he will make them victorious here, and crown them with glory hereafter.* The greater and the subtler the enemies of the children of Israel were, the more did divine power, wisdom, and goodness, sparkle and shine; and that, notwithstanding all their power, plots, and stratagems, yet to Canaan he would bring them at last. When Paul had weighed this, he sits down and glories in his infirmities and distresses and Satan's bufferings, that the power of Christ might rest upon him (2 Cor. 12:7-9).

V. CONCLUSION:
CHIEFLY, TEN SPECIAL HELPS AND RULES
AGAINST SATAN'S DEVICES

The use of the point.

If Satan hath such a world of devices and stratagems to ensnare and undo the souls of men, then, instead of wondering that so few are saved, sit down and wonder that any are saved, that any escape the snares of this cunning fowler, who spreads his nets and casts forth his baits in all places, in all cases and companies.

But this is not the main thing that I intend to speak to; my main business shall be, to set before you some special rules and helps against all his devices.

The first help. If you would not be taken by any of Satan's devices, then *walk by rule.*[1] He that walks by rule, walks most safely; he that walks by rule, walks most honourably; he that walks by rule, walks most sweetly. When men throw off the word, then God throws off them, and then Satan takes them by the hand, and leads them into snares at his pleasure. He that thinks himself too good to be ruled by the word, will be found too bad to be owned by God; and if God do not, or will not own him, Satan will by his stratagems overthrow him. Them that keep to the rule, they shall be kept in the hour of temptation. 'Because thou hast kept the word of my patience, I also will keep thee from the hour of temptation, which shall

[1] Prov. 12:24; Gal. 6:16.

come upon all the world, to try them that dwell upon the earth' (Rev. 3:10).

The second help. As you would not be taken with any of Satan's devices, *take heed of vexing and grieving of the Holy Spirit of God.*[1] It is the Spirit of the Lord Jesus Christ that is best able to discover Satan's snares against us; it is only he that can point out all his plots, and discover all his methods, and enable men to escape those pits that he hath digged for their precious souls. Ah! if you set that sweet and blessed Spirit a-mourning, who alone can secure you from Satan's depths, by whom will you be secured? Man is a weak creature, and no way able to discover Satan's snares, nor to avoid them, unless the Spirit of the Lord gives skill and power; therefore, whoever be grieved, be sure the Spirit be not grieved by your enormities, nor by your refusing the cordials and comforts that he sets before you, nor by slighting and despising his gracious actings in others, nor by calling sincerity hypocrisy, and faith fancy, nor by fathering those things upon the Spirit, that are the brats and fruits of your own hearts.[2] The Spirit of the Lord is your counsellor, your comforter, your upholder, your strengthener. It is only the Spirit that makes a man too great for Satan to conquer. 'Greater is he that is in you, than he that is in the world' (1 John 4:4).

The third help. If you would not be taken with any of Satan's devices, then labour for more heavenly wisdom.[3] Ah, souls!

[1] *Spiritus sanctus est res delicata.* The Divine Spirit is a very tender thing: if you grieve him, he will certainly grieve and vex your precious souls (Lam. 1:16).

[2] Isa. 63:10; Psa. 73:23; 1 Thess. 5:19; Acts 2:13.

[3] If men could but see the fair face of wisdom with mortal eyes, they would be in love with her, saith Plato.

you are much in the dark, you have but a little to that others have, and to that you might have had, had you not been wanting to yourselves. There are many knowing souls, but there are but a few wise souls. There is oftentimes a great deal of knowledge, where there is but a little wisdom to improve that knowledge. Knowledge without wisdom is like mettle in a blind horse, which often is an occasion of the rider's fall, and of his bones being jostled against the walls. It is not the most knowing Christian, but the most wise Christian, that sees, avoids, and escapes Satan's snares. 'The way of life is above to the wise,' saith Solomon, 'that he may depart from hell beneath' (Prov. 15:24). Heavenly wisdom makes a man delight to fly high; and the higher any man flies, the more he is out of the reach of Satan's snares.[1] Ah, souls! you had need of a great deal of heavenly wisdom, to see where and how Satan lays his baits and snares; and wisdom to find out proper remedies against his devices, and wisdom to apply those remedies seasonably, inwardly, and effectually to your own hearts, that so you may avoid the snares which that evil one hath laid for your precious souls.

The fourth help. If you would not be taken with any of Satan's devices, then *make present resistance against Satan's first motions*. It is safe to resist, it is dangerous to dispute. Eve disputes, and falls in paradise (Gen. 3); Job resists, and conquers upon the dunghill. He that will play with Satan's bait, will quickly be taken with Satan's hook. The promise of conquest is made over to resisting, not to disputing: 'Resist the devil, and he will fly from you' (James 4:7). Ah, souls! were you better at resisting than at disputing, though haply you were not very

---

[1] A serpent's eye is a singular ornament in a dove's head.

expert at either, your temptations would be fewer, and your strength to stand would be greater than now it is.

The fifth help. If you would not be taken with any of Satan's devices, then labour to be filled with the Spirit. The Spirit of the Lord is a Spirit of light and power; and what can a soul do without light and power 'against spiritual wickedness in high places'? (Eph. 6:12). It is not enough that you have the Spirit, but you must be filled with the Spirit, or else Satan, that evil spirit, will be too hard for you, and his plots will prosper against you. That is a sweet word of the apostle, 'Be filled with the Spirit' (Eph. 5:18);[1] *i.e.* labour for abundance of the Spirit. He that thinks he hath enough of the Holy Spirit, will quickly find himself vanquished by the evil spirit. Satan hath his snares to take you in prosperity and adversity, in health and sickness, in strength and weakness, when you are alone and when you are in company, when you come on to spiritual duties and when you come off from spiritual duties, and if you are not filled with the Spirit, Satan will be too hard and too crafty for you, and will easily and frequently take you in his snares, and make a prey of you in spite of your souls. Therefore labour more to have your hearts filled with the Spirit than to have your heads filled with notions, your shops with wares, your chests with silver, or your bags with gold; so shall you escape the snares of this fowler, and triumph over all his plots.[2]

The sixth help. If you would not be taken in any of Satan's snares, then *keep humble*. An humble heart will rather lie in the

---

[1] Be filled with the Spirit, as the sails of a ship are filled with wind.

[2] Luther saith, a holy gluttony is to lay on to feed hard, and to fetch heart; draughts, till the; be even drunk with loves, and with the abundance of the Spirit. Oh that there were more such holy gluttony in the world!

dust than rise by wickedness, and sooner part with all than the peace of a good conscience. Humility keeps the soul free from many darts of Satan's casting, and snares of his spreading; as the low shrubs are free from many violent gusts and blasts of wind, which shake and rend the taller trees. The devil hath least power to fasten a temptation on him that is most humble. He that hath a gracious measure of humility, is neither affected with Satan's proffers nor terrified with his threatenings.[1] I have read of one who, seeing in a vision many snares of the devil spread upon the earth, he sat down, and mourned, and said in himself, 'Who shall pass through these?' Where upon he heard a voice answering, Humility shall. God hath said, that 'he will teach the humble,' and that 'he will dwell with the humble,' and that 'he will fill and satisfy the humble.'[2] And if the teachings of God, the indwellings of God, if the pourings in of God, will not keep the soul from falling into Satan's snares, I do not know what will. And therefore as you would be happy in resisting Satan, and blessed in triumphing over Satan and all his snares, keep humble; I say again, keep humble.

The seventh help. If you would not be taken in any of Satan's snares, then keep a strong, close, and constant watch (1 Thess. 5:6).[3] A secure soul is already an ensnared soul. That soul that

---

[1] It is reported of Satan that he should say thus of a learned man: 'Thou dost always overcome me; when I would exalt and promote thee, thou keep eat thyself in humility; and when I would throw thee down, thou liftest up thyself in assurance of faith.'

[2] Psa. 25:9; Is. 57:15; James 4:6.

[3] We must not be like Agrippa a dormouse, that would not awake till cast into boiling lead, but effectually mind these following scriptures, wherein this duty of watchfulness is so strictly enjoined:—Matt. 26:40; Mark 13:33-35, 37; 1 Cor. 16:13; Col 4:2; I Pet. 4:7; Rev. 3:2.

will not watch against temptations, will certainly fall before the power of temptations. Satan works most strongly on the fancy when the soul is drowsy. The soul's security is Satan's opportunity to fall upon the soul and to spoil the soul, as Joshua did the men of Ai. The best way to be safe and secure from all Satan's assaults is, with Nehemiah and the Jews, to watch and pray, and pray and watch. By this means they became too hard for their enemies, and the work of the Lord did prosper sweetly in their hands. Remember how Christ chid his sluggish disciples, 'What! could you not watch with me one hour?' what, cannot you watch with me? how will you then die with me? if you cannot endure words, how will you endure wounds? Satan always keeps a crafty and malicious watch, 'seeking whom he may devour,' or whom he may drink or sip up, as the apostle speaks in 1 Peter 5:8. Satan is very envious at our condition, that we should enjoy that paradise out of which he is cast, and out of which he shall be for ever kept.

Shall Satan keep a crafty watch, and shall not Christians keep a holy spiritual watch?[1] Our whole life is beset with temptations. Satan watches all opportunities to break our peace, to wound our consciences, to lessen our comforts, to impair our graces, to slur our evidences, and to damp our assurances. Oh! what need then have we to be always upon our watch-tower, lest we be surprised by this subtle serpent. Watchfulness includes a waking, a rousing up of the soul. It is a continual, careful observing of our hearts and ways, in all the turnings of our lives, that we still keep close to God and his word.

[1] Hannibal never rested, whether he did conquer or was conquered. It is so with Satan. Learn, for shame of the devil, said blessed Latimer, to watch, seeing the devil is so watchful.

Watchfulness is nothing else but the soul running up and down, to and fro, busy everywhere; it is the heart busied and employed with diligent observation of what comes from within us, and of what comes from without us and into us. Ah, souls! you are no longer safe and secure than when you are upon your watch. While Antipater kept the watch, Alexander was safe; and while we keep a strict watch, we are safe. A watchful soul is a soul upon the wing, a soul out of gun-shot, a soul upon a rock, a soul in a castle, a soul above the clouds, a soul held fast in everlasting arms.

I shall conclude this seventh head with this advice: Remember the dragon is subtle, and bites the elephant's ear, and then sucks his blood, because he knows that to be the only place which the elephant cannot reach with his trunk to defend; so our enemies are so subtle, that they will bite us, and strike us where they may most mischief us, and therefore it doth very much concern us to stand always upon our guard.

The eighth help. If you would not be taken with any of Satan's snares and devices, then *keep up your communion with God.*[1] Your strength to stand and withstand Satan's fiery darts is from your communion with God. A soul high in communion with God may be tempted, but will not easily be conquered. Such a soul will fight it out to the death. Communion with God furnisheth the soul with the greatest and the choicest arguments to withstand Satan's temptations. Communion is the result of union. Communion is a reciprocal exchange between Christ and a gracious soul. Communion is Jacob's

[1] 1 Cor. 6:19. The words are very significant in the original. There are two *ins*, as though God could never have near enough communion with them.

ladder, where you have Christ sweetly coming down into the soul, and the soul, by divine influences, sweetly ascending up to Christ. Communion with Christ is very inflaming, raising and strengthening. While Samson kept up his communion with God, no enemy could stand before him, but he goes on conquering and to conquer; but when he was fallen in his communion with God, he quickly falls before the plots of his enemies. It will be so with your souls. So long as your communion with God is kept up, you will be too hard for 'spiritual wickedness in high places'; but if you fall from your communion with God, you will fall, as others, before the face of every temptation.[1] David, so long as he kept up his communion with God, he stands, and triumphs over all his enemies; but when he was fallen in his communion with God, then he falls before the enemies that were in his own bosom, and flies before those that pursued after his life. It will be so with your souls, if you do not keep up your communion with God. Job keeps up his communion with God, and conquers Satan upon the dunghill; Adam loses his communion with God, and is conquered by Satan in paradise. Communion with God is a shield upon land, as well as an anchor at sea; it is a sword to defend you, as well as a staff to support you; therefore keep up your communion.

The ninth help. If you would not be taken in any of Satan's snares, then *engage not against Satan in your own strength,*

---

[1] The sea ebbs and flows, the moon increases and decreases; so it is with saints in their communion with God. Plutarch tells of Eudoxus, that he would be willing to be burnt up presently by the sun, so he might be admitted to come so near it as to learn the nature of it. What should not we be content to suffer for the keeping up communion with Christ?

but be every day drawing new virtue and strength from the Lord Jesus.[1] Certainly that soul that engages against any old or new temptation without new strength, new influences from on high, will fall before the power of the temptation. You may see this in Peter; he rested upon some old received strength—'Though all men should deny thee, yet will not I' (Matt. 26:35)—and therefore he falls sadly before a new temptation. He curses and swears, and denies him thrice, that had thrice appeared gloriously to him. Ah, souls! when the snare is spread, look up to Jesus Christ, who is lifted up in the gospel, as the brazen serpent was in the wilderness, and say to him, Dear Lord! here is a new snare laid to catch my soul, and grace formerly received, without fresh supplies from thy blessed bosom, will not deliver me from this snare. Oh! give me new strength, new power, new influences, new measures of grace, that so I may escape the snares. Ah, souls! remember this, that your strength to stand and overcome must not be expected from graces received, but from the fresh and renewed influences of heaven.[2] You must lean more upon Christ than upon your duties; you must lean more upon Christ than upon your spiritual tastes and discoveries: you must lean more upon Christ than upon your graces, or else Satan will lead you into captivity.

The tenth help. If you would not be taken in any of Satan's snares, then *be much in prayer.* Prayer is a shelter to the soul, a sacrifice to God and a scourge to the devil. David's heart

---

[1] There is a remarkable saying of Moses (Exod. 15), God is my strength, and my praise, and my salvation, all in the abstract. It is but, Look up and live; look unto me, and be saved, from the ends of the earth (Isa. 45:22).

[2] John 15:5. Separate from me, or apart from me, ye can do nothing.

was oft more out of tune than his harp. He prays, and then, in spite of the devil, cries, 'Return unto thy rest, O my soul.' Prayer is the gate of heaven, a key to let us into paradise. There is nothing that renders plots fruitless like prayer; therefore saith Christ; 'Watch and pray that ye enter not into temptation' (Matt. 26:41). You must watch and pray, and pray and watch, if you would not enter into temptation.[1] When Sennacherib and Haman had laid plots and snares to have destroyed the Jews, they prayed, and their souls were delivered, and Sennacherib and Haman destroyed. David had many snares laid for him, and this puts him upon prayer. 'Keep me,' saith he, 'from the snares which they have laid for me, and the gins of the workers of iniquity.' 'Let the wicked fall into their own nets, whilst that I escape' (Psa. 141:9, 10). 'The proud,' saith he, 'have hid a snare for me, and cords: they have spread a net by the wayside; they have set gins for me. Selah. I said unto the Lord, Thou art my God: hear the voice of my supplication, O Lord!' (Psa. 140:5, 6). Saul and many others had laid snares for David, and this puts him upon prayer, and so the snares are broken and he is delivered.[2] Ah, souls! take words to yourselves, and tell God that Satan hath spread his snares in all places and in all companies; tell God that he digs deep, and that he hath plot upon plot, and device upon device, and all to undo you; tell God that you have neither skill nor power to escape his snares; tell God that it is a work too high and too hard for any created creature to work your deliverance, unless he put under his own

[1] It was said of Charles the Great that he spake more with God than with men. Ah! that I could say so of the Christians in our days.

[2] O Lord! saith Bernard, I never go away from thee, without thee. Let us, saith Basil, with a holy impudence, make God ashamed, that he cannot look us in the face, if he do deny our importunity: Jacob-like, 'I will not let thee go, unless thou bless me.'

everlasting arms; tell God how his honour is engaged to stand by you, and to bring you off, that you be not ruined by his plots; tell God how the wicked would triumph, if you should fall into Satan's snares; tell God of the love of Christ, of the blood of Christ, and of the intercession of Christ for you, that a way may be found for your escape; tell God that if he will make it his honour to save you from falling into Satan's snares, you will make it your glory to speak of his goodness and to live out his kindness. Christians must do as Daedalus, that when he could not escape by a way upon earth, went by a way of heaven,[1] and that is, the way of prayer, which is the only way left to escape Satan's snares.

Use. The next use is a use of *thankfulness to those that escape Satan's snares, that are not taken by him at his will.* Ah! Christians, it stands upon you with that princely prophet David, to call upon your souls, and say, 'Bless the Lord, O our souls; and all that is within us, bless his holy name! Bless the Lord, O our souls, and forget not all his benefits!' (Psa. 103:1, 2); who hath not given us to be a prey to Satan, and to be ensnared by those snares that he hath laid for our souls. The sense of this great favour did work up David's heart to praises: 'Blessed be the Lord,' saith he, 'who hath not given us a prey to their teeth. Our soul is escaped as a bird out of the snares of the fowlers: the snare is broken, and we are escaped' (Psa. 124:7). Ah! Christians, remember that the greatest part of the world, yea, the greatest part of professors, are taken in Satan's snares. Can you think seriously of this, and not blush to be unthankful? What are you better than others? and what have ye deserved of God, or done for God more than

---

[1] The well-known legend of the 'wax-fixed wings' of Daedalus and Icarus.

others, that you should by the help of a divine hand escape the snares, when others are taken and held in the snares of the devil to their eternal overthrow?

Will you be thankful for the escaping the snares that men spread for your lives or estates, and will you not be much more thankful for escaping those snares that Satan hath laid for your precious souls? (Psa. 71:14).[1]

Remember this, that deliverance from Satan's snares doth carry with it the clearest and the greatest evidence of the soul and heart of God to be towards us. Many a man by a common hand of providence escapes many a snare that man hath laid for him, but yet escapes not the snares that Satan hath laid for him. Saul, and Judas, and Demas, doubtless escaped many snares that men had laid for them, but none of them escaped the snares that the devil had laid for them. Many men are lifted up above the snares of men by a common hand of providence, that are left to fall into the snares of the devil by a hand of justice; your deliverance from Satan's snares is a fruit of special love. Can you thus look upon it and not be thankful, O precious soul? I judge not.

Use. The last use of this point is, *to bespeak Christians to long to be at home.*[2] Oh! long to be in the bosom of Christ!

[1] The ancients use to say: Say a man is unthankful, and say he is anything. Psa. 71:14, 'I will yet praise thee more and more.' In the original it is, I will add to thy praise. The stork is said to leave one of her young ones where she hatcheth them; and the elephant to turn up the first sprig toward heaven, when he cometh to feed, out of some instinct of gratitude. Ah! souls, that these may not bear witness against you in the day of Christ.

[2] Augustine wished that he might have seen three things: Rome flourishing, Paul preaching, and Christ conversing with men upon the earth. Bede comes after, and, correcting this last wish, saith, Yea, but let me see the King in his beauty, Christ in his heavenly kingdom.

long to be in the land of Canaan! for this world, this wilderness, is full of snares, and all employments are full of snares, and all enjoyments are full of snares. In civil things, Satan hath his snares to entrap us; and in all spiritual things, Satan hath his snares to catch us. All places are full of snares, city and country, shop and closet, sea and land; and all our mercies are surrounded with snares. There are snares about our tables and snares about our beds; yea, Satan is so powerful and subtle that he will oftentimes make our greatest, nearest, and dearest mercies to become our greatest snares. Sometimes he will make the wife that lies in the bosom to be a snare to a man, as Samson's was, and as Job's was. Sometimes he will make the child to be a snare, as Absalom was and Eli's sons were; and sometimes he will make the servant to be a snare, as Joseph was to his mistress. Ah! souls, Satan is so cunning and artificial[1] that he can turn your cups into snares, and your clothes into snares, and your houses into snares, and your gardens into snares, and all your recreations into snares. And oh! how should the consideration of these things work all your souls to say with the church, 'Make haste, my beloved, and be like a roe, or a young hart upon the mountain of spices,' and to love, and look, and long for the coming of Christ (Song of Sol. 8:14). Shall the espoused maid long for the marriage day? the servant for his freedom? the captive for his ransom? the traveller for his inn, and the mariner for his harbour? and shall not the people of the Lord long much more to be in the bosom of Christ? there being nothing below the bosom of Christ that is not surrounded with Satan's snares (Phil. 1:23, and 2 Cor. 5:2-4).

[1] 'Artful.'

What Paul once spake of bonds and afflictions, that they attended him in every place (Acts 20:23), that may all the saints say of Satan's snares, that they attend them in every place; which should cause them to cry out, Let us go hence, let us go hence; and to say with Monica, Augustine's mother, 'What do we here? why depart we not hence? why fly we no swifter?' Ah! souls, till you are taken up into the bosom of Christ, your comforts will not be full, pure, and constant. Till then, Satan will still be thumping of you, and spreading snares to entangle you; therefore you should always be crying out with the church, 'Come, Lord Jesus! ' (Rev. 22:20). Is not Christ the star of Jacob, that 'giveth light to them that are in darkness'? that Prince of peace who brings the olive branch to souls that are perplexed? Is not the greatest worth and wealth in him? Are not the petty excellencies and perfections of all created creatures epitomized in him? Is not he the crown of crowns, the glory of glories, and the heaven of heavens? Oh then, be still a-longing after a full, clear, and constant enjoyment of Christ in heaven; for till then, Satan will still have plots and designs upon you. He acts by an united[1] power, and will never let you rest till you are taken up to an everlasting rest in the bosom of Christ.[2]

[1] Qu. 'untired'?

[2] It is as easy to compass the heavens with a span, and contain the sea in a nutshell as to relate fully Christ's excellencies, or heaven's happiness.